EATING DISORDERS

EATING DISORDERS
The Journey to Recovery Workbook

Laura J. Goodman, M.Ed., LMHC
Mona Villapiano, Psy.D.

BRUNNER-ROUTLEDGE
ALERE FLAMMAM
Taylor & Francis Group

USA	Publishing Office:	BRUNNER-ROUTLEDGE *A member of the Taylor & Francis Group* Taylor and Francis Books 29 West 35th Street New York, NY 10001
	Distribution Center:	BRUNNER-ROUTLEDGE *A member of the Taylor & Francis Group* Routledge/Taylor and Francis c/o Thomson Distribution Center 10650 Toebben Drive Independence, KY 41051
UK		BRUNNER-ROUTLEDGE *A member of the Taylor & Francis Group* 27 Church Road Hove E. Sussex, BN3 2FA Tel.: +44 (0) 1273 207411 Fax: +44 (0) 1273 205612

EATING DISORDERS: The Journey to Recovery Workbook

3 4 5 6 7 8 9 0

Printed by George H. Buchanan Co., Bridgeport, NJ, 2002.
Cover design by Claire O'Neill
A CIP catalog record for this book is available from the British Library.
∞ The paper in this publication meets the requirements of the ANSI Standard Z39.48-1984 (Permanence of Paper).

Library of Congress Cataloging-in-Publication Data
Goodman, Laura J.
    Eating disorders : the journey to recovery workbook / Laura J. Goodman, Mona Villapiano.
       p. cm.
    Inludes bibliographical references and index.
    ISBN 1-58391-058-1 (pbk. : alk. paper)
     1. Eating disorders. 2. Eating disorders—Treatment. 3. Eating disorders—Patients—Anecdotes. I. Villapiano, Mona.

RC552.E18 .G655 2001
616.85'20606—dc21

00-052946

ISBN 1-58391-058-1 (paper)

DEDICATION

To our many courageous clients, we dedicate this book.
You have taught us much about your unique journeys to recovery.
As others traverse their roads, know that your wisdom will guide
and your hope will light their way.

Contents

Preface   **xi**

Acknowledgments   **xiii**

Introduction   **xv**

How This Workbook Works   **xvii**

Chapter 1   *Guiding Your Journey: The Tree and the Web*   **1**

The Tree / 1
The Web / 3

Chapter 2   *What You Need to Know About Eating Disorders*   **5**

Set Point Theory or Regulated Weight / 7
Dieting, Emotions, and Cognition / 9
Physical Changes / 12
Conclusion / 15
Preview to Improving Your Relationship with Food / 15

Chapter 3   *Your Relationship with Food*   **17**

The Food Pyramid / 18
Common Eating Problems / 18
Food Restriction / 19
Compulsive Overeating / 20
Binge Eating and Purging / 23
What Stage Are You In? / 28
Exploring Belief Systems / 31
Safe Foods, Potential Foods, and Risk Foods / 33

Chapter 4   *The Female Body: Spirituality and Religion*   **37**

Questions About Religion and Eating Disorders / 39

Chapter 5   *The Female Body: History of Size and Thinness*   **41**

Questions About Body Image / 43

Chapter 6   *Body Image*   **47**

Exploring Body-Image Distortion   /   48
My Body . . . My Story   /   58
Your Body Roadmap   /   59

Chapter 7   *Your Relationship with Exercise*   **63**

Rate Your Relationship with Exercise   /   64
Exercise Guidelines   /   65
Physical Benefits of Exercise   /   65
Identifying Common Exercise Problems   /   67
Exercise and Identity   /   73

Chapter 8   *Women's Issues*   **75**

Not Good Enough: Body Distortion   /   77
Looking for Love: Appearance and Body Image   /   78
The Power of Positive Self-Talk and Affirmations   /   80
Infertility and Pregnancy   /   84
Osteoporosis   /   90
Sexuality   /   91
Women's Issues Survey   /   92

Chapter 9   *Men's Issues*   **93**

Diagnosis: How is it Different for Men?   /   94
Incidence: How do Men Stack Up?   /   96
Profile: Are Men's "Make-Ups" Any Different?   /   96
Men's Weight History Questionnaire   /   97
What About Feelings?   /   105
Communication   /   107
Men's Issues Survey   /   110

Chapter 10   *Substance Abuse and Eating Disorders*   **111**

The Cyclical Road to Addiction   /   112
Alcohol Abuse   /   117
Drug Abuse and Addiction   /   119
Laxative Abuse   /   122
Diuretics   /   124
Diet Pills   /   124
Ipecac Abuse   /   125

Chapter 11   *Trauma and Abuse*   **131**

Physical Abuse   /   132
Sexual Abuse   /   132
Emotional Abuse   /   133
Exploring Your History of Abuse   /   133
Trauma   /   134
How Has Food Helped You Survive?   /   134

Chapter 12 *Special Circumstances: Obsessive-Compulsive Disorder,*   **147**
Depression, and Diabetes

Obsessive-Compulsive Disorder / 147
Depression / 155
Diabetes / 161
Conclusion / 164

Chapter 13 *The Treatment Team*   **165**

The Physician / 166
The Therapist / 170
The Nutritionist / 175
The Pharmacologist / 181

Chapter 14 *Media Madness*   **185**

Chapter 15 *For Families, Friends, and Loved Ones*   **195**

Education / 197
Common Myths About Eating Disorders / 202
What To Do If You Suspect Your Loved One Has an Eating Disorder / 204
How To Be Supportive of Recovery / 211

Chapter 16 *Concluding Your Journey: The Tree and the Web Revisited*   **213**

Resources and References   **217**

Index   **219**

Preface

Over the years we have worked with hundreds of people with eating disorders. For many of our clients, the struggle to overcome these illnesses was intense, exhausting, and immensely challenging. For others, the battle for health and life continues.

What we noticed was that many clients have the energy, will, and motivation to work between sessions to learn new information, practice strategies, and master skills for living. Some clients are able to find and assimilate information on their own. Others are lost and out at sea, not knowing what to do. Many are so seduced by the eating disorder's voice that they cannot learn or try anything which might challenge the eating disorder's preeminence in their lives.

Furthermore, many treatment providers are trying to get more done in less time. They do not have the availability of intensive treatment programs that introduce clients and their loved ones to the psychoeducational information about their illnesses or the strategies and skills needed to combat the eating disorder's control over their lives. People with eating disorders don't have as much time to practice their newfound skills in safe treatment settings.

Therefore, we wanted to develop a workbook which would encourage self-paced learning and practice for people with eating disorders. If you are in therapy you might discuss with your therapist whether or not to use this workbook between your therapy sessions to augment information-gathering and the process of your therapy. For those of you who are attempting to understand whether or not you may have an eating disorder, or if you do not have access to treatment, this workbook may help you better understand your illness and guide you to steps you might take on your own journey to recovery.

For therapists and other treatment providers, this workbook offers: ready-made between-session tasks for your clients to practice, topics for discussion within the session, and opportunities to help your clients widen their network of support in the community. For many, this workbook, with its anecdotes and personal accounts from many people who have struggled with eating disorders, may offer hope, a sense of connection, and direction.

For those of you who provide treatment and know that your clients need more than you, or any treatment provider, could provide, the use of this workbook could help your clients proceed with their work, develop a sense of mastery and accomplishment outside of the therapeutic office, and foster connection with the outside world in meaningful and supportive ways. Such an adjunctive piece of work will likely enhance your clinical work and foster each client's efforts at recovery in the world.

We hope clients and therapists alike will find this workbook a helpful adjunct to your work together.

To those of you for whom this workbook is your first effort, or one of many efforts, at understanding or confronting your eating disorder, we hope it will guide you toward the help and compassionate understanding that you need to begin your Journey to Recovery.

Acknowledgments

Approximately two years ago I approached my colleague and friend, Mona Villapiano, with an idea for a book. I had a vision, and needed some help turning this vision into a reality. With Mona's interest, we began to pursue this vision. Thanks to many people, we have successfully turned this vision into a reality. I would like to personally thank all the people that helped make this happen.

First of all, I would like to thank my former and current clients for all you have taught me over the years. Without you, I could not have made this happen. I would also like to thank all those individuals who devoted their time and energy to share their personal stories, poems, and illustrations. Your works are truly inspiring and are an invaluable component of this book. To Susan Christopherson, Beth Mayer, and Linda Gelda, thank you so much for the time spent editing our manuscript. Your insights and comments were greatly appreciated. To Albert Villapiano, I thank you for your knowledge of computers and your patience with Mona and me. You have been a lifesaver on more than one occasion! Tobin, I thank you for your understanding, compassion, and love. If it hadn't been for your encouraging words and *incredible* patience, I don't know if I could have completed this project. Soon our lives will be able to return to "normal" (whatever that may be). Taylor, you are too young to understand how you have helped me with this project, but thoughts of you inspired me to keep working. My desire to spend time with you kept me writing whenever I felt the need to procrastinate! Finally, to my dear friend and colleague, Mona Villapiano. Writing this book has been an experience I will always treasure! I thank you for your commitment to the field of eating disorders, and all I have learned from you over the years.

—LAURA J. GOODMAN

During the preparation of this book many people were helpful, encouraging, and supportive. To my own and my colleagues' clients who wrote personal stories and shared their poetry, and to those I don't know but who were willing to share their personal stories with me, I wish to express my sincerest thanks for your courage and generosity. I would like to thank my colleagues, Sue Christopherson, Beth Mayer, and Linda Gelda who took the time and care to review and edit this manuscript. Your comments and suggestions only made it better. To my wonderful oldest daughter, Allison, thank you for rendering such clear and powerful illustrations. Your artistic and creative talent and your wisdom never cease to amaze me. To my wonderful youngest daughter, Alexandra, your loving support and reminders to live in the moment always brought me back to earth when I got too deeply into this process. Your ability to connect with people never ceases to amaze me. And finally, to my loving and supportive husband, Albert, your patience, guidance, and professional and personal support in the preparation of this manuscript made everything possible. Without question, the many Saturdays and Sundays you spent sharing your professional and technical know-how and computer expertise with me made the challenges of manuscript submission a possibility.

To my co-author and dear friend, Laura Goodman, thank you for asking me to participate in this project with you. It was an arduous but exceedingly worthwhile journey.

—MONA VILLAPIANO

We would like to thank Jared Epps for his work on the illustrations throughout this book. Now a freshman in college, majoring in interior design, Jared has spent these past three years recovering from his battle with anorexia nervosa. Determined to find recovery, Jared is now able to use his illustrations to share the powerful experiences he faced in his journey. In addition to his expression through art, Jared has volunteered his time to help others better learn about eating disorders. His interviews can be seen in *Good Houskeeping Magazine* (August 2000), and as a part of a film developed for the First National High School Eating Disorders Screening Program. He has also provided local television interviews on WCVB TV-5 in Boston. We wish Jared well in his future endeavors, and thank him immensely for his work on the books.

We would also like to thank Allison Villapiano for her illustrations. A senior in high school, Allison has had the honor of having her artwork chosen for display in her town's education center and here in this book. We appreciate your willingness to use your creative talents to document our ideas.

Introduction

When we began to think about writing this workbook, it was with these thoughts in mind. People with eating disorders need more support than we, as therapists, can give due to the restrictions on available time and resources. Even if all the time and resources needed were available to each client, much of the work to be done must be the work of learning, reflection, practice, integration, and connection within each person's outside world. All of this cannot be done in the therapist's office. People with eating disorders need to feel empowered in their recovery process and in their world. They need to own and embrace their steps toward recovery; otherwise, gains and movement toward health will be fleeting and environmentally dependent.

People with eating disorders, like all people, flourish when they feel a sense of agency. This means they feel empowered as agents of their own change process while accepting and understanding the natural process of things. Recovery is personal. It unfolds at the pace and timing of the individual guided by some predictable and understandable principles of change. Each person benefits if she is supported at each stage of her recovery process. She must be allowed and encouraged to experience the full impact of her feelings and needs at each step along the way. She will not benefit if her process is short-circuited or circumvented by those who are in too much of a hurry to let the process unfold. The caveat to this, of course, is if she is in medical or psychiatric crisis, treatment providers, families, or the courts must take over to protect her life until she is ready to protect her own. Except in cases of imminent risk, she will travel her journey to recovery at her own pace and in her own time. Each treatment provider and loved one's task is to support and enhance the process . . . the unfolding of this journey.

Our second thought was, how can we help each person with an eating disorder understand where she is along the stages of change? Where is she in her process? What is the natural unfolding that should occur if we support her at each stage? If we are loved ones, how can we know what will be supportive and helpful at each stage? If we are treatment providers, how can we adapt our interventions to her needs at each step along her personal journey?

Our answers came from the work of James Prochaska (Prochaska, Norcross, & DiClemente, 1994) and his colleagues. Dr. Prochaska determined through years of research on people who were trying to overcome smoking and alcohol addictions, that all people change in expectable ways. The stages of change are the same no matter what problematic behavior people are trying to overcome. Most importantly, all people must go through each stage. No one stage is more important than another, and often people need to cycle through the stages multiple times before change for good can occur.

This stage theory, with its research support, seemed to bolster what we already knew but lacked empirical support for until now. This stage theory gave credence to those most uncomfortable stages of change where clients want and need to hold onto their symptoms in the face of declining health. It gave solace and support to treatment providers, loved ones, and even to those with eating disorders themselves that wanting and needing a symptom, despite powerful evidence of its destructive quality, must be understood, affirmed, and digested before it is possible to move onto the next stage of change.

Along with this theory and empirical evidence, we also embraced the work of another pioneer in the world of treatment. This is the work of Dr. Marsha Linehan (1993). Dr. Linehan concluded, after years of research and clinical study, that many of her clients did not know how to tolerate and cope with the distress of life. Although she was looking specifically at clients with Borderline Personality Disorder, her conclusions are relevant to many people with other psychiatric diagnoses or other problematic behaviors. In fact, learning to tolerate distress is a skill all people need to learn. One need not have been diagnosed with a psychiatric disorder to find benefit from her work. So too, a psychiatric diagnosis is not needed to find benefit and relevance in the work of Dr. Prochaska and his colleagues.

We, therefore, set out to provide in workbook form, information, exercises, and growth-producing challenges for people with eating disorders. People at all stages of change will find strategies and skills to enhance their ability to tolerate the distress of life without reverting to the destructive and hurtful behaviors and conclusions of the past.

We also wish to provide hope to those of you who are now suffering with eating disorders. We hope this workbook will be your benevolent companion as you work to counteract the negative and destructive internal voices of the eating disorder. We encourage you to use this workbook between therapy sessions (or as one of your supports if you are not in therapy), to assist you in becoming the loving and caring agent of your own life.

How This Workbook Works

Workbooks are meant to provide you with information and practice. This workbook asks you to be an active participant in your recovery process. If you read this book it may be helpful. If you read and *interact* with it, doing the exercises and sharing some of the tasks with a family member or loved one, it will be even more helpful.

Because this workbook is meant to provide information and participatory exercises to many different people at many different stages of change, all the information and all of the exercises may not be relevant or helpful to you at this time.

We encourage you to read and do what you are ready to read and do—to sample what the workbook has to offer. We do not encourage you to attempt to digest this workbook all at once. Interestingly, this workbook can be rejected, ingested, spit out, or thrown up like food. You can eat too much at once and feel ill or you can long for more and refuse yourself another bite. Watch your approach to this workbook—it may parallel your approach to food. Know that you can come back to certain sections at a later date; if some of it is too hard, you either need help and support with it, or you need to leave it and take in a part of it that is more digestible. It is best eaten in small and manageable chunks.

Eventually you may ingest the whole thing, if it is the right thing for you. Or you may take in the portions that are right for you and leave the rest. Invite others you trust to sample it with you.

As you sample this and other offerings in your life, you will find the right pace and timing for your work. We wish you a safe and productive journey to recovery.

Guiding Your Journey: The Tree and the Web

Before you begin your own journey to recovery, it is important to understand the role your eating disorder has served. That is, although coined an *illness*, eating disorders are *coping mechanisms*. As destructive as they are, eating disorders serve individuals by leaving them feeling protected from something larger and more terrifying than the eating disorder itself.

THE TREE

Eating disorders themselves are never the issue; they are *symptoms* of a larger issue. On the following page, you will find the diagram of a tree (Figure 1.1). In the diagram, you will notice the tree has many roots; some will be exposed (like those in the deep woods), and some will be covered (like those in a landscaped yard). We have placed the eating disorder in the middle of the trunk of the tree.

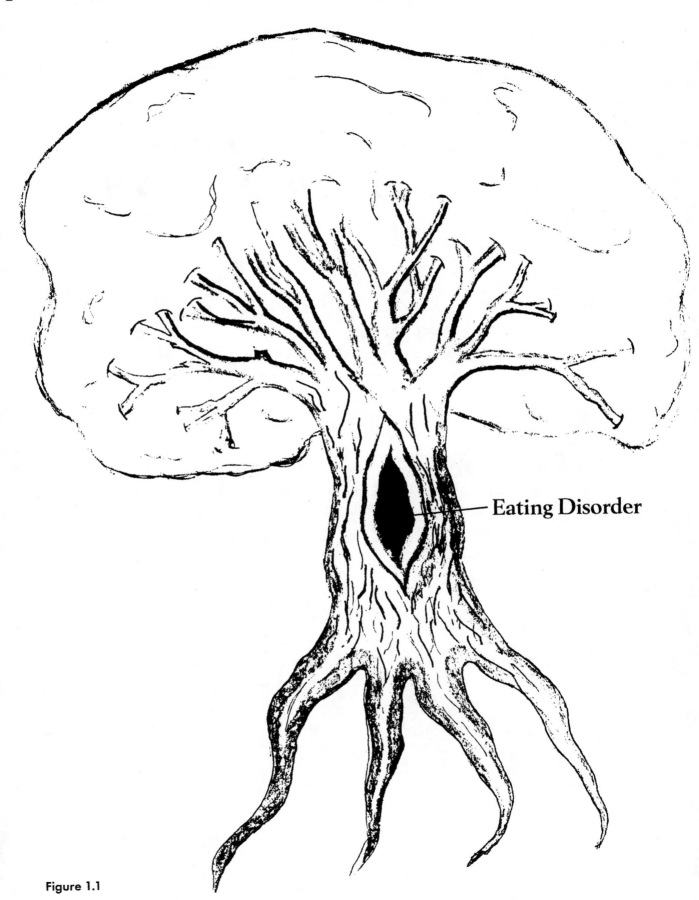

Eating Disorder

Figure 1.1

In the spaces provided, write what you believe are the roots (some underlying issues) of your eating disorder. Some may be well hidden like the covered roots. Others may be easily seen and understood like the exposed roots. Please feel free to draw grass to cover those roots you feel are not exposed. On the branches write how the eating disorder has had an impact on you (e.g., weight loss, weight gain, isolation, diminished sexual thoughts and feelings, greater control). Also on the branches write the purposes of the eating disorder. For example: "it decreases my sexual thoughts and feelings"; "I feel powerful and superior when eating less than others"; "I feel finally in control of something in my life"; "now my 'outside' matches my 'inside'"; "I feel empty and devoid of warmth"; "I feel fat and repulsive"; "I'm drying up and dying"; and "I finally feel free of others' expectations." At the end of your journey, you will find another tree. Record what you believe are the *roots* and *branches* of your eating disorder again. Did you learn anything new as you progressed through your journey? Do you now have a better understanding of your eating disorder and its purposes? These are only a few of the questions you may want to consider.

Once you have diagrammed your tree, look carefully at the words that you have written on the roots. These are the reasons for the eating disorder, as you understand them. The eating disorder has protected or shielded you from these issues. Now look carefully at the words you have written on the branches. The branches represent the purposes or the "pros" of the eating disorder. This is why your eating disorder may be hard to give up. It has served one or many purposes.

Sadly, your eating disorder (i.e., your protection . . . your shield) does not come without cost. For some its cost weighs in forms such as loss of friends, or a missed prom or other events. For others it results in lost wages, financial distress, or miscarriages. Although it serves a purpose, its costs can be dear and long lasting.

THE WEB

On the next page you will find the beginnings of a *web* (Figure 1.2). At its core is your eating disorder. The boxes growing out of the core of the web depict its various "costs." The illustration will help you draw your web. Our goal is to help you see the costs, or the "cons," of your eating disorder. What have you lost as a result of your eating disorder?

The web will help you see what price you pay for the eating disorder. We hope your *Journey to Recovery* will eliminate the costs and reap you bountiful rewards in health, safety, and happiness. However, this won't happen until you find another, more healthy and adaptive way, to protect and shield yourself (as represented by the roots) and meet the purposes or pros the eating disorder was meant to meet (as represented by the branches). Your journey through this workbook will help you find more healthy ways to protect yourself while furthering these purposes. As well, it will eliminate the costs you now pay for meeting these needs.

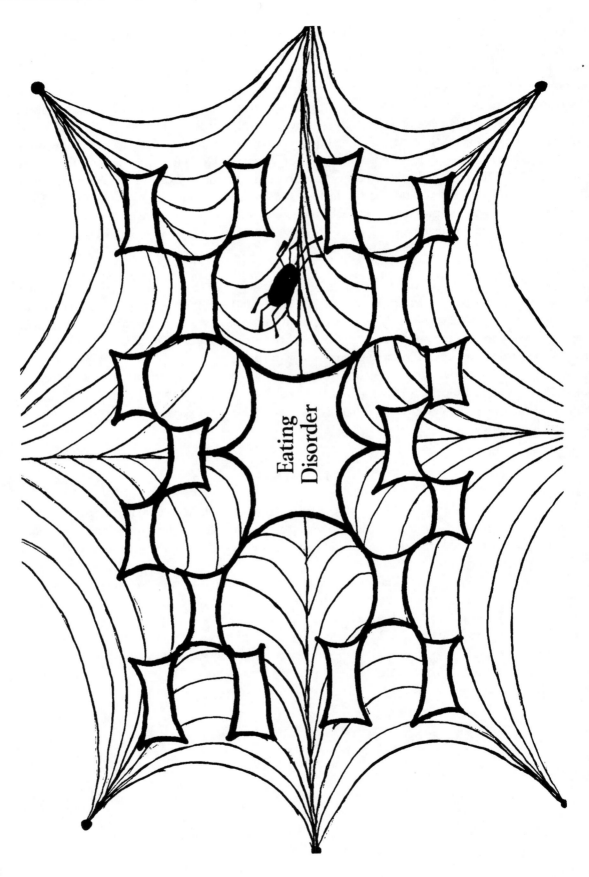

Figure 1.2

What You Need to Know About Eating Disorders

We're pretty sure you know a lot about your body and nutrition. You know the calorie content and numbers of fat grams of almost all foods. You probably know about every imaginable diet, and perhaps some we've never heard of. You've tried many of these diets, and it's likely you're on a diet or thinking of going on a diet right now.

Although you may have much information about nutrition, we want to make certain that you have all the facts. We're also hoping that if you have any misperceptions or misinformation, we can correct them for you. Our hope is that you will make choices about how you nourish yourself and take care of your body based on all the facts.

First, an important questionnaire begins your journey. Then there are a few True or False questions to start. All the answers are included in this chapter.

Answer **"yes"** or **"no"** to whether you've experienced any of these thoughts, feelings, or behaviors when you've been on a diet.

When I'm on a diet . . .

1. I feel more depressed, low or blue than when I'm not on a diet.

                    yes   **no**

2. I get easily irritated or annoyed by little things that might not otherwise irritate me.

                    yes   **no**

3. I cry more easily than usual.

                    yes   **no**

4. I sometimes choose not to go out or be with my friends because I'm worried that I'll eat.

                    yes   **no**

5. I think about food and what I'm going to eat all the time.

                    yes   **no**

6. I think I'm "good" if I eat very little and I feel ashamed and disgusted with myself if I eat more than I've told myself I should eat (or if I eat a food which I think is "bad"; i.e., not on my diet).

                    yes   **no**

7. I have trouble concentrating on my studies. I don't remember anything I read. It seems I have to work harder to do as well as I did in school or at work in the past.

                    yes   **no**

8. I feel more tense and anxious. I notice that I might smoke, pace, shake my leg or foot, or bite my nails more than I did before the diet.

                    yes   **no**

9. I find myself drinking more coffee, tea, or diet soda than I did before.

                    yes   **no**

10. I find myself chewing more gum than I did before.

                    yes   **no**

11. I don't have as much interest in my partner/significant other or I'm just not as interested in dating.

                    yes   **no**

12. I don't have as much interest in sex.

                    yes   **no**

13. I sometimes hide or sneak food because I feel so guilty wanting more.

                    yes   **no**

14. My friends, family, peers, or coworkers tell me I'm more short-tempered, less patient, or just not as easy to be around.

                    yes   **no**

15. I don't care that much to have family, friends, peers or coworkers around. I'd rather be left alone.

                    yes   **no**

16. I sometimes shoplift.

                    yes   **no**

17. I sometimes binge eat (i.e., eat a large amount of food in a small amount of time), and I feel ashamed when I do this.

                    yes   **no**

Read on and you'll see why these questions are so important.

SET POINT THEORY OR REGULATED WEIGHT

Set Point Quiz

1. All people can weigh what they want to weigh if they are motivated to diet and exercise.

         T   F

2. We are meant to be a certain weight (within a range) like we are meant to be a certain height.

         T   F

3. The less you eat, the less you'll weigh.

         T   F

According to research, our bodies, like furnaces or air conditioners, work to maintain a set point. The set point is the range of weight that our body seeks to maintain—usually a range of 5 to 10 pounds. Anything over or under this range is fiercely defended against. Our bodies resist changes in weight—up or down—just like furnaces and air conditioners set at a particular temperature resist changes in temperature up or down. They work to maintain their set point (i.e., the temperature at which they are set) just like bodies work to maintain the weight at which they are biologically set. Bodies, like thermostats, can have low, medium, and high set points. Set points don't change with fashion and cultural trends. Therefore, if your biological set point is ectomorphic (naturally thin) you will fit in with the fashion and cultural norms without much effort today. If your biological set point, however, were mesomorphic (naturally heavy) you would have fit in more naturally during the Impressionistic era when rounded, voluptuous female forms were admired. Sadly, most women (90+%) are unhappy with their body size because the cultural ideal (extremely thin) is not even possible for the vast majority of women. Their biological set point for weight is not extremely thin.

Set point is a range. With changes in diet and exercise we may seek to attain the lowest weight within our set point, but only by taxing and stressing our bodies will we achieve a weight lower than the lowest point in our set point range. Trying to weigh less than your set point compromises physical and emotional health. With no attention to diet and exercise, we may achieve the highest weight within our set point. To move over *that* weight, however, compromises physical and emotional health. In conclusion, set point theory tells us that although our weight is not as immutable, or unchangeable, as our height, our set point—or healthy weight—is changeable only within a certain range, and that range is unique to each of us. To push our bodies to gain or lose above or below that range will be heartily resisted, and likely will cause physical and emotional health consequences.

Set Point Answers

1. **False.** You can't weigh what you want to weigh and be healthy *unless you have a set point which puts you in your desirable weight range.* Motivation, diet, and exercise can help, but your body has a chosen set point, a weight that it wishes to be. A healthy diet and exercise can help you reach

the lowest point in your set point, but to get below it, you may need to severely restrict your food intake, excessively exercise, or engage in other dangerous weight loss practices. What is your body's set point? What is the weight it wishes to be? Your genetic make-up, your size, height, and age all help to determine your set point.

2. **True.** Weight can be changed . . . but if you want to be healthy, it's best to allow your body to stay within its set point. Your set point is determined by your genetic make-up, your frame size, height, and age. Healthy eating and exercise will help you to stay within your set point weight. You cannot change your height once it is reached. Factors which can interfere with your genetically determined height, however, are poor nutrition and smoking. Osteoporosis, which is bone loss or thinning, can cause a person to "shrink" in stature because bones start to "shrink" or thin. Osteoporosis usually occurs in post-menopausal women, but girls who have anorexia nervosa can also develop osteoporosis.

3. **False.** Those who eat less do not necessarily weigh less. People who eat very little may weigh less but they may also weigh more. Your metabolism and your genetic make-up may be more important in determining what you weigh than how much you eat. Also, the less you eat the slower your metabolism becomes. This is sometimes why people stop losing weight even though they're dieting. The less you eat, the slower you metabolize (burn calories).

Diet-Induced Thermogenesis

Diet-Induced Thermogenesis Quiz

1. Low-calorie diets increase metabolism (speed up the body's efforts to burn calories).

T   F

2. Low body temperature could be a sign that the person's body weight and food intake are too low.

T   F

If we turn the heating or cooling system off completely (i.e., provide it with no fuel) our homes will become too cold or too hot. If we don't give our bodies enough fuel, they will "shut off" (i.e., stop all nonessential functions) to conserve energy (i.e., "cool down"). If we give them too much fuel, they will speed up (i.e., increase metabolism by producing heat, profuse sweating, etc.) to "spill" the unneeded energy. *This process is called diet-induced thermogenesis.* This means that our metabolism (i.e., the speed and rate at which we use our calories or burn our fuel) appears to increase when we take in more calories, and decrease when we take in fewer calories.

If you are cold all the time, it may mean that you are not taking in enough fuel to warm your body. That's why your physician takes your temperature when you come in for a check-up. He wants to see if you have enough fuel to keep your temperature at about 98.6 degrees. If your temperature falls, and your weight is low, it may mean you're not taking in enough fuel (i.e., calories) to heat your body and remain healthy. Using your fuel to heat your entire body is not as essential as using your fuel to heat your vital organs. Therefore, you may experience cold, especially cold hands and feet, which are further away from your trunk where most of your vital organs exist. Once your temperature falls, it is dangerous to your health, not merely uncomfortable.

If you are hot all the time, it may mean that you are taking in too much fuel. To "waste" or get rid of the excess fuel coming in, your body burns the extra calories and produces heat. If you are taking in too much fuel (calories) regularly, you may perspire more than others to "waste" the fuel.

Therefore, if you are not taking in enough calories or fuel, your metabolism, or energy expenditure, will slow down to conserve fuel. This probably will mean that you will experience feeling cold. Your temperature may also be lower than it should be. Finally, it may mean your weight loss has stopped or slowed tremendously. Your body is fighting to survive! It does not want to lose more weight. It may be hard to believe, but a person who is perceived as overweight may experience the same symptoms as a person who appears severely underweight. Each is defending her set point. Their set points may be dramatically different, yet their experiences are the same.

This is why, no matter what some people do, they cannot lose more weight even on low-calorie diets. Or if they lose the weight, as soon as they stop the diet they regain the lost weight and sometimes more. This is the body's way to restore set point—and sometimes add a little extra—to protect against weight loss in the future. So too, if a person's weight has increased dramatically as a result of overeating, despite continued overeating, the person may not gain any more weight.

In summary, diet-induced thermogenesis is the technical explanation for why the body doesn't constantly gain weight beyond normal weight or set point even when the person continues to eat. And it explains why many people cannot lose weight beyond their normal weight or set point despite continuing to diet. The body either turns the thermostat (or metabolism) down to conserve calories when one is trying to lose weight below one's set point, or the body turns up its metabolism to "waste" or "spill" unneeded calories when one is pushing one's weight above set point. It takes great effort (extreme dieting or extreme overeating) to push one's body beyond its set point. Usually when extreme measures are halted, the body returns to its regulated weight or set point.

Although people can get their weights above or below set point with extreme measures, these measures take a toll on physical, emotional, social, and cognitive health and functioning, as will be explained in the next section.

Diet-Induced Thermogenesis Answers

1. **False.** Low-calorie diets slow down metabolism because the body attempts to conserve fuel (protect against weight loss below the person's set point). The metabolism of the men in the Keys' experiment (described in the following section) went down 40% by the end of 6 months of semi-starvation.
2. **True.** People who have lost too much weight and are taking in too few calories are likely to have low body temperature as well as other low vital signs such as blood pressure and heart rate. These are signs of the body's responses to semistarvation. The body attempts to slow down all non-vital (and *even vital*) bodily functions in an attempt to conserve fuel.

DIETING, EMOTIONS, AND COGNITION

You may believe you possess a great deal of information about the effects of dieting. Here's your chance to find out. Answer the following questions True or False. All the answers are included in this chapter.

Dieting, Emotions, and Cognition Quiz

1. Restrictive eating (dieting) and weight loss intensifies our thinking and focus on food and eating.

    T   F

2. Physically and emotionally healthy people can tolerate prolonged, low-calorie diets with no adverse side effects.

    T   F

3. People who are on prolonged, low-calorie diets exhibit the following: greater accuracy and speed on tests, good judgment, and social competence.

    T   F

4. Restrictive eating (dieting) causes binge eating.

    T   F

5. Purging behaviors like vomiting, and diuretic and laxative abuse will help you stop binge eating.

    T   F

In 1950, a scientist named Dr. Ancel Keys published a study on the effects of restrictive eating and weight loss. His subjects were 36 physically and psychologically healthy young men who were chosen among many whom had volunteered for the study as an alternative to military service. For the first 3 months of the study the experimenters closely observed the men's eating, attitudes, and behavior. During the next 6 months of the study, the men had their rations of food cut in half. So, for example, a man who had been consuming 4,000 calories per day was now allowed only 2,000 calories per day. Most of these men lost about 25% of their body weight during this 6-month period. During the next 3 months the men were gradually refed. Most of the men were followed for 9 months after the refeeding process.

What is most noteworthy about this study is that these men, although displaying a range of responses to the semistarvation study, experienced the same physical, psychological, cognitive, and social changes often seen in people who suffer from eating disorders.

We once attributed the emotional, social, and thinking changes observed in clients with eating disorders to the psychiatric diagnosis of an eating disorder. Now, we know many of these changes may be due to the semi-starvation. This means many of these changes can be corrected with refeeding and weight gain. By this, we mean, they may not *be enduring psychiatric conditions.*

This section goes through the changes that the men in the Keys study experienced and compares them to those experienced by people diagnosed with eating disorders.

Thoughts and Behaviors Related to Food and Eating

The men in the study were preoccupied with *food thoughts*. They began reading women's magazines to study the recipes. They began reading cookbooks and discussing food and recipes with the other men in the study. Many of them developed interests in food-related occupations (although none of them had these occupations prior to the study). Some of them even changed their occupations after the study was over.

The men spent most of their waking time thinking about how they would eat their allotment of food. Once eating, much of their focus was on the food, not socializing. They would design elaborate rituals to make the food last, such as by mixing, cutting, and pushing the food around their plates, as well as by eating very slowly to make each bite last. Some of the men would make their meals last up to two hours so they could extend the experience of eating. This would often alternate with the desire to ravenously gulp the food down to assuage their mounting hunger. The men often felt pulled in both directions—either to devour everything in sight as quickly as they could, or to make each morsel last as long as they could by extending the meal over hours. These competing desires created great distress and anxiety around eating.

To make the experience of eating more salient and satisfying, many of the men began to use spices excessively or mix incongruous combinations of foods together. Some of the men also increased their consumption of coffee and tea dramatically . . . so much so that the men were limited to 9 cups per day. Gum chewing also increased dramatically to the point where one man was chewing 40 packs per day. He chewed so much that his mouth began to hurt and, thus, he was no longer allowed gum. It seems as if the men felt so deprived of adequate food that keeping their mouths busy with chewing or swallowing—or filling their stomachs with non nutritive substances like coffee and tea or air from chewing—were small ways to assuage the pain and deprivation of their mounting hunger.

Some of the men found the restrictive eating intolerable. They could not follow the diet and they smuggled food. Sometimes men ate such large amounts that they experienced nausea and vomiting. All the men who reported binge-eating episodes reported feeling disgust and guilt because they could not adhere to the diet.

Some of the men experienced such extreme episodes of binge eating once the refeeding phase of the study began, that they needed to be removed from the experiment. In one case a man's binge eating was so extreme that he became sick, aspirated his vomit, and had to be hospitalized. Some of the men reported that no matter how much they ate they could not feel satisfied; others reported that they felt hungrier after eating than before. Some began to believe that the only way to control their binge eating was not to eat at all.

For some of the men, binge eating persisted for 9 months. Within 5 months, most men had their eating under control and returned to baseline eating (meaning the way they were eating during the first 3 months of the experiment when they could eat what and how much they wanted).

What we have learned about the behaviors, thoughts, and attitudes we see in those who suffer with eating disorders is that many of the symptoms that we might think of as primary psychiatric symptoms, may actually be artifacts of the restricted eating and weight loss. The diet itself (which is often akin to semistarvation) may cause the extreme binge eating behaviors observed in the men in Keys' experiment and in clients who suffer from eating disorders. In sum, restricted eating and weight loss over prolonged periods may precipitate thoughts, behaviors, and attitudes that are often interpreted as the psychiatric symptoms of eating disorders.

Emotional and Personality Changes

As we said before, the men chosen for Keys' study were psychologically healthy. Yet even these psychologically robust men experienced marked emotional distress during this experiment. Many of the men reported feeling their emotional changes were severe enough to interfere with their functioning. As the experiment went on, the men reported feeling more and more depressed. Mood swings, irritability, outbursts of anger, and episodes of tearfulness became more prominent with the continuation of the experiment. Many of the men reported feeling more anxious and began biting their nails or smoking. Men who had normally experienced interest and joy in activities became apathetic, no longer showing interest or joy in anything.

For some men the restricted eating and weight loss phase of the experiment became so intolerable, they developed disturbing psychiatric symptoms and had to be removed from the experiment. One compulsively looked through garbage cans for food scraps and another began shoplifting and became violent and suicidal. Both were psychiatrically hospitalized.

Although they experienced emotional deterioration during the period of restricted eating and weight loss, *some men became more depressed, angry, difficult, and negativistic during the refeeding phase of the experiment.* One man reported feeling so depressed, that he felt the only thing that would help would be release from the experiment. However, before that could occur, he chopped off three fingers in response to the stress.

Changes in Thinking

During the restricted eating and weight loss phase of the experiment, the men reported that their concentration and focus were impaired. They also experienced a decrease in alertness and exhibited poor judgment. According to formal intellectual testing, however, their intellectual abilities remained intact.

This means that although the men retained all of their intellectual capabilities, they struggled more to use them, as they could not concentrate as they had in the past; they were often "foggy" and fatigued and their choices and behaviors no longer showed good judgment.

Social and Sexual Changes

Men who had been gregarious began to isolate. Men who had enjoyed social activity no longer sought others out and felt that it was burdensome to socialize. Interestingly, one man mentioned that the only thing he enjoyed when he went to a movie was watching the scenes where people were eating.

Men who would have formerly enjoyed visits from their partners, no longer cared to see them. Those who continued their relationships saw them deteriorate and become strained. Men who had sexual interests prior to the experiment, no longer experienced any sexual desire. Perhaps most noteworthy was Dr. Keys' finding that many of the men felt relieved to be free of the sexual tensions and frustrations normally present in young adult males. Freedom from growing sexuality, and the concomitant choices and responsibilities, is hypothesized to be one of the reasons that anorexia nervosa may take hold in young women. Some believe that Dr. Keys' experiment on semistarvation suggests that restrictive eating is one of the factors that lead to the development of anorexia nervosa.

PHYSICAL CHANGES

Most of the men experienced the physical changes often reported by people suffering from eating disorders: (a) feeling cold, especially cold hands and feet; (b) hair loss; (c) dizziness; (d) headaches; (e) sleep disturbances; (f) weakness; (g) edema (swelling caused by fluid retention); (h) sensitivity to light and noise; and (i) stomach upset and general gastrointestinal discomfort.

Metabolism

As discussed earlier, so often, people with eating disorders think that continuing to restrict their intake will lead to decreased weight. This does happen for a while, and, tragically, for some it happens until they die. The body, however, is working to compensate for the restricted eating by slowing its physiological processes (like decreasing its heart rate and temperature) which means there will be greater and greater reductions in metabolic rate (i.e., the body is using fewer and fewer calories to stay alive). So, the less food you take in, the fewer calories the body will burn. This means that eating more increases the body's metabolism, and therefore burns more calories. Read on and you will see the proof.

Dr. Keys found in his study that *by the end of the semistarvation phase of the study (6 months of restricted eating) the metabolism of the men had been reduced by 40%.* This means that the men's bodies, in response to the deprivation imposed by semistarvation, burned 40% fewer calories than they did when they were eating normally (e.g., double what they were eating during the restriction phase of the experiment). Their bodies compensated for restrictive eating by burning fewer calories. So, the more you restrict your food, the fewer calories you will burn. Even more interestingly, Dr. Keys found that those who ate larger amounts during the refeeding phase of the experiment (as opposed to those who increased their eating only by small increments) had the greatest increases in metabolism. When they ate more, they burned more.

Dr. Keys also found that it took up to 9 months following the refeeding phase of the experiment for many of the men to return to normal eating (the eating they engaged in during the first 3 months of the experiment) and to normal weight. Many of the men experienced the same discomfort with their bodies that we see in people with eating disorders who regain lost weight. Many reported feeling "fat" and uncomfortable. The majority of the men regained their pre-experiment weight plus 10%, which they gradually lost over the next 6 months.

This experiment indicates how strongly the body resists weight loss below set point; how devastating restrictive eating and weight loss over a prolonged period of time are on psychological, cognitive, and social functioning; and how many of the symptoms associated with weight loss and restrictive eating disappear with gradual return to normal weight and normal eating.

Stopping restrictive eating and regaining lost weight is the cure for many of the psychological, cognitive, and social symptoms associated with eating disorders, even when the period of refeeding brings with it tremendous emotional turmoil. Staying the course gradually brings about physical and emotional health.

Dangers Associated with Purging Behaviors

Some clients with eating disorders believe the way to combat the effects of overeating or binge eating is through vomiting, excessive exercising, or abuse of diet pills, diuretics, and laxatives.

These are, at best, temporary solutions; at worst they could be fatal. Purging reinforces binge eating because it provides a short-cut solution to addressing the problem of binge eating. This short-cut never solves the problem; usually it makes it worse. Binge eating can be lessened by normal eating; by this we mean, no more restrictive eating, such as eating too little or skipping meals.

Vomiting is very harsh and stressful to your gastrointestinal system. In effect, you are teaching your GI tract to work backwards. The more you push it to work backwards, the more difficulty it will have working in the way it was intended—taking food and drink from the mouth and moving it through the body to the point of elimination. Instead, you are telling it to expel what it has taken in by mouth.

Eventually, you may notice several things will happen to you because of vomiting. First, you may develop mouth sores, a sore throat, burning in your throat, and reflux (the food comes up in your mouth naturally). You may also notice that you are developing swollen parotid glands (the glands under your jawbone, which gives the appearance of "chipmunk cheeks"), and bloodshot eyes because the purging is so forceful it will break blood vessels in your eyes. When you go to the dentist he may find many cavities and, because the vomit is so acidic and corrosive and has worn the enamel off your teeth, you'll likely need extensive dental work or cosmetic dentistry to restore your teeth.

If you haven't already, you may begin to develop stomach pains and you may become constipated. This occurs because your food is not moving through your system normally. Basically, your GI system (gastrointestinal system) no longer knows how to work. It's out of practice and in distress because of it.

Diuretics and diet pills rid your system of needed fluids. The fluid loss makes it look as if you've lost weight, but you haven't. You have merely lost needed fluid, which puts you at risk for dehydration. The primary symptoms of dehydration are: (a) dizziness, (b) fainting, (c) heart arrhythmias, (d) mental distress, and (e) kidney and liver problems. Vomiting and laxative abuse also lead to dehydration, a potentially severe consequence of purging.

Laxative abuse causes severe discomfort, profuse diarrhea, and nausea. At it's most lethal, it destroys bowel function, rendering a person unable to eliminate on her own. Before it is that damaging, a person abusing laxatives often becomes dependent on them, needing more and more for regular elimination. Laxatives also cause severe dehydration leading to the symptoms described in the prior paragraph.

Excessive exercise, especially in a person already engaging in other purging behaviors or restrictively eating, may lead to severe dehydration, muscle tears, and bone fractures.

In conclusion, purging is a short-cut attempt to ward off the negative effects of binge eating. It is not a long-term solution, and often leads to more binge eating, medical complications, and psychological debilitation. Now check the answers to the Dieting, Emotions, and Cognitions Quiz below.

Dieting, Emotions, and Cognitions Answers

1. **True.** According to Dr. Keys' study, men who didn't normally think about food started reading women's magazines to focus on the food and recipes, or started enjoying movies solely for the purpose of watching the scenes of people eating. Prolonged dieting, or semistarvation, caused these changes.

2. **False.** Dr. Keys found that men who had been psychologically healthy (they had no emotional symptoms or psychiatric histories) developed mood swings, became depressed, apathetic, irritable, argumentative, and, in a few cases, developed symptoms so severe they had to be removed from the experiment and hospitalized. In sum, physically and psychologically healthy men developed emotional, personality, social, cognitive, and physical changes as a result of prolonged semistarvation, weight loss, and refeeding.

3. **False.** According to the data in Dr. Keys' study, some of the cognitive changes experienced by the men were slowed down response time, slowed alertness, and poor judgment. Some of the social and sexual changes experienced were isolation (a desire not to be with people and socialize) and decreased sexual desire, which negatively impacted on their relationships with their partners.

4. **True.** Many of the men in the Keys study could not continue on the semistarvation diet without episodes of binge eating, for which they felt terrible remorse and guilt. During the refeeding phase of the experiment, some of the men regularly engaged in binge eating as a response to the prolonged food deprivation.

5. **False.** Purging by vomiting and abuse of diuretics and laxatives promotes continued binge eating. To stop binge eating, one must return to regular, consistent eating and stop restrictive eating and dieting.

How did you do? Did you learn anything new? Were you surprised by any of the data from the study by Dr. Keys?

CONCLUSION

Here's a re-cap of the major points of this chapter along with a preview activity for the next chapter.

You have learned about *set point theory*, the body's tenacious seeking of it's unique weight range and its intense defense of weight loss below or weight gain above set point.

You have learned about *diet-induced thermogenesis*, the body's tendency to "shut down" all energy expenditures (i.e., calorie burning) that is nonessential until the body is taking in more food (i.e., fuel) at which point it will "spill" unneeded calories and burn calories at a faster pace.

We discussed *Dr. Ancel Keys' study* where prolonged restrictive eating, weight loss, and eventual refeeding caused physically and psychologically healthy men to develop many of the social, emotional, cognitive, and behavioral changes experienced by people with eating disorders. Refeeding and return to normal weight eventually restored most of these men to physical and psychological health.

We covered the *dangers of purging behaviors* and how they promote binge eating and lead to potentially dire medical and psychological consequences.

We also began to look at the power of affirmations in improving our relationship with food.

The goal of the next chapter is to help you develop your own personal plan for normalizing your eating, normalizing your weight, stopping purging behaviors, and restoring your physical and emotional health. It may be difficult at first but the strategies and plans provided have been proven to help people with eating disorders move into recovery.

PREVIEW TO IMPROVING YOUR RELATIONSHIP WITH FOOD

First, get some file cards and get ready to write your way to healthier thinking and behavior!

Your behavior follows your thinking. Try to do some cognitive restructuring (change your thinking) by writing down some of these affirmations and posting them around your house. If you practice these and refer to them often, you might find your thinking and behavior around food changing for the better.

Affirmations

1. I am lovable no matter what my size.

2. Food is neither good nor bad, but in moderation all foods provide nourishment for my body, mind, and soul.

3. I deserve to eat 3 normal-sized, well-balanced meals per day.

4. If I am thinking only of food, what am I avoiding thinking?

5. My body will find its normal, healthy weight as I eat normally.

6. Treating myself well may feel uncomfortable at first, but as I continue to do it, day by day, it will feel right and good.

7. Too much or too little food numbs my feelings and erases my ability to be free and alive. Eating in a balanced way makes me feel great.

8. If I feed my brain appropriately, I will think clearly, and I will be able to function optimally at school, work, in my therapy, and even in this workbook.

Your Relationship with Food

So far you have learned about the various eating disorders to be addressed in this book, and the clinical criteria associated with each disorder. Through this awareness, we see why the medical profession coins eating disorders as "illnesses." As you travel through this workbook, you should have a better understanding that eating disorders are not necessarily illnesses, but rather, faulty coping mechanisms. Though destructive in nature, your eating disorder has developed as a way to help you tolerate painful experiences/feelings in your life. Successful recovery comes when the eating disorder no longer serves the benefit that it once served. In other words, recovery from anorexia nervosa, bulimia, and compulsive overeating takes place when the individual becomes aware that what has appeared to be serving a beneficial purpose has now become more of a detriment than a benefit.

How "ready" are you to recover? Are you ready to let go of the behaviors that you now see as harmful to yourself, and allow yourself to sit with those uncomfortable feelings that are underneath the eating disorder? Are you feeling strong enough to begin to fight back to the bullying of the eating disorder voice and risk change? If you are feeling ready, but don't know how to proceed, this book will help you. You will begin by looking at your relationship with food and the behaviors and thoughts that you want to change. Before you can successfully begin your recovery, you need to explore your relationship with food. In doing so, you will take some important steps in this chapter. First, you will identify behaviors and thoughts that you want to change, and second, you will develop strategies that will make those changes happen. Begin by answering the following questions. As you continue with this workbook, you will explore these questions in greater depth. Refer to the illustration of the food pyramid if you're not sure what groups the foods that you eat or avoid are from.

THE FOOD PYRAMID

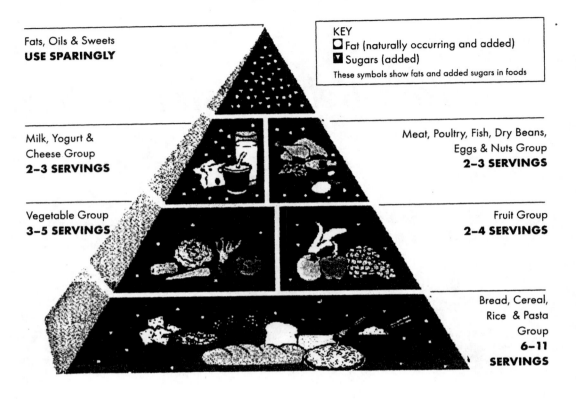

Fats, Oils & Sweets
USE SPARINGLY

KEY
▢ Fat (naturally occurring and added)
▼ Sugars (added)
These symbols show fats and added sugars in foods

Milk, Yogurt &
Cheese Group
2-3 SERVINGS

Meat, Poultry, Fish, Dry Beans,
Eggs & Nuts Group
2-3 SERVINGS

Vegetable Group
3-5 SERVINGS

Fruit Group
2-4 SERVINGS

Bread, Cereal,
Rice & Pasta
Group
6-11
SERVINGS

Do you eat foods from all the food groups at each meal? _____

What foods do you avoid? Why? _____

_____

Are you eating enough to satisfy your hunger?	____ Yes	____ No
Are you skipping meals?	____ Yes	____ No
Are you eating 1-3 healthy snacks per day (depending on your need to reduce bingeing urges at low times of the day like late afternoon or evening before bed)?	____ Yes	____ No
Are you spacing your meals appropriately (at about four hour intervals)?	____ Yes	____ No

COMMON EATING PROBLEMS

What are your current eating problems? Using the list below, circle the eating problems that you are having now. Put an asterisk (*) next to the eating problems that you once had but no longer have.

unconscious eating (unaware that you are eating) eating too quickly skipping meals

eating late at night binge eating compulsively overeating fasting

eating too much of a certain food eating for emotional reasons

closet eating eating to prevent hunger eating when too hungry

eating in response to the clock eating while preparing meals

eating in rooms other than the kitchen or dining room eating more on the weekends

eating on the run eating to fall asleep at night restrictive eating

restricting fats restricting protein restricting dairy restricting carbohydrates

counting calories difficulty eating with others eating more when alone

other (please explain): _____

Now, list behaviors and attitudes around food and eating that you would like to change. Here is an example: *Stop eating out of cartons and boxes while standing up.*

1) _____

2) _____

3) _____

4) _____

5) _____

6) _____

7) _____

Congratulations! You have just completed the first step on your journey to recovery. Now let's look at the behaviors and attitudes you want to change. If restrictive eating is an area of concern for you, please complete the questionnaire on Restriction. If compulsive overeating is an area of concern for you, refer to the Compulsive Overeating questionnaire, and if binge eating is of concern, refer to the questionnaire on Binge Eating and Purging. If you are aware that all are areas of concern for you, please complete each section.

FOOD RESTRICTION

Restriction: an act of limiting. People with eating disorders restrict in many different ways. Some may restrict fat intake, yet eat a large amount of "fat free" foods. Others may restrict their intake of calories. This exercise is designed to help you clarify how your difficulties with restriction get expressed, and develop alternatives to "fight your urge to restrict." Balance and moderation in eating are the goals. List your restrictive behaviors and attitudes. Write what you might do to challenge these behaviors or attitudes. Here are two examples:

(1) **Restrictive behavior or attitude:** *I can't eat anything with fat. I believe one mouthful of a food with fat will make me fat.* **How to challenge this behavior:** *Other people eat foods with fat in them and they don't gain weight with every mouthful. I've been told I need some fat in my diet. I will try to eat low-fat instead of no-fat yogurt and tell myself this is good for my health.*

(2) **Restrictive behavior or attitude:** *I should never eat cookies. I am overweight and I don't feel deserving of even one. People who see an overweight person eating something like a cookie think she has no willpower.* **How to challenge this behavior:** *I like cookies and I feel angry and deprived when I feel I can't have even one. So, in the presence of others, I eat none; but when I'm home alone I eat the whole bag. Then I feel disgusted with myself. If I told myself I could have one serving of cookies when I want them—even when in the presence of others—I would feel less like eating the whole bag when I'm alone. I'm sure it is worse for my physical and emotional health to eat a whole bag than one serving of cookies. This plan will help me take better care of myself.*

1) Restrictive behavior or attitude: _____

Things to do to challenge this behavior: _____

_____

_____

_____

_____

2) Restrictive behavior or attitude: _____

Things to do to challenge this behavior: _____

_____

_____

_____

_____

3) Restrictive behavior or attitude: _____

Things to do to challenge this behavior: _____

_____

_____

_____

_____

Strategies for Reducing Restrictive Eating

1. Eat with someone to help challenge yourself, while minimizing the focus on food.
2. Listen to soft music during mealtime/snack time.
3. Measure foods to make sure you aren't skimping on the serving size.
4. Plan meals/snacks ahead of time.
5. Plan to do something after the meal/snack to help with any feelings that may surface.
6. Write your feelings and observations in a journal after meals/snacks.
7. Practice allowing the "healthy voice" to have the last word over the "eating disorder voice."

COMPULSIVE OVEREATING

Compulsive overeating is defined as eating more than what the body requires to satisfy physical hunger. Although seen as a "choice," people who struggle with compulsive overeating do not feel in control of their behaviors. The difference between compulsive overeating and bingeing will be described on page 23. The questions below should help you understand what factors might contribute to your compulsive overeating. After answering the questions you'll find a list of recommendations to help combat compulsive overeating. We've allowed extra space for you to add to the list of recommendations.

Compulsive Overeating Questionnaire

1. Where do you do your eating (e.g., kitchen, bedroom, closet, car, etc.)?

_____

2. What are you doing when you are eating (e.g., watching TV, driving, etc.)?

_____

_____

_____

_____

_____

3. How are you positioned when you are eating (e.g., standing, eating on the run, sitting, lying on the bed, etc.)?

_____

4. What percentage of the time would you say you are eating out of physical hunger?

_____

5. Do you think you might be eating to "stuff down" emotions?   ___Yes ___No
   If "yes," what do you think you are feeling when you choose to eat?

_____

6. Can you taste your food when you are eating?   ___Yes ___No

7. Do you have a tendency to overeat at meals?   ___Yes ___No

8. Do you have a tendency to snack a lot between meals?   ___Yes ___No

9. Do you eat quickly, or do you eat slowly and savor every bite? _____

Now write down the behaviors and attitudes you want to change and the ways you might try to challenge yourself. Here is an example. **Overeating Behavior:** *As soon as I get home from work, I climb into bed, turn on the TV, and snack non-stop until I fall asleep. I never make myself dinner. I know I'm snacking all the time because I never feel satisfied.* **Things to do to challenge this behavior:** *Maybe I'd feel better if I made dinner. It seems such a waste to make dinner just for me. Maybe that's the problem! I don't think I'm worth a good, healthy dinner, but I am!*

1. Overeating behavior: _____
   Things to do to challenge this behavior:

   _____

   _____

   _____

   _____

   _____

2. Overeating behavior: _____
   Things to do to challenge this behavior:

   _____

   _____

   _____

   _____

   _____

3. Overeating behavior: _____
   Things to do to challenge this behavior:

   _____

   _____

   _____

   _____

   _____

BINGE EATING AND PURGING

Binge eating is similar to compulsive overeating. In both behaviors people eat more than what they need to satisfy physical hunger. The key difference between binge eating and compulsive overeating is that binge eaters will eat a large amount of food in a brief period of time, and will feel very much out of control. Although many compulsive eaters do not feel "in control," they appear to have a greater ability to "stay present." Binge eaters often report feeling "not present"; it is as if they are in a trance when they are eating. This trance-like condition is usually followed by feelings of tremendous guilt when they "re-connect" with their bodies. This reconnection tends to take place when the binge eater is feeling so physically full and uncomfortable that she/he again feels "in his/her body."

Purging is an attempt to "get rid" of food, and therefore calories. Purging methods include vomiting, laxative and diuretic use, enemas, and excessive exercise. Some people with binge eating disorder or bulimia fast following binges to get rid of calories. If you are struggling with binge eating and/or purging, answer the following questions before continuing on.

Think of the last time you had a binge-eating episode.

1. What were you feeling before you ate?_____

2. How did you feel after eating?   Satisfied _____   Full _____   Stuffed _____

3. Did you feel "present" while you were eating, or did you feel somewhat disconnected from your actions?
                          Present _____   Disconnected _____

4. Where do you generally do your binge eating? (please check all those that apply)
   kitchen _____   living room _____   family room _____   dining room _____
   bedroom _____   bathroom _____   car _____   alone _____
   with friends/family _____

5. When you are binge eating, are you physically hungry?   Yes _____ No _____

6. If you answered "No" on question 5, do you know what you are really hungry for?   Yes _____ No_____
   If "yes," please explain: _____

7. How uncomfortable are you with your binge eating behaviors?
   Not at all uncomfortable _____   Somewhat uncomfortable _____
   Uncomfortable _____   Very uncomfortable _____   Extremely uncomfortable ___

Challenging Binge Eating Behaviors

Write down the binge eating behaviors you would like to change. After each behavior, please record at least three strategies you can practice to delay/prevent binge eating. Example: **Binge eating behavior:** *If I have one bite of chocolate or some other food I think is "bad," I feel like a failure, and say 'who cares, I blew it anyway!' and, I eat everything in sight because I'm just going to throw it up anyway.* **Strategies to delay/prevent binge eating:** *I don't have to 'eat everything in sight' because I've had one bite of a "bad" food. I will try to tell myself its o.k. to eat foods I like and crave. Once I've eaten them I need to tell myself its o.k. to let my stomach digest them. This will be hard, so I'm going to take a walk, call my friend, or write in my journal so I won't binge or purge.*

1. Binge eating behavior: _____
   Things to do to challenge this behavior:

   _____
   _____
   _____
   _____
   _____

2. Binge eating behavior: _____
   Things to do to challenge this behavior:

   _____
   _____
   _____
   _____
   _____

3. Binge eating behavior: _____
   Things to do to challenge this behavior:

   _____
   _____
   _____
   _____
   _____

For Your Information!

Laxatives, vomiting, diuretics, and diet pills are not effective methods of weight loss. This is why many people suffering from bulimia are of average or above-average weight. These are the reasons:

1. Laxative abuse rids the body of *at most* 12% of caloric absorption—that is, the changes in weight due to laxative abuse are the results of diarrhea and water loss . . . not calories.
2. Vomiting is not entirely effective in removing food from the body. What vomiting does do, however, is perpetuate hunger by eliminating the fuel (food) we need to keep our bodies running. Thus, people who induce purging through vomiting may be more likely to set themselves up for binge eating as they are deprived of necessary fuel.
3. Diuretics have absolutely no impact on weight loss other than temporary water loss.
4. Diet pills have also been found to offer absolutely no proof of weight loss . . . the only weight loss as a result of diet pills will be in your wallet!

If you have ever engaged in any purging behaviors, please answer the following questions:

1. Had you binged before purging?   Yes _____ No _____

2. How often do you engage in purging behaviors?
   1–3 times weekly _____   4–7 times weekly _____   8 or more times weekly _____
   1–3 times per month _____   1–3 times every three months _____
   1–3 times every six months _____   1–3 times every nine to twelve months

3. Please check all those methods of purging in which you engage.
   self-induced vomiting _____   laxative use _____   diet pills _____
   diuretics _____   enemas _____   excessive exercise _____
   starvation _____   other (please explain): _____

4. How do you feel after purging?_____

5. How uncomfortable are you with your purging behaviors?
   Not at all uncomfortable _____   Somewhat uncomfortable _____
   Uncomfortable _____   Very uncomfortable _____   Extremely uncomfortable _____

Recommendations for Controlling Overeating and Binge Eating

1. Arrange to eat in one room only.
2. Do not eat while watching TV, reading, or engaging in emotional discussions.
3. Purchase individual-serving-sized snacks instead of regular or family-sized bags.
4. Do not "diet"—diets are a set-up for failure. Instead, work on "legalizing" food; this means incorporating "risk" foods into your meal plan on a regular (scheduled if necessary) basis.
5. Do not skip meals.
6. Sit down when eating, and focus on the food you are eating. Feel the texture of the food in your mouth. Take your time while eating; placing your utensils down between bites can be helpful.
7. Do not allow yourself to get too hungry before eating. Allow yourself snacks between meals as a way to prevent overeating.
8. The meal should have offerings from protein, grains, dairy, vegetable, and fruit groups, and should consist of adequate caloric intake.
9. Normalized eating, not dieting, is the first rule of recovery for all including those who are significantly overweight.
10. Meals should be spaced appropriately. Spacing may have to be rigidly tied to specific times during the day to reduce the tendency to delay eating or to overeat at certain times of the day.
11. Rigid spacing meets the goal of reducing hunger, but also it takes advantage of *diet-induced thermogenesis*. Frequent "stoking of the furnace" with fuel burns more calories. Consuming the same number of calories in fewer meals appears to lead to a greater accumulation of body fat. For example, rats fed two large meals a day gained as much as three times as much body fat as those allowed to freely "nibble" those same calories spread throughout the course of the day.

Three important steps have been accomplished: You have begun to explore your relationship with food; you've identified behaviors that have led to the development and maintenance of your eating disorder; and you have also begun to explore alternative strategies to combat these destructive patterns. The next step is to understand *why* you abuse food and your body. Before beginning, let's try to understand what purpose the eating disorder has served. Intellectually, you understand the pros of change, meaning you understand the reasons why you *should* change your eating behaviors. But, do you understand the *cons* of change, meaning the reasons why you *should not* change? It may feel odd to discuss why you should *keep* your eating disorder. It's unhealthy. It's costly. It's shameful. It's deadly. Yes, these things are true. However, at some point in your life it helped you survive. Understanding the *cons* of change means honoring and respecting the purpose the eating disorder served in the beginning. Only when you understand this, can you begin to give up the eating disorder. It is always difficult to leave a *friend*, even a *hurtful friend* like the eating disorder. We're going to introduce you to a theory of change discovered by Dr. Jim Prochaska and his colleagues. We believe this theory will help you understand why you must go through the stage of Contemplation (the stage where you explore *why you should not change*, or the *cons* of change, before you can prepare to change).

MY JOURNEY OUT OF COMPULSIVE OVEREATING AND OBESITY

When asked to write my story, I was faced with telling the facts of a 40-year history and the feelings I have come to understand at 52 years old. Learning to make choices and take control has enabled me to replace the numb third person I had created to cope with pain I was unable to feel.

I am now able to release and acknowledge the person I had buried 40 years ago. I had remained a child in an adult body up until the past few months. I now realize that the past can not be re-cycled, the present can not be changed; only the future can be affected. I can not recover the lost years when my compulsive overeating gave me a safe place to hide—most of all from myself. I ate secretly; I hid and ate in my car and in toilets in restaurants late at night. I was burying myself alive. I chose never to grow up, because that would have meant becoming responsible for my own choices, actions, and decisions. I would have had to stop running.

I have no recollection of my early childhood. Why that is, for now, remains in the past. From my adolescence to 19 years old, I started to discover that living my life for and through others was safe. Remaining a child enabled me to accept the unacceptable. I was 19 years old and pregnant—my parents, together with the social workers, decided for me that I had no choice. I signed away my son, the only child I would ever have. I never shed a tear, but I did eat my way from 232 pounds to 405 pounds in 6 years.

The person I had created cried in anger, never in pain. While introducing 16 successful romantic relationships among my friends, I never even dreamed of a wedding for myself. I was surrogate mother to my friends and family. I had become skilled at living in my counterfeit lifestyle; at 32 years old I was diagnosed as morbidly obese.

As a last-ditch effort I turned to a surgeon to have my stomach stapled. When he informed me that this procedure was not medically sound for me, I considered this a death sentence. He had slammed the door on my last hope and I openly blamed him for my inevitable death. After my accusation he did open a door for me, by offering to surgically treat my recurrent bleeding ulcer. If I were ever to find my way out of the spin cycle of abuse and failure this was a necessary step.

At 34 years old, my father had his first heart attack. Like myself, he lived a 25-year history of illness. Frequently accused of immaturity and told to be serious and grow up, he would respond, "If I took my life seriously, I would not be able to take it." The night before my ulcer surgery he said encouragingly, "Believe you will make it. Never lose your sense of humor. Fight for life one step, one moment at a time." Upon being told that I almost had not survived the surgery, I was faced with what I now recognize as my first conscious choice. I now had a chance for physical as well as emotional recovery and the responsibility to embark on a path to control my own recovery. This served as the catalyst, I chose to fight back and live.

The path was not without detours and roadblocks. The years surrounding the surgery were filled with personal tragedies—both my parents died within 2 years of each other (at 57 years old), I also lost my grandmother and sister-in-law (two best friends to me). I cried my way to and from work, and then there were those lonely, empty nights filled with my secret life. I was in the spin cycle and screamed out, "Stop the merry-go-round, I want to get off!" Too much pain, too many empty bags, the third person declared to the world, "get off my back, my life, my choice. No more diets—too many failures!"

Continued

There was no specific light-bulb moment; only minor commitments, which involved learning to make choices, then only minor changes. I never felt deprived, I never denied myself. I made absolutely no change in my choice of foods—I would just leave a little over on my plate every time I ate. Within a few short months, just reducing my portions was resulting in weight loss.

That success led to my second life-long commitment, to eat on a small plate whatever I wanted. No longer living on remote control was not an overnight transition. With success came strength—each minor change lead to awareness of my triggers for eating and compulsive behavior.

In the next 10 years following the surgery, I learned to apply these new skills to gain control. In hindsight, I realize that only 3 years ago did I cease being controlled by the abusive codependant world I created. I had truly finally learned that power of choice was the path not the destination.

My real success is knowing that I can still fumble and even fail in making good choices, but I am now aware of the difference. This process has led me to freedom to grow, to let go of the anger and pain.

At 50 years old, I was finally ready for new beginnings—finally ready to cross the finish line and change my choice of foods. The 250 pounds I have lost is a by-product of this metamorphosis. I no longer live life as a third person. I am aware of my feelings, I can cry when I hurt, but most of all, I have been able to love and be loved in return. I now have goals and the power to achieve them!

Yvonne, age 52

WHAT STAGE ARE YOU IN?

Before we begin, let's take a brief look at Prochaska's stages of change theory. Prochaska and colleagues (1994) set out to understand why some people—those who do and do not seek professional help—either succeed in changing unwanted and problematic behaviors, or do not. What they found was that most treatment programs, for a large number of problems, meet people at the *Action* stage of change, yet less than 20% of people who seek change are actually at that stage of change. Therefore, excellent programs often fail . . . not because they are not good, but because they are good only for the small segment of the population that is ready to change *now*. In Stages of Change theory, it is known, accepted, and understood, that most people who are in treatment are not ready for change at the Action stage. But they may be ready for an intervention at an earlier stage of change. According to Prochaska and colleagues, there are six stages of change: Precontemplation, Contemplation, Preparation, Action, Maintenance, and Termination.

These stages are predictable, follow for all people no matter what problematic behavior they want to change, and are of equal importance in the change process. The researchers have found that matching the intervention to the client's stage of change yields better results than does imposing an intervention that does not match the client's stage of change. Why do we feel this information is important for you? Because it is important that you understand what stage you are in for the various problematic eating behaviors *before* you take action. Understanding your stage will yield increased understanding, and ultimately a greater likelihood of recovery. Below you will find brief definitions of each of Prochaska's stages of change. Write down what stage you think you're in for each of the eating-disordered behaviors. Here is an example of what we mean: You may know others think you should stop eating so restrictively, but you may like your restrictive eating. You may want to keep it. If this is the case, you are in Precontemplation about your restrictive eating. This means that even if everyone else thinks it's a problem, you don't. You are not even ready to think about changing it. However, you can't stand your binge eating. You want to stop it and you want to stop it now, but you don't know how. In this case you may be in the stage of Preparation for your binge-eating behavior. This means you want to stop it but you need help knowing how to do it. You need help in developing strategies and structures which will help you change this behavior.

You can be in Precontemplation (not at all ready to change) regarding one of your eating-disordered behaviors like restrictive eating, while you are in Preparation (ready to change but not knowing how) for your binge eating behavior. This means that you can be in different stages of change for different behaviors. Why this is so important, is that you will need to do different things (and your support network or treatment providers will need to do different things) to help you change depending on what stage of change you are in for each behavior.

Prochaska et al.'s Stages of Change

Precontemplation Stage: *There is either denial of a problem, or an awareness of a problem with an unwillingness to change. For example, a person with anorexia nervosa who knows she has a problem, but doesn't want to change.*

Contemplation Stage: *There is awareness of a problem, an understanding of the pros of change, yet fear of change. For example, the person who binge eats at night in order to fall asleep may be aware of his problem, but he may be terrified that if he doesn't binge at night he won't be able to sleep and, therefore, he will not be able to function the next day.*

Preparation Stage: *There is an awareness of a problem and the need to learn how to change. For example, the person with bulimia may want to delay a binge/purge but doesn't know how to do this and needs to explore alternatives.*

Action Stage: *This is the stage where the person puts the "how to's" she's learned in the Preparation stage into practice.*

Maintenance Stage: *This is the stage where actions are practiced and continually reinforced until the person can do them automatically.*

Termination Stage: *This is the stage where mastery has occurred.*

Now list your eating disordered behaviors. For each behavior list the corresponding stage of change.

<table>
<tr><td></td><td>Eating-Disordered Behavior</td><td>Stage of Change</td></tr>
<tr><td>1)</td><td>_____</td><td>_____</td></tr>
<tr><td>2)</td><td>_____</td><td>_____</td></tr>
<tr><td>3)</td><td>_____</td><td>_____</td></tr>
<tr><td>4)</td><td>_____</td><td>_____</td></tr>
<tr><td>5)</td><td>_____</td><td>_____</td></tr>
<tr><td>6)</td><td>_____</td><td>_____</td></tr>
<tr><td>7)</td><td>_____</td><td>_____</td></tr>
<tr><td>8)</td><td>_____</td><td>_____</td></tr>
</table>

For each behavior, even those for which you believe you are in one of the later stages of change (i.e., Preparation through Termination) list the pros and cons of change. We'd like you to do this because even when preparing to change or actually changing (i.e., in Action), many people often forget to deeply and thoroughly explore their ambivalence about change. It is this ambivalence which often interferes with lasting change, what Dr. Prochaska calls, "Changing for Good." The goal of this exercise is to help you understand how the eating disorder is going to "challenge" you . . . how it is going to fight you in your recovery. You will see this as you explore the cons, or the reasons *not* to change.

    When you understand your ambivalence, or the cons of change, you will better understand your fears. When you understand your fears, you will be better able to develop alternative, healthy ways to address those fears. We hope this task will lessen ambivalence and facilitate change. Now write the pros and cons for changing all of your eating disordered behaviors.

Eating Disordered Behaviors

Example: **Behavior:** *Frequently leaving my desk at work to purchase snacks at the vending machine.*
    Pros: *decreases tension, alleviates stress, keeps me from leaving work entirely.*
    Cons: *increases guilt, increases shame, contributes to poor reviews by boss, increases weight, increases health risks (i.e., high blood pressure, high cholesterol).*

Behavior #1 _____

Pros	Cons
_____	_____
_____	_____
_____	_____
_____	_____

Behavior #2 _____

Pros	Cons
_____	_____
_____	_____
_____	_____
_____	_____
_____	_____

Behavior #3 _____

Pros	Cons
_____	_____
_____	_____
_____	_____
_____	_____
_____	_____

Behavior #4 _____

Pros	Cons
_____	_____
_____	_____
_____	_____
_____	_____
_____	_____

EXPLORING BELIEF SYSTEMS

Paying close attention to detail is important for recovery. As such, let's take this exercise one step further. You have begun to identify your eating-disordered behaviors and the pros and cons of those behaviors. You have identified the stages of change for each identified behavior. You have taken the first step toward acknowledging the "benefits" of your eating disorder, as well as its harmful effects. Now, we would like you to explore the thoughts that, although maladaptive, have helped you to survive. We want to teach you how to begin to challenge these thoughts by using your nurturing, compassionate "voice." Remember that the eating disorder voice is the voice of a charlatan: It promises to be your "friend"; it promises to alleviate your emotional pain. But *true friends do not destroy you.* Left to its own devices, the eating disorder will destroy you. This exercise will help you counter your faulty belief system regarding the eating disorder. It will help you challenge the eating disorder voice which tells you that to be spared your pain you must suffer and die from the eating disorder. Now write down your beliefs.

My Belief System

Example: **Current belief system:** *If I don't binge at night, I won't be able to sleep.*
Counter belief: *I understand I may be anxious that I won't sleep if I don't eat at night, and I may need to consider other alternatives to help me sleep, but the eating at night really isn't helping me.*

1) Current belief: _____

_____

Counter belief: _____

_____

2) Current belief: _____

_____

Counter belief: _____

_____

3) Current belief: _____

_____

Counter belief: _____

_____

4) Current belief: _____

_____

Counter belief: _____

_____

5) Current belief: _____

_____

Counter belief: _____

_____

The exercise you just completed may help you *know* that your counter belief is true—even if you do not *feel* that it is. As you continue to challenge your thoughts, even though they will not be felt on an emotional level, practice will eventually allow you to feel their truth. Speak in your *counter belief voice*, even if you do not believe it. Ask others to reinforce this counter belief voice. Write your counter beliefs down and post them in all the important places in your world (e.g., on your bedroom mirror, in your medicine cabinet, in your dresser drawer, on the dashboard of your car, in your wallet, on your computer clipboard, on your refrigerator, etc.).

Now let's begin to address some of your issues with food. Most individuals with eating disorders have *safe foods*. Safe foods are those foods that feel emotionally and physically comfortable to eat. Usually those with eating disorders also have *risk foods* or *unsafe foods*. These are the foods that the individual doesn't feel comfortable eating. She will either restrict or avoid eating these foods altogether, feel guilty if she consumes them, or purge them if she eats them. The third category of foods, which is often overlooked, is a category that we call *potential foods*. Foods in the potential list are those foods that are on some occasions safe to eat, and on other occasions unsafe to eat. At the end of this exercise, you should be able to differentiate your safe, potential, and risk foods. This information will be invaluable in your attempt to *legalize* or *make peace* with food. Write down all your safe, potential, and risk foods.

SAFE FOODS, POTENTIAL FOODS, AND RISK FOODS

Make a list of all your safe, potential, and risk foods in the columns below. The column marked **N/A** is for those foods that are not palatable to you.

Safe Foods	Potential Foods	Risk Foods	N/A

Incorporating risk foods can be terrifying. Many people have convinced themselves that they just cannot eat certain foods without dire consequences. To them, *indulgence feels sinful.* If you have an eating disorder, you believe that food is not something you should want or enjoy. It might be okay for others to want or enjoy food; but not for you. To deny yourself what you want and enjoy (and we must not forget that you also *need* food) often results in feelings of deprivation when you don't have the food and guilt when you do. Denial of wants and needs and guilt also increase the likelihood of binge eating and purging if you do eat the food.

However, if you can allow yourself the foods you want and need, there will be fewer chances that you will binge eat or purge. Enjoying food does not mean indulging and eating everything in sight. Enjoying food means making peace with food, eating all foods in moderation, and differentiating physical, emotional, and social hungers. It means giving yourself permission to eat a piece of cake, without being terrified that cake is going to go directly to your hips! Before you begin to incorporate potential and/or risk foods, make sure you understand the difference between how you experience physical, emotional, and social hunger.

Physical hunger: *If you think hard enough, you should be able to recall times you were physically hungry. When we are physically hungry, our body lets us know. Some people get lightheaded and shaky; others have stomachs that cry for food. Regardless of what your body does, if you do not feed it enough, it is going to let you know.*

Emotional hunger: *This hunger is prompted by feelings such as sadness, anger, boredom, etc. Emotional eating may provide comfort, numbing, or escape from emotional pains. A person who eats for emotional reasons also may be using food as a source of self-punishment for having done or felt something viewed as "negative."*

Social hunger: *This is the hunger that emerges because those around you are eating. You are not eating out of physical hunger, nor are you eating for emotional reasons. You are eating because the food is there and everybody else is eating.*

Why Am I Eating?

Using the definitions just listed, record your intake for the next three days. Pay close attention to *why* you are eating. If you find yourself eating for emotional reasons, it will also be important that you follow up with Part II of this exercise.

Part I: Record Hunger

Type Of Hunger (P, E, or S)	How Hungry Were You (rate 1 – 10)	What Did You Eat (list foods and meal, snack, or binge)	How Did You Feel (rate: full, satisfied, stuffed)	Urge To Purge, did you? (yes, no)
_____	_____	_____	_____	_____
_____	_____	_____	_____	_____
_____	_____	_____	_____	_____
_____	_____	_____	_____	_____
_____	_____	_____	_____	_____
_____	_____	_____	_____	_____
_____	_____	_____	_____	_____
_____	_____	_____	_____	_____
_____	_____	_____	_____	_____
_____	_____	_____	_____	_____
_____	_____	_____	_____	_____
_____	_____	_____	_____	_____
_____	_____	_____	_____	_____

Part II

If you noticed a tendency toward emotional eating, circle the feelings you were trying to *assuage, stuff down,* or *punish yourself for having.*

anger	aggression	anxiety	boredom	confusion
disappointment	disgust	exhaustion	fear	frustration
grief	guilt	horror	hurt	jealousy
loneliness	misery	negativity	paranoia	puzzlement
regret	sadness	terror		

other: (explain) _____

Incorporating Risk Foods

What do you think will happen if you begin to incorporate your risk foods?

_____

_____

_____

_____

_____

Are your concerns realistic, or do you need to take a minute to challenge these thoughts? If so, please challenge them and write your counter beliefs in the space below.

_____

_____

_____

_____

_____

Are you ready to introduce a risk food? Whether the food is risky because you're afraid to eat one bite, or because you're afraid you'll eat the whole bag, follow the preparation instructions below. Preparation includes the following:

1. Work with your therapist, nutritionist, or a support person. Do not take this step alone. Let this person know you are ready to attempt this feat. Strategize with her how to do this.
2. Create a safe environment. This may include setting the stage for with whom and where you are going to introduce this risk food. It must also include a plan for what to do after introducing your risk food (e.g., going for a walk). Journal writing can also be helpful; writing can help you better understand the feelings associated with the risk food.

Risk-Food Preparation

Step I:

Risk food I am going to introduce: _____

Where I am going to introduce this risk food: _____

Who I am going to be with when I introduce this risk food: _____

What I am going to do after I have introduced this risk food: _____

Step II:

How I feel *before* introducing this risk food? _____

What I am thinking *before* introducing this risk food? _____

_____

Do I need to challenge this thinking *before* introducing this risk food? _____

If so, please "challenge": _____

What am I feeling *as* I introduce this risk food? _____

What am I thinking *as* I introduce this risk food? _____

_____

Do I need to challenge this thinking? _____

If so, please "challenge": _____

_____

For example, **Original Thought:** "I'm scared that this veggie burger will go to my hips." **Challenge:** "This veggie burger is fuel. It's not going to cause me to gain weight."

What am I feeling *after* introducing this risk food? _____

What am I thinking *after* introducing this risk food? _____

_____

Do I need to challenge this thinking? _____

If so, please "challenge": _____

You may photocopy this exercise and use it repeatedly as you continue to introduce new foods. It can also be used to work with "potential" foods, if you are not ready to tackle the risk foods.

The Female Body: Spirituality and Religion

Why is it that our bodies seemingly convey such powerful messages about our character, strength, weakness, goodness and evil? Why is it that some people feel more holy, stronger in character, and more worthy if they denounce their bodies' needs and desires? Why is it that some hide their bodies, wound their bodies, and sacrifice their bodies to experience a sense of spirituality and goodness?

In this chapter, you will read about how attitudes toward the body have evolved over the centuries with the advent of Christianity. You might be able to see how your own religious and spiritual upbringing may have influenced your feelings and experience of your body. You may be able to better understand whether you treat your body in certain ways to enhance your strength of character, your spirituality, or your feelings of goodness and worthiness. Are you longing for spirituality? Is there a connection between how you treat your body and your spiritual or religious life? Read on and then answer the questions to see how your treatment of your body might connect with your spiritual or religious life or longings.

Elizabeth, a lovely, bright, talented young woman grew up in a home of two cultures, Pakistani and American. Her mother, a Caucasian American, was a very thin woman who ate almost nothing. Her father, of Pakistani descent, was an average-sized man. Elizabeth's older sister resembled their mothers, being naturally very thin and eating very little. Elizabeth seemed to resemble her father more.

As Elizabeth tried to understand why she wished to be like her mother and not her father, it seemed that it was because mother's austerity . . . needing and taking very little for herself as evidenced by her thin appearance and insignificant intake of food—as well as mother's pronounced veins which protruded from her hands—conveyed strength to Elizabeth. She, herself, wished to have protruding veins, especially in her arms, so she could convey strength.

Her mother had had such serious bouts of depression while Elizabeth grew up that there were times she believed her mother would commit suicide. Her father had always been stable and highly functioning. As well, her parents had a relationship characterized by estrangement and bitterness. Why would she choose to emulate her mother? Because, in Western culture, thinness, protruding veins, muscles, and eating very little (if one is a woman) conveys strength of character. Might it also convey goodness and even holiness? Her mother was a devout Christian and believed that denouncing bodily urges produced strength of character and holiness.

Another young woman, Gretchen, spoke with pride of bruises and gashes received during athletic competition. She saw these visible marks as signs of her strength and endurance . . . like badges of courage. Gretchen felt this too when she would get scratches or gashes from cleaning out the stables where she volunteered her time.

Why is it that many young women with eating disorders feel more assured of their inner strength of character, their very goodness, through bodily hurts or deprivation?

Religious history may unearth some of the reasons. Before Christianity, most religious and holy symbols and icons were very large, corpulent, or voluptuous figures. They carried no wounds or signs of physical hurt. Largeness conveyed greatness, wealth, bounty, and fertility. In China, corpulence is associated with prosperity and good fortune as protrayed by the Buddha. In Hinduism, Lord Ganesh, part man and part elephant, is one of the most popular and corpulent gods. His ample stomach contains all known universes, and he is the god of success, wisdom, and the remover of all obstacles. Enjoying life's pleasures, including food, is one of the main principles written in the Vedas, the Hindu holy writings. In an archeological dig in Willendorf, Austria in 1908, a statue of a very corpulent female with enormous breasts, hips, belly, and vagina was found. It was judged to be 26,000 years old and was, thus, named after the goddess Venus, the goddess of sex. If, in fact, this was early man's vision of a goddess, she was most certainly a representation of fertility.

With the birth of Christianity, the most popular and widespread religion of the Western world, came the advent of austerity in appearance and principle (Mondadori, 1998). Believing poverty to be holy, many religious followers of Christianity take a vow of poverty. Poverty, not wealth, is conveyed through an austere and thin appearance as evidenced by the representation of Jesus on the cross, where every rib protrudes from his skin. He is also a visual sign of suffering and strength. Blood drips from his wounds from the lashing of the whips, the crown of thorns , and the nails through his feet and hands on the cross.

Christian saints suffered to affirm their holiness. Saint Joan of Arc was burned at the stake for her religious beliefs. Saints fasted as signs of their holiness. They fasted, became emaciated, and grew in saintliness. With the conquest of goddess-worshipping societies where fertile, round female forms were revered, came Christianity where the female was denied a holy place in the religion unless she was an ascetic, mystic, virgin, or saint. And the way to holiness was through fasting and the consequent loss of the female form. Even Christ's mother, Mary, was po. trayed as a virgin—as the chaste bearer of the Christ child. Women, therefore, had to renounce their fertility, their ability to bear children, in order to be holy. In Christianity, it was only through the repudiation of procreation—through celibacy, effected by the obliteration of sexual desire via fasting and emaciation—that women could share some place of holiness with men. Men, by virtue of their maleness, could attain holy places without such asceticism.

QUESTIONS ABOUT RELIGION AND EATING DISORDERS

Are there religious overtones to *your* quest for thinness?_____ Yes   _____ No

Do you think your beliefs about goodness, holiness, and strength have religious underpinnings and if so, how and why?

_____

_____

_____

_____

_____

What female images are depicted in your religion? How do you understand these images?

_____

_____

_____

_____

_____

Does the goodness or strength of these female religious images lie in their thin appearance or their renouncement of their sexuality?

Explain: _____

_____

_____

_____

_____

Do these female religious images achieve greatness through physical suffering? Give examples:

_____

_____

_____

_____

_____

Write about your views. Write about your earliest memories of your religious teachings. Do your religious beliefs support the health and goodness of women? Once you have written your beliefs, find a friend or two and ask them to respond to these questions as well. Are your beliefs and experiences the same or different? Are there ways to attain goodness and religious fulfillment without denying and hurting your body? What are they?

_____

_____

_____

_____

_____

_____

_____

_____

_____

_____

_____

_____

_____

_____

_____

_____

_____

_____

_____

_____

_____

Now that you have considered whether there are any religious or spiritual underpinnings to your belief system about your body, let's look at the history of the human body to see what else you might discover about your beliefs.

The Female Body: History of Size and Thinness

By World War II, the penchant for the slim, bare-boned female form began to be formed. By the 1960s Twiggy—all 5'7" and 98 pounds of her—was the model to emulate. By her standards, normal-sized women were considered fat. The health industry began to follow the "ideal weight" charts established by the insurance industry. These "ideal" charts proposed that people should fit into ideal weight categories. From this point onward, health and morality were merged into a shared prejudice: that fat was bad and the inability or unwillingness to lose fat became a sign of weakness of character and will power.

Interestingly, from earlier times, a rounded, fuller form was considered the picture of health and thinness was a sign of illness. Today, the opposite is true.

In the animal world, thinness is a sign of ill health and diminishes chances for survival. The larger members of the species usually wield more power and live longer. Animal experts also know that different breeds yield different builds and sizes. Although Siberian Huskies and Pekinese are both dogs, no one would expect them to be the same size. Actually they are about as different in size as any two members of the same species could be. Although some people might prefer the Siberian Husky over the Pekinese, and vice versa, people would not ridicule or chastise one dog for not matching the size of the other. We would think that was preposterous if it were to happen. Does it not follow that ridiculing people for being unable or unwilling to starve themselves into a certain size is also preposterous?

Actually, in the animal world there is an appreciation for the unique size, color, and personality of each member of the species. In the world of people, those of certain colors, sizes, and qualities have always been more appreciated than others, usually depending upon the particular historical and cultural period.

We might wonder whether in this land of plenty we must bridle our appetite for food now that most in Westernized societies are adequately nourished. In fact, this restraint might show that we have triumphed over our instincts to eat. Similarly, in the Victorian period of the 19th century, bridling the appetite for sex occurred as infant mortality rates had decreased and sex for procreation was no longer as vital for the survival of the species.

A group of American college-aged men participating in a focus group in Boston (Budman & Villapiano, 1999) acknowledged that for women in our culture there is no substitute for beauty, as primarily represented by slenderness. Yet, for men, age and increased weight can be compensated for by money and power, as evidenced by a flashy new sports car, a boat, or a powerful position or profession. Women with these attributes, but without trim physiques, are no match in most men's eyes for their slender cohorts who do not have the trappings of material success. Interestingly, Prince Phillip of England said Princess Diana would breed height into the royal lineage. Men—at least those from Western cultures—it seems, wish to breed thinness into their lineages.

In focus groups with American college-aged women in this same research study, we learned that women knew that their physical appearance, most importantly embodied by thinness, would attract men. To promote this attraction women acknowledged that they would purposely eat less in the presence of males and would worry more about their table manners as well. They reported that they did not draw negative opinions about men who ate large amounts in their presence. In fact they saw it as laudable. Table manners, again, were not things which would significantly detract from a man's attractiveness.

Bridling appetites appears to be women's lot. Today, in the land of plenty, restraining one's appetite for food is the moral equivalent to restraining sexual appetite in the 19th century. As Roberta P. Seid said in *Too Close to the Bone: The Historical Context for Women's Obsession with Slenderness*, "In the 19th century, the control of sexual instincts was the acme of virtue; sexual behavior was the yardstick of goodness. Today, eating habits and body weight have become the yardsticks of virtue, and food rules have become as dour and inhibitory as the sex rules of the 19th century" (p. 8).

It is not that men do not feel these pressures as well. Many men do and have reported the same. However, there is more room for them to fit into Westernized cultures if they do not contain their appetites. There is less room for women, and the sanctions for not doing so could be ridicule, low self-esteem, and fewer choices and opportunities personally, professionally, and socially.

QUESTIONS ABOUT BODY IMAGE

Do you feel pressure to fit into your culture's ideal of thinness? If so, explain how you feel the pressure. What do you do to deal with the pressure?

_____

_____

_____

Write a story about your body during the Baroque period when the nudes chosen by famous artists such as Rubens were ample, voluptuous forms. How would you have felt about your body if you had lived during this time? Would it be different than how you feel about it today? Give examples that show the difference.

_____

_____

_____

_____

_____

Write a story about how you feel about your body under today's physical standards. Is it a more positive feeling than the ones you would have had if you had lived during the Baroque Period? Is it less positive? Give examples that show the difference:

_____

_____

_____

_____

_____

What is your cultural and genetic heritage? Do you know about the cultures from which your ancestors descended? Do you know about their traditions with food? Do you know how they cared for, adorned, and appreciated their bodies? If you do not have grandparents or great grandparents who could give you some of this important information, ask if you could talk with the elderly of your heritage in a nursing home or in an assisted living facility. Perhaps there is a gathering place for the elderly in your community or you could speak with elders in your church or synagogue. Find out about the culture from which you descended. Its amazing how much information and knowledge our elders have, but how seldom we ask them to share their wisdom and knowledge with us. While you're speaking with the elders, notice the beauty in their wrinkled faces and hands. Notice the wisdom and depth in their eyes. Write about your experience with your's or other's elders and notice whether you have gained a deeper appreciation of different cultures . . . their food . . . their practices . . . and their bodies. Notice whether you have expanded your definition of beauty. Once you're done, ask a friend to do this too and share your stories.

_____

_____

_____

_____

_____

_____

_____

_____

_____

MORE ON MY JOURNEY FROM COMPULSIVE OVEREATING AND OBESITY TO MODERATE EATING AND HEALTHY WEIGHT

Recently I said that writing my story and digging into the past was opening Pandora's box. Facing that was a debilitating lifetime fear. I am thrilled to say that what I have discovered is a treasure chest of understanding and at last, closure.

I have been asked how and why I realized that diets don't work. The reason is because diets are external-control and quick-fix solutions, both of which reinforce the pattern of not being responsible or in control. Here are just a few examples of programs that were not able to make me lose weight: Weight Watchers, Optifast, behavior therapy, hospitalization, Losers are Winners, diet pills.

Overeaters are always hungry—both physically and emotionally starved. Diets mean deprivation which leads to bingeing when you can't take it anymore. Each failed weight-loss attempt only reaffirms failure, over and over again. Smooth and manipulative, I customized myself to suit the program that was going to do it for me. No amount of humiliation, embarrassment, disappointment, desperation (internal pain 24/7), desire, bribery, motivation, or solution that was forced on me by others, or myself, could lose the weight for me. I was too deeply buried in the third person I had created to live the life I could not face.

That is why long-term success can not be achieved by external control. The process is like peeling an onion—layer by layer each new layer brings you closer to the inner core. Starve = deprivation, physical and emotional; Binge = immediate gratification, a quick fix for the need of the moment. What a great excuse lack of willpower was to the third person, who believed that lack was why the scale showed 405 pounds. I had to learn how to re-wire will power which had short-circuited. In fact, it took tremendous willpower to resist pressure from those around me who would never get off my back. As long as I could find excuses why the current approach was failing, I was not responsible. As long as the program of the moment was either the magical answer or the cause for failure, I was not responsible.

Unable to assume personal responsibility, I became the master of denial. Getting stuck in a booth in a restaurant, being told by a stewardess that I should be responsible for using two seats, needing double extensions for seatbelts on the plane, children laughing and pointing, are just a few reasons for the protective third person I created.

Weight Watchers was a group program which controlled portions (weighing on a kitchen scale), had rules as to protein intake, snacking, etc. Unable to be externally motivated or controlled, I refused to have my weight loss announced or celebrated by the group, so I only went to weigh-in (after all, weight loss was the goal), thereby appeasing others. With neither behavior change nor an awareness that I still had no clue what feeling hunger was, I was equally unaware of being full.

With each diet, I hung in until it became apparent that this was just one more camouflage for what others expected me to do. Repeated attempts with psychologists failed because I knew they were not good therapists; or I got them to open up to the decoy I had worked. Optifast (liquid protein—no solid food) was so much easier than trying to make changes or choices.

Then one day I saw a Coffee Crisp commercial—seeing that chocolate being poured over crisp wafer—triggered my having my first solid food in 5 months. This then led to me "outwitting" the program because I discovered that if I binged for one or even two days and starved the other days of the week, I could still lose weight. Immediately after weigh-ins, my friend (also on the program) and I would methodically binge. There was great comfort in not having to gain control by just abstaining from solid food. After breaking our fast with chocolates across from the hospital we were now ready to embark on our journey to the East end of the city where we were not known. There we would binge to the point of throwing up and then starve and binge again. This process resulted for me in an ulcer bleed.

No price was too high to pay for immediate gratification. Yet I was not a real lover of food, as would be shown by my dipping 8–10 slices of bread in mayonnaise rather than bother to make sandwiches; I remember frantic midnight searches for mayonnaise, eating an entire Pepperidge Farm chocolate cake in one sitting (always in hiding), or chocolate pudding pack, all 6 portions, at one sitting.

I ate in cycle patterns—the same foods for month-long cycles at a time. Coffee shops to restaurants all started my order automatically—for breakfast: western sandwich, milkshake, cheese Danish; mid-morning snack of Coffee Crisp or Kitkat; then lunch: club sandwich with French fries and dessert; snacks in between; supper: soup, meat, potatoes; salad, dessert: late night trips to Dunn's 24-hour restaurant open all night for smoked meat, French fries, milkshake, and cheesecake—eaten, in toilet stall downstairs (so alone, so controlled by a habit that ruled my world). Compulsive, addictive behavior which was unthinking, unfeeling, and that was caused by too much pain and loss.

As I lived life on automatic pilot, the only course change possible was to make only very minor changes at first. I started by throwing a piece of the Danish or pastry out the car window (mobile eating). Every day I would stop for three pastries and the first minor change I made was to take a piece from each and throw it in the garbage. This now became as routine as buying and eating. In time this led to always discarding half. These were minor changes but I was beginning to make choices and gradually ate with conscious decisions. Eventually I reduced down to one, and then only the icing. I was learning to be satiated by taste rather than quantity. I did not restrict my choice of foods in any way and I would eat whatever I wanted, which included a steady menu of cheeseburgers, French fries, hot dogs, and General Tao's chicken. Gradually, as I got comfortable with always having half portions, I also committed to always having one slice of bread at a time. I strictly had open-faced sandwiches or a cheeseburger on half a bun and learned to have any number of slices as long as never more than one at a time. This freedom of choice allowed me to remain comfortable with portion awareness. As children, we were rewarded with dessert if we finished all the food on our plates. If we didn't, this meant we did not appreciate or like the food. Eating on a small plate helped me learn awareness and to make choices rather than behave on automatic pilot.

Simultaneously, not sequentially, I started the process to emotional recovery and image change. My issues were now becoming secondary and my survival and well-being became the focus. Image change is not necessarily on the same timetable. There, too, I had to discover new worlds. At 50 years old I was able for the very first time in my life to wear a belt and jeans. Shopping in normal, not over-size, stores contributed as a positive re-enforcement of changes. I faced the life-long feared age "50"—it was now or never.

Armed with new learned skills, I finally was ready to make changes in food choices—I gradually cut fat, then fried, then fatty foods. No longer being an overeater and growing in emotional strength enabled me to discover eating by preference, being in control of my eating, and acknowledging my hunger.

I still eat in cycles and very routinely. I accept and work with this pattern rather than being ruled by it. In fact I have found that because I achieved my 250-pound weight loss with no feelings of deprivation, I never starve, and that is a large factor in why I have never even once binged in 20 years once I quit dieting.

This having been said, now I want to say that the hardest part has been moving on since I became aware that achieving goals and attaining control does not automatically equal happiness. I had to deal with adjusting to image change externally and internally—teaching others as well as myself how to deal with this adult who was chronologically out of place. Socially, I was now in the game—being single and realizing that I had missed a lifetime of progressive growth, I tried to recapture the lost years.

Only this summer I experienced my first real emotional commitment and communication—I discovered that if all I had accomplished were a true metamorphosis then to move forward I would have to stop this new spin cycle. I had to accept and be proud of my new self-image and maturity. I had to overcome my fear of being vulnerable, independent, and responsible. I have come to understand that revenge and holding on to the pain does not allow for healing. In hindsight, that is why I first let go of the issues, got over it, and took steps toward life-long recovery.

Inner and outer self-love needs to happen simultaneously, not sequentially. Forgiveness allowed me to learn unconditional love for others and myself. No more "mea culpa." With this final acceptance I finally have mourned and laid to rest the "third person" who protected and shielded me all my life. Each and every relationship in my life is brand new—most of all, my relationship with myself. I have explored the history and am discovering the present with the knowledge that I can affect the future.

Three absolute ingredients for long term success: recognizing the point of no return; acknowledging that you have reached the point to do or die; recognizing that the solution like the cause stems from within; although I must emphasize that discovering and adjusting remains a daily struggle—I know I can.

Yvonne, age 52

Next we'll look specifically at your body image. Is it positive? Is it negative? Do you want to feel better about your body? Read on.

Body Image

Our bodies are our roadmaps. We have signposts and landmarks identifying our movements through the world. We have detours and construction sites warning where work is unfinished or where it is dangerous to tread. Our bodies hold memories our words cannot speak.

In the previous chapters, you explored your relationship with food and the influence of your religious and cultural heritage in regard to food and eating. With the help of the exercises in those chapters, you began to identify some of your common eating problems and strategies you could use to change those behaviors. You began to understand your different hungers, and you identified your risk foods and strategies you could use to introduce them into your eating repertoire.

You have also considered how your religion and your views on spirituality may have affected your perception of your body. Finally, you have looked at how historical events and culture have influenced body attitudes and behaviors over the centuries.

The next step in your journey is to explore the relationship you have with your body right now. Our goal is to help you reconnect with your body in understanding and caring ways . . . to take a body journey that is gentle and compassionate.

This chapter will help you complete unfinished work regarding your body and decrease the numbers of detours you take to avoid, ignore, and occlude potentially dangerous body terrain. Body image issues are usually symbolic of issues that are much more deeply rooted. For those with eating disorders, it is more comfortable to focus on the body than the underlying feeling. The goal of this chapter is to help you put a plan in place for practicing body care and connection, so that hurting your body through disordered eating is no longer the route chosen on your body roadmap.

EXPLORING BODY-IMAGE DISTORTION

It is difficult to believe that our eyes are capable of deceiving us. The deception is profound for those with eating disorders. They often "see" their bodies as "fat," "ugly," and "unacceptable" no matter what their size. Rate how your eyes see you by first looking at how others see you.

How does _____ see my body? _____

_____

_____

Do I believe this person's perception? _____

How does _____ see my body? _____

_____

_____

Do I believe this person's perception? _____

How does _____ see my body? _____

_____

_____

Do I believe this person's perception? _____

If you find yourself not trusting the feedback of the chosen person(s), continue with the exercises in this chapter. The discrepancy may be the result of body-image distortion. Do not fret! Most people have some form of body-image distortion. However, people with eating disorders or disordered eating tend to have greater distortion. It is not the goal of this chapter to convince you to see yourself more accurately. You will reach this goal as you achieve greater physical and emotional health. Instead, by the time you have completed this chapter, we hope you will understand the concept of body-image distortion so you can minimize the degree to which it interferes with your recovery.

The Power of Distortion

Directions: Get a tape recorder and a blank tape. Record a conversation you have with a friend or group of friends. Once the conversation is over, play the tape back, listen to it with your friends, and answer the following questions.

1) Do you think you sounded the way you expected to sound? Explain.

_____

_____

_____

2 Did your friends sound the way you expected them to sound? Explain.

_____

_____

_____

3) Did your friends think you sounded the way they expected you to? Explain.

_____

_____

_____

4) Did your friends think they sounded the way they expected themselves to sound? Explain.

_____

_____

_____

As you can see from this exercise, our ears can deceive us; we have a *distortion in hearing*! Just as our ears deceive us about our own voices, our eyes deceive us about our bodies. Okay! Now that you understand distortion, you're probably wondering what you can do about it. The next exercise is designed to help you answer that question.

Correcting Misperceptions

How do you go about correcting misperceptions in your life? For example, has anyone ever interpreted something you said in a way that was different than how you meant it? How did you know that you and the other person had different understandings about what you said? What did it feel like to be misunderstood? What did it feel like when you and the other person had a better understanding of each other? After you answer these questions, ask a friend to answer them, too. Compare how you each responded to these questions. What did you learn about yourself/your friend? What did your friend learn about herself/you?

_____

_____

_____

_____

_____

_____

_____

_____

_____

_____

_____

_____

_____

_____

_____

_____

What three things could you do to find out if you are misperceiving what you see (e.g., your body) or what you hear (e.g., your voice; the words of another)?

1) _____

2) _____

3) _____

One way we can challenge our misperceptions is by asking others to interpret our statements in their words. Then we use our words to clarify any inaccurate perceptions. Unfortunately, although we may ask others to help us clarify our misperceptions of our voices or our bodies, seldom do _we_ change our minds about our misperceptions. Perhaps it's because our misperceptions are between parts of ourselves, not ourselves and another. This does not mean, however, that you are not able to challenge your own misperceptions. Please continue with the following exercises. At the end of this chapter, we will provide you with some tools to help you challenge your body-image distortion.

How Do You Measure Up?

Directions: Using no tape measures, "guestimate" and record the measurements of the body parts listed below. Then choose a person you feel comfortable working with, and "guestimate" and record his/her measurements (under **G**). Once recorded, use a tape measure to find *actual* measurements for you and your "safe" person (under **A**).

My Measurements (G)   My Safe Person's Measurements (G)

chest _____   chest _____

upper arms _____   upper arms _____

waist _____   waist _____

hips _____   hips _____

thighs _____   thighs _____

My Measurements (A)   My Safe Person's Measurements (A)

chest _____   chest _____

upper arms _____   upper arms _____

waist _____   waist _____

hips _____   hips _____

thighs _____   thighs _____

Reflections:

1) Were your guesses about your own measurements accurate? _____
_____.

2) Were your guesses about your safe person's measurements accurate? _____
_____

3) Were you surprised by your findings? Explain _____
_____
_____

4) Do you feel any differently about yourself as a result of this exercise? Explain _____
_____
_____

5) Comparing the above exercise with the exercise of the voice recording on the tape recorder, were you surprised by how you "see" and "hear" yourself when compared to how the tape measure and tape recorder "see" and "hear" you? Explain _____
_____
_____

6) Do you feel any differently about your "safe person" as a result of this exercise? Explain
_____
_____

7) What three things could you do to correct your perceptions about your body (if your guesses were not accurate)?
A) _____
B) _____
C) _____

8) Have your feelings about yourself or your body changed as a result of this exercise? Explain
_____
_____
_____
_____
_____

9) Have your feelings about your friend or her body changed as a result of this exercise? Explain
_____
_____
_____
_____
_____

WORDS FROM AN EX-ANOREXIC

If you secretly fear and try to hide from some imagined "Anorexia Gestapo," you should, because I have developed hawk-eye vision for those with anorexia; I can pick 'em out of a crowded dining hall in a flash. It takes one to know one!

I'd like to emphasize what I think will be most useful to you and increase your chances of getting lucky like me; and that is the vital importance of having confidence in and sticking up for your own self-worth. I think the only tragedy in my situation is that I ever came to like myself so little. Nowadays, I can't stand to see others not have faith in themselves; that was a one-way track to death for me. Even if not physical death, then joining the living dead, never reaching the potential of myself, not because someone or something got in my way, but because I limited myself and forfeited my own chance. To the aforementioned end, I'd like to focus upon my recovery.

About five months after transitioning from depression to anorexia (and after passing through those first couple months of "happy" weight loss), I had suppressed the voice of myself almost completely. Being 14 and having no previous experience as an adult to use for reference, I was unaware that there were any alternatives to this new existence that I had entered upon, an existence that I suppose I felt I deserved. I recall a camp leader I knew and respected greatly asking me about my eating habits; I said I was fine because I honestly believed I was! In my experience, the sickness is wholly a mind-game (the body can't become addicted to being starved), and the decay of your body only represents a pain screaming to be noticed, a pain that your mind refuses to acknowledge.

Finally my camp director put me on the scale one day (I hadn't been weighing myself), and my reaction was one of penetrating terror. I was dying, and I did not want to die. In this realization, that deeply buried voice of my healthy consciousness had managed to speak out, even if it was only a whisper, and its struggle with the disordered part of my mind had begun. My mind and my will became split between the rational notion that I needed to do something about myself, and this fierce, unrelenting intensity of needing to control. So I had to really 'transcend' myself. *I had to bypass other thoughts, focus only on the larger picture of me getting better, and just put in my mouth, chew, and swallow what the nurse gave me to eat. I had to release control and give it all to her, because I knew I couldn't trust myself with any.*

For me it was all about self worth. I felt disgusted with my own worthlessness, and I believe that I subconsciously lost weight so that I would ultimately die. I was trying to kill myself without even knowing it! I couldn't trust myself to take care of myself—now that's frightening. Talk about out of control . . . when you thought you were so in control! It's amazing that the mind can work itself into such a predicament.

This was the most difficult time, as the healthy part of my thinking began to drive a thin wedge into the side of my mind, slowly forcing out that disordered mentality that gripped me. A couple of weeks later, I returned home from camp, determined to eat as much as possible to gain weight. I then returned to boarding school, knowing that if I took care of my mind, my body would easily follow; it did!

I see an eating disorder as a flu that attacks you when your mental immunity (your self worth) is weakened. This mental immunity makes you sick and later leaves you as you build up your mental strength. It's a disease you have to pull out by this essential problem. Dealing only

Continued

with the eating aspect or body image or some other distracting manifestation will not be successful; that is like putting a Band-Aid over the splinter.

I'm very glad no one held me back from school or forced this to become a piece of my identity among my friends. The healthy people around me treated me as if I was healthy, too. This gave me a sense of 'normalcy' in my life. Meanwhile, my therapist was leading me into the war zone that helped me dig my true self out of the rubble! The experience made me feel sorriest for those with subclinical eating disorders; I wonder if they ever get fully addressed.

Others believed in me more than I believed in myself. Always in those who were important to me, did I sense a crucial open-ended, patient expectation rather than a resolved attitude that I might not ever be able to recover. At the time, I had no idea how hard it is to fully recover, and in looking back, I'm glad I didn't!

For probably two-thirds of the school year, I ate the exact same 'acceptable' breakfast, lunch, and dinner in the cafeteria. In the spring, and after overcoming the weirdness of being in the same place in such a different mentality, I was able to eat different things and experiment, hence returning the needs of my body back to regulation by my body. I learned to quell 'control attacks' by focusing on the priority of taking care of myself and on 'letting go' of the feelings. From there on, eating was happily and rightly divorced from my emotional issues!

I take comfort in the idea that fooling with eating or your body beyond what is necessary for real health reasons is *never* a good solution and *never* worth it. And to those with anorexia out there, I hate to break it to you, but one day you, too, may discover that the tasks of dwelling on food and trying to remember what you ate—are SO tediously BORING!!

Sure, I still battle with some of this crap. I still have trouble feeling good about myself and what I do and, since I don't have much built-in faith and confidence in myself to ride on, I have to build them in myself. But hey, I've come a long way!

You need to be on your own side in life; goodness knows there will be enough external obstacles to deal with! There isn't time to be your own worst enemy. Cheer for yourself! There's so much out there to enjoy and to live for! And hey, taking yourself out of the game by avoiding living, or having an eating disorder, isn't fair play; it's a cheap and crappy substitute for attempting to live 'a real life' in the long run. Getting rejected by others hurts, but at least you took the risk! Learn . . . move forward . . . live today as if it were your last and as if you'd live forever.

I'm a vastly stronger person for surviving this. And for every personal step of progress I've made in communicating, expressing myself, and relating to others, the reward is a real, wonderfully enriched experience.

If you are determined, disciplined, and hardworking enough to get into being 'good' at having anorexia, you're automatically determined enough and strong enough to get out of the pain of anorexia. But, YOU HAVE TO WANT IT FOR YOURSELF. And YOU'RE WORTH IT; so take care and good luck!!

Anne, 21

In our years of work with clients with eating disorders, we have found that the majority have accurate perceptions of others' measurements, yet tend to over-estimate their own.

Following such an exercise, many clients can finally "see" the concept of body-image distortion and how it affects their perceptions of their own bodies.

Now you should be more able to see the *tricks* your eyes and ears play on you. These tricks often leave people feeling frustrated. Unfortunately, there are no glasses or special hearing aids to "fix" these tricks. Learning to challenge and compensate for your misperceptions, however, can lead to a better body image. Try the next exercise to see if it helps you challenge your typical way of "seeing" your body.

Dear Body . . . Dear Self

Before you begin this exercise, please consider the following questions:

- How do you "speak" to your body?
- How does your body "speak" back to you?
- Do you and your body know each other well?
- Do you and your body treat each other well?
- Would you want the relationship between your body and your self to change? If so, how?

Once you have considered the questions above, we would like you to write a letter to your body. Say everything you've wanted to say to it; do not edit your feelings or thoughts. Once completed, sign your name.

Dear Body,

_____

_____

_____

_____

_____

_____

_____

_____

_____

_____

_____

_____

_____

_____

_____

_____

_____

Sincerely,

_____

Now it's time for your body to write a letter back to you. Let your body say everything it has wanted to say to you. Do not edit your body's feelings or thoughts.

Dear _____,

_____
_____
_____
_____
_____
_____
_____
_____
_____
_____
_____
_____
_____
_____
_____
_____
_____
_____
_____
_____
_____

Sincerely,
Your Body

If you responded like many other people with eating disorders you probably wrote a very harsh and critical letter toward your body. Did your body's letter back to you help you soften your harshness? Did your body's letter back to you help you to appreciate your body more?

Recovery is going to mean silencing that harsh, critical voice and substituting it with one which is nurturing and compassionate. We care more for the things that we treat well. The corollary is also true. We treat well the things for which we care more. Before moving on to the next exercise, please answer the following questions:

1) How did you feel about your letter to your body?

_____
_____
_____

2) How did your body feel about your letter to it?

_____

_____

_____

3) How did you feel about the letter your body sent back to you?

_____

_____

_____

_____

4) Do you and your body know each other well?   _____ Yes   _____ No

5) What did you learn about yourself from this writing exercise?

_____

_____

6) What did you learn about your body from this writing?

_____

_____

7) Do you think any differently about your body after doing this writing exercise? If so, how?

_____

_____

_____

8) What are the ways you could think and act differently to enhance your appreciation of your body? (Please list at least 5 ways.)

_____

_____

_____

_____

_____

Before we end our body-image journey, think about whether you feel your feelings in your body. When you are sad, do you feel an ache in your throat, as if you are stifling tears? When you are angry, do you feel your stomach churning as it does when you are about to be sick? When you are tense or anxious, do you feel your jaw clenching and your back muscles tightening as if you are steeling yourself for an attack? We are asking you this because you, like many of our clients, might be finding yourself saying, _"I feel fat."_

"Fat" is not a feeling. It is a description of a negative feeling state. Finding out what feelings lurk _beneath_ the "fat feeling" will be an important step in your recovery process.

Valerie, a young woman with whom we worked, learned that when she felt most fat she was feeling more burdened by her mother. She described feeling as if she were constantly carrying her mother on her back. Of course, it was the emotional burden and responsibility of her mother which _weighed_ on her, not her mother herself. But to Valerie, the _burden_ of her mother felt like _fat_. What are the feelings that _fat_ hides from you?

MY BODY . . . MY STORY

Our bodies have a lot to say to us. Unfortunately, many of us don't pay enough attention to our bodies; we have cut our bodies off and treat them as if they do not belong to us.. The following exercise may help you recapture your body feelings. It may be difficult for some of you to do. Recapturing old feelings can be painful; it can also be life saving. You may want to use a candid photo of yourself or allow yourself to go through a photo album of childhood to help you reconnect with your body.

This assignment asks your body to write a story about its feelings. Have its "body feelings" changed as your body has matured? If so, what were the feelings and where did they reside, and what are the feelings now? Allow your body to talk about whether there are positive feelings that it would like to recapture, or whether it, for the first time, would like to experience positive feelings. Write without censoring or editing; let your body be without bounds in its expression. Once you have finished this writing, please take the opportunity to consider three things you could do to help your body recapture, or experience for the first time, positive feelings. You may also discover, why your body does not want to feel, and what feelings you escape with your food and weight obsession.

_____

_____

_____

_____

_____

_____

_____

_____

_____

_____

_____

_____

_____

_____

_____

_____

_____

_____

_____

_____

_____

_____

_____

YOUR BODY ROADMAP

On the following page is a timeline/roadmap; it comes with suggested symbols for your body's journey over time. We ask that you map your body feelings and experiences from your earliest memories to the present. You can draw major life events on billboards; indicate high points, good feelings, and physical successes with reaching the top of a hill. Low points, disappointments, physical defects, failures, illnesses, injuries, or surgeries can be expressed through valleys. Confusion, indecision, or frustration may be depicted by a fork in the road. Expressing fear can be conveyed by being lost in the woods. Flowers can depict gentleness, kindness, and caring ministrations from you or others. Falling rock, washed out bridges, or other road hazards could depict hurt or abuse by others. Times of acceptance, quiet, and serenity could be depicted by rural, tree-lined roads, bubbling brooks, or an expanse of ocean as you pass.

As you can see, this map can take you through green pastures and tree-lined lanes. It can also take you over rough and rocky terrain, over mountains and deep into valleys. Any possible conditions are available here. You just need to use your imagination to illustrate your body's journey over time. The key below will provide you with some ideas about how to depict your body experience. But you might have metaphors, signs, and symbols of your own which can more accurately depict your body experience. Use them! Our goal is to help you recognize and visualize *your* body's experiences over time. Has your body had a placid or arduous journey? Was your body's journey idyllic until it hit puberty and then did the journey grow rocky and dangerous? Put plenty of billboards indicating important events, messages, or memories that illustrate your body's experience over time. Once you are through you can turn the page and continue the timeline and map in a futuristic plan for the rest of your body's life. What would you like the rest of your body's journey to be like? How could you lead your body down a path of care, kindness, confidence, and esteem?

Mapping your body's past, present, and future journey could take a long time. Give yourself the time to do this. Do not rush it. You can come back to this exercise over and over again. If this task feels overwhelming, do it with a trusted friend or therapist. Or leave it. Respect your pace and timing. This will be here for you at a later date as well as now. If you're ready to proceed, go on to the roadmap exercise. We have included an example, but you may want to draw your own roadmap to illustrate your body's journey.

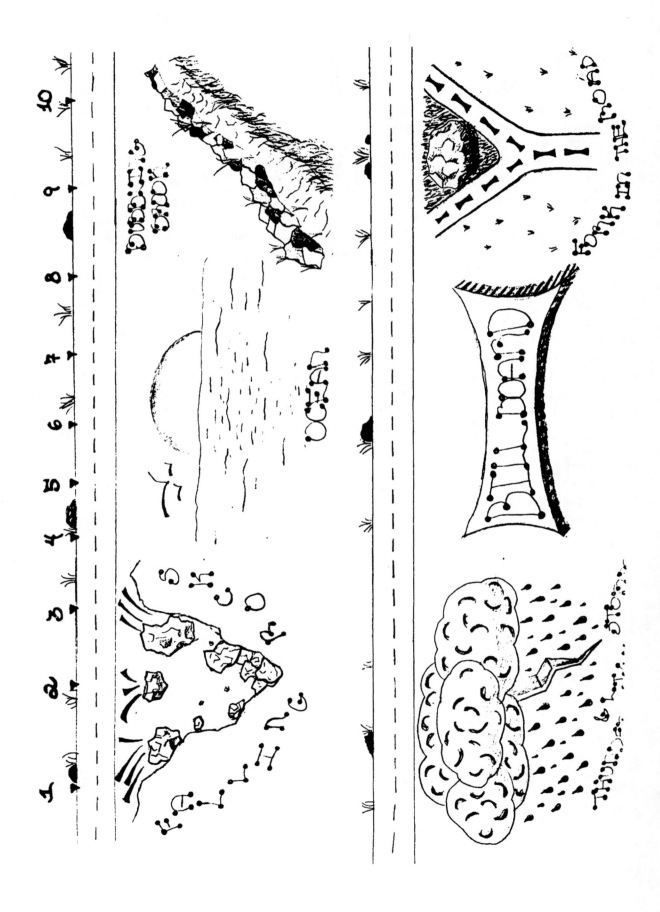

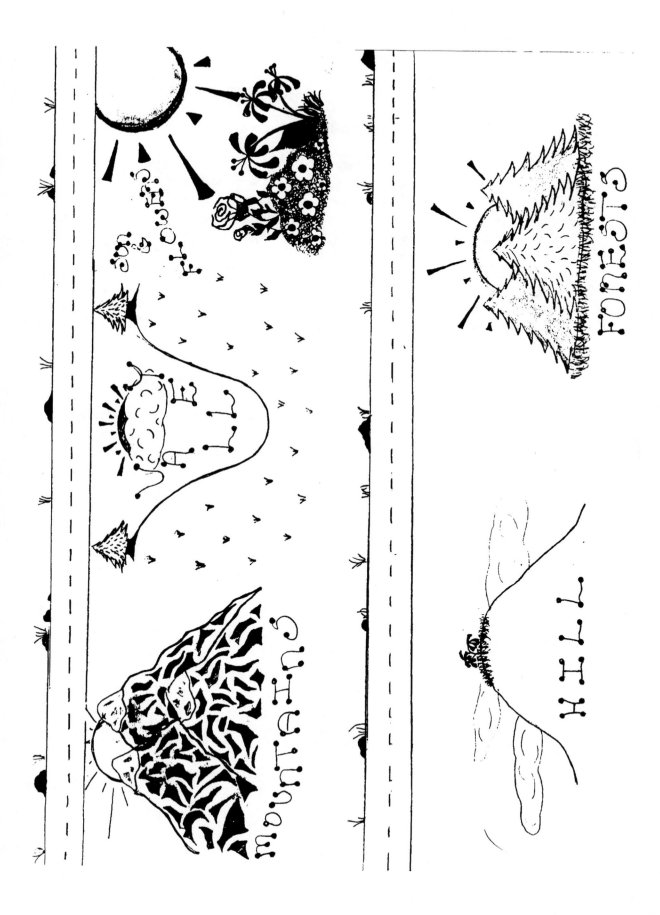

By now you have made significant headway on your body journey. We hope you understand the power of body-image distortion and its impact on your use of food. Before we move on to the chapter on exercise, consider some of the following suggestions in your efforts to combat body-image distortion.

Challenging Body-Image Distortion

1. Limit the amount of time you spend looking at yourself and your body in the mirror. Remind yourself of the concept and power of body-image distortion, and repeat this question to yourself: "When I am *feeling fat,* what am I feeling *beneath* the fat feeling?"

2. Refuse to buy or read magazines that emphasize thinness, and pay close attention to the messages society and the media give us. Be proactive with this information, not reactive. Consider writing letters to the editor stressing your concerns, or boycotting the magazines once and for all.

3. Begin to focus the concept of *inner beauty* for yourself and others. Look for beauty in personality and attitude and decrease the focus on physical appearance.

4. Fuel your body as you would fuel your car. Calories are energy; deprivation of calories can result in greater body-image distortion.

5. When you find yourself focusing on your body, vision a *stop sign*, and do not allow this focus to continue. "Thought stopping" will also lead to decreased focus and distortion.

Your Relationship with Exercise

Exercise! This word means so much. In addition to its definition of "exertion made for the sake of training," exercise also means: creating health, creating happiness, creating an identity. In another context, it may also mean creating un-health, unhappiness, and losing one's identity. In this chapter, we will help you to explore and understand your use of exercise, and explain how to incorporate a healthy, balanced exercise regime into your life.

As you have seen in the previous chapters, body-image concerns can encourage unhealthy relationships with food. When people don't like their bodies they fill their heads and hearts with negative self-statements, deny themselves relationships, and avoid loved activities. If the loved activity was exercise, instead of avoiding it, they may turn it into an "exercise in abuse." What was once loved becomes yet another means of self-flagellation, pushing the limits of what the body can endure. Sadly, once one forms a negative opinion of one's body, often a hurtful relationship with exercise ensues.

What is *healthy* exercise? How do we know how much exercise is good for health reasons, and when we have crossed the line into "over-exercising"? These questions are difficult for many of us to answer. It can be even more challenging and complicated for someone with an eating disorder. If you have a history of exercise, even if you believe it is strictly for health reasons, it is important to assess whether it is in balance. If you are struggling with food issues and a negative body image, your relationship with exercise bears exploration. Before we begin our journey through exercise and the role it plays in the development *and recovery* from eating disorders, take a moment to answer the following questions.

RATE YOUR RELATIONSHIP WITH EXERCISE

How healthy is your relationship with exercise? After you answer the questions, use the scale to assess the *health* of your relationship with exercise.

1) Why I exercise (please check all those that apply)
   a) I exercise for health maintenance and/or prevention (score 1)
   b) I exercise for weight management and/or weight loss (score 1)
   c) I exercise as a means of releasing emotions (score 1)
   d) I exercise as a means of body sculpting (score 1)
   e) I exercise for fun (score 1)
   f) I exercise in an attempt to create a body similar to someone I see on TV or in magazines (score 2)
   g) I exercise as a way to get rid of calories (score 2)
   h) I exercise as a way to give myself permission to eat (score 2)
   i) I exercise as a way of punishing myself (score 2)
   j) I don't exercise (score 2)

2) I exercise (choose only 1)
   a) Not at all (score 0)
   b) Less than 3 times per week (score 1)
   c) 3–5 times per week (score 2)
   d) 5–7 times per week (score 3)

3) The amount of time spent during an aerobic exercise session is (choose only 1)
   a) Not at all (score 0)
   b) Less than 30 minutes (score 1)
   c) 30–60 minutes (score 2)
   d) 60 minutes or more (score 3)

4) When I look in the mirror, I like what I see.
   a) False (score 0)
   b) True (score 1)

5) If I couldn't exercise on a particular day that I had planned on, I would (choose only 1) . . .
   a) be okay (score 0)
   b) feel a bit guilty but overall be okay (score 1)
   c) feel very guilty and uncomfortable and feel the need to compensate (but not actually compensate) (score 2)
   d) feel very guilty and uncomfortable and find a way to compensate (score 3)

If you have scored 0–8, chances are you do not exercise enough, and you have not developed an exercise regime for health maintenance. As a result, your relationship with exercise is non-existent, and therefore, not healthy. You are more susceptible to developing complications as a result of lack of exercise, and may be more susceptible to obesity. We recommend you consult your physician and consider developing a healthy exercise routine (in moderation).

If you have scored 9–11, you have a good relationship with exercise, however, there may be some room for improvement. Make sure you are not leaning toward a pattern of disordered eating, and that you keep your exercise consistent and fun. It is important that you be realistic with your particular body type, and not strive for unrealistic goals. You may want to consider meeting with a nutritionist and/or personal trainer as a means to keeping your attitude toward exercise, food, and weight in balance.

If you have scored 12–14, you have a very healthy relationship with exercise.; it looks as if you have found the healthy balance between exercise and health, and you are exercising for all of the right reasons. Keep up the good work!

If you have scored 15 or more, you do not have a healthy relationship with exercise. You are more likely to be struggling with over-exercising or exercise as a result of body-image issues. You are more likely to be struggling with disordered eating, if not an eating disorder, and you are at risk for physical and emotional difficulties. It is strongly recommended that you contact your physician for further evaluation.

EXERCISE GUIDELINES

Although research varies, it can be assumed that the recommendations for healthy exercise consist of 5–7 days per week of exercise for a duration of 30–40 minutes per episode. Unlike what many of us have been told, this exercise does not have to be aerobic in nature. What is more important is the *quantity* and *frequency* of prescribed exercise; less attention is paid to the intensity of exercise. This is good news for many of us, for we have now found that we were exercising when we had not necessarily been aware of it. For example, taking the stairs to your place of employment or parking away from the shopping mall now provides exercise . . . exercise toward our weekly requirements. Playing ball with our children, gardening, pushing a baby stroller are all forms of exercise that are part of a regular day for many. Yet many people do not realize that they are keeping healthy while having fun.

For many sedentary people, this has been welcome news to their ears! No longer do you need to sweat it out at the gym in order to be on a physical fitness plan. However, even with these new guidelines, many people do not get nearly enough exercise to maintain their health; and many people over-exercise in a way that compromises their health.

PHYSICAL BENEFITS OF EXERCISE

What does exercise do for us when incorporated regularly? Here are some specific physical benefits of exercise:

Heart: The human heart is a muscle. As with other muscles, the more we work our heart through exercise, the stronger it is going to become. This strength is equated with efficiency, which results in a decreased likelihood of heart disease or heart attacks. The athletic heart has an average heart rate of 60 beats per minute. This slow heart rate speaks to its efficiency.

Lungs: Regular exercise helps the lungs to move air in and out. Therefore, more oxygen is brought into the body, and more carbon dioxide and other wastes are expelled. Regular exercise helps keep oxygen intake up which challenges the body's natural response to decreased oxygen intake as we age and become increasingly sedentary.

Cholesterol: Regular exercise reduces our level of low-density lipoprotein (LDL) or "bad cholesterol" and fats in our blood. In addition to this, exercise also increases high-density lipoprotein (HDL) or "good cholesterol." Exercise increases the flexibility of the walls of blood vessels, which works to reverse hardening of the arteries. This, in turn, helps to lower blood pressure. By lowering LDL and increasing HDL, there is less likelihood of cutting off blood flow, or clogged arteries, which are major causes of stroke and heart attack.

Weight: In order to run, our bodies need fuel, just as our cars need gasoline. This fuel that we use is called calories. We need calories in order to "run" effectively, however excess calories become converted into fat. Our working muscles help burn off this fat. Thus, the more we exercise, the more likely we are to burn the necessary calories for weight loss or maintenance. If, however, we do not take in enough calories, and require our body to use our "fuel" through exercise, the result is going to be that our metabolism is going to slow down in order to help us continue to "run." Thus, exercise alone is not sufficient for weight loss; the combination of healthy eating and exercise is going to result in the greatest likelihood of weight loss and health. Each person's body has its own set point weight. Set point refers to the weight range each body seeks to maintain. For further information on set point theory refer to Chapter 2.

Cancer: Studies have shown that regular exercise helps lower occurrences of cancers of the breast, colon, uterus, and prostate. Exercise speeds digestion of food through the colon, which results in a decrease in the time it can cause irritations that can create cancer. For women, exercise can help reduce body fat. Body fat produces estrogen, and higher levels of estrogen have been found to increase the risk of female cancers, including endometrial and breast cancer, and to facilitate the growth of already existing cancers.

Bones: Exercise increases bone density which helps prevent osteoporosis.

Emotional health: Regular exercise increases a neurochemical in the brain called serotonin. Increased levels of serotonin are associated with decreased depression, increased focus and concentration, increased energy, and an increase in overall well-being. In addition to this, exercise releases endorphins into the bloodstream, which have also been shown to result in feelings of well-being.

As you can see, regular exercise can be a vital ingredient of health and happiness. If you are reading this book, however, chances are you are struggling with how to incorporate *healthy* exercise into your lifestyle. Regardless of your score on the exercise quiz, please read on. **Remember, these guidelines are for people whose physicians have determined they are capable of a regular exercise regimen. If you are underweight, overweight, or suffering from other medical complications, your physician may restrict or prohibit exercise. Consult your physician before starting or continuing any exercise regimen.**

IDENTIFYING COMMON EXERCISE PROBLEMS

exercising more than 7 times per week
exercising less than 5 times per week
exercising when in physical pain
exercising without enjoyment
exercising to rid body of calories
exercising more than prescribed by physician
choosing elevators over stairs
exercising for permission to eat
obsessive-compulsive attitude
ritualistic behaviors with exercise
restrictive eating as a result of exercise

exercising more than 2 hours per episode
exercising less than 30 minutes per episode
exercising when injured
feelings of guilt when not exercising
exercising to acquire an unrealistic body
exercising less than prescribed by physician
parking close to building
excessive exercise
behaviors toward exercise
binge eating as a result of exercise
other: _____

Do you recognize any of these behaviors or attitudes in yourself? Write down all that you recognize and mark with an asterisk (*) those you'd like to change.

1)_____
2)_____
3)_____
4)_____
5)_____
6)_____
7)_____
8)_____

Remember, writing down your challenges with exercise and wanting to change does not mean that you are going to be able to change immediately. Successful change occurs when you want to change and when you understand what fears you will face as you change.

It is important to distinguish between two important concepts—*want* and *need*. This distinction is important, for in order to facilitate healthy change, you are going to need to focus on what you *need*, despite what you may *want*! The following example and exercise will help you with this process.

WEIGHT LOSS: MY PATH TO DESPAIR AND DESTRUCTION

I was an overweight child, so weight has always been an issue for me. As a matter of fact, I cannot remember a time in my life when I was not concerned about my weight. My diet history goes back to the tender age of 8; at that time, I attended Weight Watchers with my mom. She believed that if I lost weight I would feel better about myself. Although I never lost weight on this first diet, I did manage to "get the message." This message was that *fat is not good; it is not normal.* If I was to be good and normal, I was going to have to find a way to get rid of my fat.

As with many overweight children, I was teased. I can remember the names I was given by my peers: fatso, fat cow, fat pig. Rarely was I referred to as Erika; I was only 8 years old, and already my identity was being determined by my weight.

As we all know, middle school years are years of awkwardness! For me, it continued to be a time of great distress. Although I did have friends, I never felt as if I was anyone's best friend. With the boys, I was a "friend." When I would express an interest in one of the boys in my class, the common response from my friends would be, "He says you are a nice girl, but you are not his type." Really what they were saying is, "What are you kidding . . . she's fat!"

By the time high school came along, I felt free from the awkwardness of preadolescence. However, I was thrown into the adolescent pack, and tried desperately to find a way to survive. As we all know, high school is a time in which relationships are based much more on physical appearance than anything else. I knew I didn't have what it took to catch any boy's eye, but what was worse was that my friends appeared to be the poster children for "perfection." I didn't fit in, and I knew why; this is when it all began.

I was a freshman in high school and determined to make a change. Never did I realize that in doing so, my life would never be the same. What started out as an innocent attempt to lose weight gradually turned into a path of despair and destruction. I began with a diet, and somehow it snowballed out of control. Before I knew it, I was stuck in the middle of a crazy obsession that controlled every aspect of my life.

My dieting began to lead to confusion. No longer was I aware of what was "good" to eat. As a result, I began to restrict what I ate, and would feel guilty when eating foods that I was uncertain about. In an attempt to deal with this guilt, I joined a gym. I believed that if I began exercising more, this could help me feel better about eating foods about which I was uncertain.

After a few months, I started to lose weight. People noticed and I began to receive compliments. This felt particularly nice, considering that I don't *ever* remember receiving compliments as a child. In order to maintain these compliments and newfound attention, I continued restricting my intake and over-exercising. Before I knew it, I had dropped 5 clothing sizes and approximately fifty pounds. My eating disorder didn't allow me to see the changes in my body. I was struggling with an intensely negative body-image distortion (I only know this now through years of therapy). This distortion left me feeling dissatisfied with my weight and myself, and reinforced my eating disorder. No matter how much weight I was losing, it wasn't enough . . . I always wanted to lose ten more pounds. As my weight loss continued, I developed excess body hair (called lanugo), muscle tears, and an obsession with food, calories, and weight that interfered with every aspect of my life.

Eventually, I succumbed to my hunger. Individuals with anorexia *do* get hungry! I was starving myself and I could feel it. I began to eat . . . and eat . . . and eat until I couldn't stop. I literally could not stop! When I finally did, I panicked. I knew I couldn't let this "YUCK" stay inside of me. In a state of panic, I marched myself off to the bathroom and made myself throw up. I continued to force my body to respond in a way that it was not wanting to until no food was remaining. When I saw blood and bile, I felt relieved. It was out of me, and I wasn't going to get fat! I had found a way to eat and not gain weight . . . or so I thought. No one had told me that vomiting does not necessarily help with weight loss. It wasn't until I was in therapy that I realized that I was gaining weight in an attempt to lose weight; she was right—it doesn't work. My head, however, didn't care. It continued to tell me to get rid of anything "bad" that I had put in my mouth, and not to stop until it was all gone.

I continued through high school living this way. I had been confronted on numerous occasions by guidance counselors, friends, and friends of my family. I thought they were all crazy; I was fine, and no one was going to convince me otherwise. By my senior year, however, I became a little anxious when I stopped and thought about what may happen when I leave for college. What was I going to do? How was I going to hide the fact that I barely ate? How was I going to get my work done *and* work out four hours a day? I was scared to death, and I didn't know how to deal with it. Obviously, I wasn't thinking about being scared of death, even though I was slowly heading in that direction.

My other question, as I thought about heading to college, was how am I going to avoid the "freshman 15"? I was constantly hearing about this, and was determined not to let it get me. It didn't; in fact, I did just the opposite. The "freshman 15" can become a self-fulfilling prophecy. With the correct balance of nutritious foods and healthy exercise, the "freshman 15" can be history. A healthy weight can be attained without taking extremes. Yes, I can say this now! Back then I was too busy fearing the "freshman 15" to conceptualize the notion of healthy eating.

My behaviors did not change my freshman and sophomore year. In fact, I was continuing to lose weight. I was also continuing to see a very distorted image of myself. There was one change, however. I now had my own bathroom. This meant I no longer had to throw up in plastic bags. I continued to believe that I'd be happy if only I was thin. All my problems would magically disappear if only I was thin. Funny, I continued to lose weight, but I did not feel I was getting closer to feelings of happiness. In fact, I was becoming even more miserable. I felt disconnected from my friends; I hardly ever went out, and when I did, I spent my time looking at how thin and/or beautiful everyone else was. It wasn't fun! It captured every part of me . . . every part of my mind, body, and soul. It felt as if everything was falling apart, and that there was nothing I could do.

My equilibrium was way off because my electrolytes were off; I constantly felt dizzy, developed an ulcer, and was fatigued all the time. I couldn't take it anymore. I felt as if I was going crazy; my head would not stop spinning and the only things I could think about were food, fat, and exercise. It was as if my head was running on a treadmill . . . even when my body wasn't! I had a choice; I could starve myself until my body began to eat my organs because it had no other source of nourishment, and literally die of starvation, or I could get help. I chose the latter.

I thought by going to a therapist I was going to miraculously get better. I believed that the therapist could take away the six plus years of obsessing about food, fat, and exercise. Boy was I in for the surprise of my life! I had never realized that eating disorders were *not* about food and weight. I began to uncover pieces of my life that had been pushed so far down that I didn't even know they had existed. I began to understand just how strongly childhood experiences, relationships with parents, friends, abusive boyfriends, and society contributes to the development

Continued

of eating disorders. I began to uncover things that I certainly never intended to uncover. Having an eating disorder isn't easy by any means; recovering is even harder! My eating disorder had been my identity since I was eight years old. Therapy meant saying "good-bye" to this identity and figuring out who I am without it. Recovery meant preparing to live in a world that I had never been in before. It was both terrifying and exciting. It was also hard work!

Recovery has also showed me things I never knew I had an interest in: poetry, writing, children. I have learned so much about my life and myself in the past two years of therapy; I believe my eating disorder helped me to do this. Although I never want it back, I do believe it has helped me to appreciate my life of today. An eating disorder is not something that just happens one day. You don't just "try it for a little while." It doesn't work that way. It is a disease—a disease that will take over your world and life. You need to know you are not alone and it can get better. But you have to want to get better, because no one can help you if you don't want to be helped.

Erika, age 23

Want Versus Need

Behavioral concern: *exercising more than five times per week.*
Want: *I want to continue to run 6 times per week . . . I will take Sundays off.*
Need: *I need to be running no more than 5 times per week for healthy exercise.*

Behavioral concern: _____

   Want: _____

   Need: _____

Behavioral concern: _____

   Want: _____

   Need: _____

Behavioral concern: _____

   Want: _____

   Need: _____

Behavioral concern: _____

Want: _____

Need: _____

Behavioral concern: _____

Want: _____

Need: _____

Behavioral concern: _____

Want: _____

Need: _____

Behavioral concern: _____

Want: _____

Need: _____

Behavioral concern: _____

Want: _____

Need: _____

This exercise may have been, or may continue to be quite difficult for you. If this is the case, we recommended that you consult with a therapist, physician, or other person who you know has a healthy relationship with exercise. They may be able to better help you with what you need.

Now that you have considered what you *need*, we ask that you go back to those needs and use a pencil, pen, or highlighter to further bring them to your attention. From this point forward, we are going to ask you to practice working toward your *needs* . . . despite your *wants*. This may be difficult for you, so we ask that you practice and that you focus on one need at a time. There is no need to change everything at once; as a matter of fact, you will be more able to create a successful lifestyle change if you do *not* attempt to change all your needs at once. The exercise below will help you in this endeavor. Patience is a virtue . . . and it facilitates change and recovery. You have successfully acknowledged your concerns with exercise, and are now in the process of exploring how to go about changing. This process is often easier said than done! Take one goal at a time. We will help you devise a strategy for accomplishing each goal, and we'll ask that you patiently practice before moving on to the next goal. It is not necessary for you to achieve mastery before moving on to the next goal; however, it is going to be important that you allow yourself many opportunities at practicing your first goal before moving on to the next (and so on).

Three Steps Toward Change

First, write each of the things that you need to change. Next, explore the 3 steps you will take—behavioral, emotional, and cognitive (thinking)—to accomplish this goal. For example:

Change: *I need to work on exercising less than 7 times per week.*
Behavioral goal: *I am going to need to stay away from the gym for one day.*
Emotional goal: *I am probably going to be irritable and anxious when I don't work out, so I will plan to be with someone to help me fight these feelings.*
Cognitive goal: *I am going to have to keep telling myself that missing one day of exercise is not going to make me fat!*

Change: _____

Behavioral Goal: _____
_____

Emotional Goal: _____
_____

Cognitive Goal: _____
_____

Change: _____

Behavioral Goal: _____
_____

Emotional Goal: _____
_____

Cognitive Goal: _____
_____

Change: _____

Behavioral Goal: _____
_____

Emotional Goal: _____
_____

Cognitive Goal: _____
_____

Change: _____

Behavioral Goal: _____
_____

Emotional Goal: _____
_____

Cognitive Goal: _____
_____

Are you more aware of how exercise can be healthy or unhealthy, a route to happiness or a route to unhappiness? Exercise can help create a person's identity or strip her of her identity. Exercise can help a person excel at a sport, which helps that person create her identity as an athlete, and thus increases her self-esteem.

Exercise to excess, however, actually strips the person of any identity, as it begins to control her life. This is because exercise becomes the primary focus, and all other aspects of her life which helped create her identity have been stripped away in order to maintain her level of exercise. If you, or those who care about you, believe exercise has interfered with your life in any way, go on to the following exercise.

EXERCISE AND IDENTITY

If you exercise on a regular basis, it is important that you complete the following. Is your exercise in balance or is it interfering with your personal development and growth?

1) Why do you exercise? _____

_____

_____

_____

2) Have you ever chosen to not participate in certain social activities in order to exercise? If Yes, please explain.

_____

_____

_____

3) Do you have *balance* in your life? Do you know what balance is (for you)? Please explain.

_____

_____

_____

_____

_____

_____

_____

If you don't have balance in your life, please use the space below to define what you need to do in order to create a healthy balance, and, therefore, find and/or maintain your identity as a complete person.

I Can Create Balance in the Following Ways . . .

1)_____

_____

2)_____

_____

3)_____

_____

4)_____

_____

5)_____

_____

6)_____

_____

You have now completed your journey through exercise. Next we'll look at special circumstances which appear to contribute to the development of eating disorders in women and men, as well as the consequences on each of the sexes.

Women's Issues

This chapter will focus on issues of particular concern to women with eating disorders. We will start with a focus on body image and appearance and move on to a section on negative self-statements which erode self-esteem and intensify body dissatisfaction. We'll teach you how to develop affirmations which will replace any negative self-talk, and which can enhance self-esteem and body care.

Other care issues discussed in the chapter are infertility, pregnancy, and the needs of the unborn fetus and the newborn baby; osteoporosis—what causes it and how to protect your bones from this devastating condition; sexuality and how eating disorder symptoms often parallel sexual issues; and, finally, we'll ask you to assess your own issues and encourage you to bring issues you discover to your therapist and physician.

> you were born a daughter.
> you looked up to your mother.
> you looked up to your father.
> you looked up to everyone . . .
> you wanted to be a princess.
> you wanted to own a horse.
> you wanted to wear pink.
> you never wanted to wear pink.

you wanted to be a veterinarian.
you wanted to be president.
you wanted to be the president's veterinarian.
you were picked last for the team.
you were the best one on the team.
you refused to be on the team.
you wanted to do well in algebra.
you hid during algebra.
you wanted boys to notice you.
you were afraid the boys would notice you.
you started to get acne.
you started to get breasts.
you started to get acne that was bigger than your breasts.
you wouldn't wear a bra.
you couldn't wait to wear a bra.
you couldn't fit into a bra.
you didn't like the way you looked.
you didn't like the way your parents looked.
you didn't want to grow up.
you had your first best friend.
you had your first date.
you spent hours on the telephone.
you got kissed.
you got to kiss back.
you went to the prom.
you didn't go to the prom.
you went to the prom with the wrong person.
you spent hours on the telephone.
you fell in love.
you fell in love.
you fell in love.
you lost your best friend.
you lost your other best friend.
you really fell in love.
you became a steady girlfriend.
you became a significant other.
you became significant to yourself.
sooner or later, you started to take yourself seriously.
you know when you need a break.
you know when you need a rest.
you know what to get worked up about, and what to get rid of.
and you know when it's time to take care of yourself, for yourself.
to do something that makes you stronger, faster, more complete.
because you know it's never too late to live life.
and never too late to change one.

—Anonymous
(sent to me [M. Villapiano] from Lisa who received
it from her dear friend, Flora)

Lisa, like so many other women, continues on her quest for recovery from a debilitating eating disorder. Knowing what she needs and knowing how to care for herself are two elusive pieces of knowledge which she seeks. Knowing that she can change, and knowing that she has the love, support, and care of others to "live life" seems to be the "fuel" that sustains her battle for her life.

Lisa, like so many other women, feels that the impediment to life without an eating disorder is acceptance of and appreciation for her body . . . and as a corollary, acceptance of and appreciation for herself.

NOT GOOD ENOUGH: BODY DISTORTION

In a study done at St. George's Hospital Medical School in London, it was found that 50 average-sized women were able to accurately estimate the width of a box, yet they over-estimated the size of their hips by 16% and waists by 25%. Women seem to have a skewed perception of their own body sizes, which, in cultures where thinness is a perceived prerequisite for a woman's worth, promotes efforts to achieve an elusive, and often unattainably small size. This puts women at risk for behaviors supportive of the development of eating disorders.

Women's efforts to sculpt, reshape, and reduce their bodies have led to an enormous increase in plastic and reconstructive surgery techniques. No longer are dieting, exercising, and other weight-reduction techniques adequate to this quest, but expensive, sometimes dangerous, and ill-conceived operations are sought in an effort to look "good enough" in the hopes of feeling "good enough."

D. W. Winnicott, a famous psychiatrist, wrote extensively about the concept of being "good enough." His "good enough" referred to mothering. He conceived that a child who saw reflected in her mother's eyes a loving and admiring gaze was receiving "good enough" mothering. This child could and would feel that she was "good enough" because that message had been reflected to her via the eyes of the love object (typically, mother, but also father or other primary caretaker). Do women continue to change, reduce, reshape, and sculpt their bodies in the hopes that they will be gazed upon with the loving and admiring gaze of their archetypal mothers . . . in the hopes that they might someday see themselves as "good enough"?

Winnicott's notion transcended the physical. Mothers of disabled, severely deformed, and homely children gazed in the same loving way as those with perfectly formed and healthy children. Their gaze was meant to convey that to their inner depths . . . and despite all physical considerations . . . these children were truly, deeply, and completely loved. Many women, it seems, are hoping that if they just *look* good enough they will be "loved enough." Because many women believe that a smaller size or shapelier figure will attract a love object—and in our society it does attract—they hope that it will attract love. Although it often does attract, it does not necessarily attract love. True and complete love reaches to the core, as it does for the "good enough" mother. This is very different from physical attraction.

But if a woman doesn't know how to *get love*, she will *attract*. Thus, women's quest to attract has moved from the newest diet which promised them weight loss, to the newest plastic surgery technique which promises them a sculpted body. They have supported the billion-dollar weight loss industry and they are now amassing a similar support for the industry of plastic and reconstructive surgery. Here are some statistics.

LOOKING FOR LOVE: APPEARANCE AND BODY IMAGE

According to the American Society of Plastic and Reconstructive Surgeons (ASPRS), in 1997 there were three times more lipoplasty (better known as liposuction) procedures performed than in 1992—47,212 in 1992, and 149,042 in 1997. Eighty-six percent of those undergoing liposuction procedures were female and 14% were male.

Although women desire to reduce their overall sizes, they seek to increase the size of their breasts to come closer to what is referred to as the "Barbie Doll look." Here are the numbers to prove it. According to ASPRS, in 1992, 32,607 women sought breast augmentation procedures while 122,285 sought this procedure in 1997—an increase of 215%.

In an article in *People* magazine, January 1992, Dr. George Semel, a Beverly Hills physician, was quoted as saying, "Plastic surgery is mandatory for a lot of what makes for successful leading men and ladies. . . . It's as much apart of the scene as taking acting lessons."

Many in our culture feel the same. It doesn't matter how you get the perfect body as long as you have it. If there are emotional or physical scars, it doesn't matter. If your health and well-being are compromised, it doesn't matter. If you feel worthless and have no self-esteem without this perfect body, it doesn't matter. Sadly, many women don't care about their "contents" as long as the "packaging" is perfect—the wrapping of the gift is more important than the gift. Yet, their essence—their unique gift to themselves and the world—is relegated to "unimportant." This leads to a tragic and profound sense of loss, an emptiness, and a self not worthy without its external trappings.

The political ramifications of this are astounding. It is no longer that women are held back because they are caring for children and homes, unable to enter the work force or college, or unable to rise in the corporate and professional ranks. Women have achieved reasonable equality . . . if not in pay or rank, then in access to the world of work and education. But the most profound cultural, societal, and political sanction to the ascent of women is the sinister and effective derailment of their energy, motivation, and tenacity. Virulent body hatred and the frenzied quest for the perfect body *at any cost* siphons off women's emotional and physical energy, vibrancy, motivation, creativity, and joy. How many times have you spoken to bright, talented girls and women who denigrate themselves or deprive themselves of opportunities because of their body hatred?

> Sally refused to let herself go for a walk for fear someone would see her. She would not go on job interviews because she was ashamed of her size. She wouldn't even attend her niece's birthday party, an event she would have loved to attend, because she felt inferior to all the other female relatives who, according to her, are "tiny." Since she did not see herself as an acceptable size, she refused to let herself go.

> Cheryl does not feel worthy of adequate food, and certainly does not feel she should have sweets, because she is "too fat" at 94 lb. So what if she is dehydrated each time she sees the doctor who threatens her with the hospital. So what if she is not allowed to drive by her doctor and parents because she is too weak. So what if she was denied a full complement of courses by her school (which she loves) because she has missed so much school due to her frequent hospitalizations. Because she did not see herself as thin enough, she missed out on all the things she said she wanted and valued. She doesn't think she is worthy of these good things because her body is "disgusting."

What are the messages you give yourself? In what forms of body dissatisfaction or hatred do you engage?

You can work at changing your negative body image if you stop saying negative things about your body and stop engaging in hurtful behaviors which promote body dissatisfaction.

Body Dissatisfaction Survey

Answer the following statements True or False to determine what attitudes and behaviors contribute to your body dissatisfaction.

1. I read women's, fashion, fitness, and movie magazines   T   F
   more than other kinds of magazines.

2. I read the fat grams and calorie contents of most foods that I eat.   T   F

3. I often look at my reflection in plate glass windows, store   T   F
   front windows, car windows, and mirrors.

4. I often compare my body to those of other women.   T   F

5. I sometimes refuse to do certain activities because I am not   T   F
   happy with my body.

6. I exercise often (or don't exercise at all) because I am not happy   T   F
   with the way my body looks.

7. I often tell myself that my body is too fat, or too large, or   T   F
   too out-of-shape.

8. I keep clothing in my closet that I cannot wear unless I   T   F
   lose weight.

9. I find myself envying women who are (or whom I perceive are)   T   F
   smaller, thinner, or in better shape than I.

10. I think that I would do things (that I do not do now) or feel better   T   F
    (than I do now) if I lost weight.

If you answered True to most or all of the statements above, you are fueling your body dissatisfaction by your attitudes and behaviors. This section will help you look at some of the ways you could work to increase your body satisfaction. Be aware that *increasing your body satisfaction does not mean decreasing your care for your body. It does not mean becoming slovenly or lazy or not caring about how you look. It means caring about your body in compassionate ways.* Some people think that if they criticize or denigrate their body enough . . . if they deprive themselves of activities, pleasure, or fun because their bodies aren't thin enough or in good enough shape, it will finally motivate them to lose weight and get into better shape. In general, this approach doesn't work. Have you ever seen a child become happier and healthier as a result of criticism? We haven't. But we have seen children and adult men and women grow happier and healthier through loving care. It is this loving care—not criticism or neglect—which fosters emotional and physical health.

Tips to Enhance Body Satisfaction

1. Read a variety of magazines such as news, travel, professional, or hobby magazines (e.g., crafts, skiing, architecture, music). Broaden your horizons!

2. If you read women's, fashion, fitness, or movie magazines, look at them more skeptically. Do they promote physical and emotional health? Do they depict all body types in equally positive ways? Do they celebrate the talent, creativity, and character of the people they write about, or do they focus primarily on physical attributes?

3. Stop making food decisions based on fat grams or calorie counts. Select foods you enjoy and foods that are healthy.

4. Don't look in mirrors unless you are applying makeup or fixing your hair.

5. Don't look at your reflection in plate glass windows, store front windows, car windows, or full-length mirrors. Decrease your *superficial focus* on your body. This may help you decrease your body dissatisfaction.

6. Look at other women with appreciation. Notice how they use color or fabric. Notice creativity. Notice facial expression. Notice how they move. Notice how they interact. Notice the differences between women and children, men and children, the young and the elderly. Notice with appreciation, not criticism or envy.

7. Engage in activities you love. Do something you love every day—take a walk, read a good book, paint, sing, dig in your garden, play the piano, ride your bike. Never let your feelings about your body restrict you from activities you love.

8. Socialize. Go out with friends, join a club (not weight loss), share dinner with a family member. Don't let your feelings about your body isolate you from nourishing relationships.

9. Discard or give away all clothing that encourages you to be an unhealthy, low weight. Someone who has very little could use it. Keeping it will "keep you unhappy."

10. Take care of your body. Bathe, exercise moderately, use cosmetics and fragrances you love, stretch, rest, eat healthfully and moderately, get enough sleep, wear clothing that is comfortable and fits well.

11. Tell your body how you appreciate it. Revel in what your body can do (e.g., walk, talk, see, hear, "smell the roses"). Tell your body it deserves loving care whatever its size; then give it that care.

12. Don't let others criticize, denigrate, or hurt your body.

THE POWER OF POSITIVE SELF-TALK AND AFFIRMATIONS

Affirmations and positive self-talk can support emotional and physical health and promote the achievement of goals. They point us in positive directions, help us conquer the difficulties in life, and help us see others and ourselves more positively. Words can hurt and words can heal.

Sometimes we don't even recognize the extent to which we engage in negative self-talk. It is amazing how debilitating it is to our self-esteem. How can we believe in ourselves and appreciate and care for our bodies or ourselves if we are constantly berating, criticizing, and unhappily talking to our bodies and ourselves? We can't. Therefore, we need to stop the negative talk and engage in positive and reinforcing talk.

The task now is to silence the critic in you that says you can't speak positively to yourself because you are "fat," "disgusting," "stupid," "lazy,"" boring," or "ugly." We would say, If you do not change the way you speak to yourself, you will always feel these things. To the inner critic who says that saying positive things to yourself means you are conceited or narcissistic, We would say learning to speak to yourself in compassionate and caring ways is nurturing, not conceited or narcissistic. Positive self-talk leads to having positive feelings about the self. Having positive feelings about the self leads to positive treatment of the self. Positive treatment of the self leads to having positive feelings about the self. Do you see how these conditions reinforce and amplify each other?

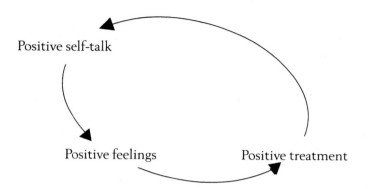

Positive self-talk

Positive feelings   Positive treatment

For one day keep a record of your negative self-talk. Write down each negative thing you say to yourself and tally up your list at the end of the day. See if the negative comments are related to one area of your life or many parts of your life. Are they just about your body or do they relate to your intelligence or competency at school or your job? Do they relate to your ability to socialize, communicate, or develop relationships? Once you have done this you will know what areas in your life need affirmation.

Situation	Negative Self-Talk	Affirmation
Late to work. Stuck in traffic.	I'm so stupid!	I did the best I could. I will leave earlier tomorrow.
Dropped tray at work. Little girl ran in front of me.	I'm such a klutz!	I did nothing wrong. Parents should not let their children run around in restaurants.
Mother wants me to take her shopping. I have an exam to study for. I tell her I can't.	I am so selfish!	It's very important that I learn to take care of myself.
Man whistles and says, "Look at that ass!"	I'm fat and disgusting!	I am healthy and attractive, and I am not going to be affected by others.
I ate a cookie at school today.	I'm a pig! Why don't I have any willpower?	I deserve foods that I like. I am learning to feed and care for myself as I would care for a child if I had one.

Now it's time to write *your* plan for positive self-talk. This means writing affirmations that you will practice many times each day. Notice if these affirmations lead you to feel more positively toward yourself. Notice if these affirmations encourage you to treat yourself better.

Set a goal to write 3 affirmations. Once you write them, make several copies and place them where you'll see them often, such as on your bathroom mirror, on your refrigerator, in your wallet, on your computer monitor, and on the dashboard of your car. Repeat them often, such as before each meal, each time you brush your teeth, before and after conversations with others, before bed, and when you wake up in the morning. Remember, it takes time to unlearn self-criticism and negative self-talk, and it takes practice to affirm yourself.

Situation	Negative Self-Talk	Affirmation

Affirmations

1. _____

2. _____

3. _____

If you're having trouble getting started, here is a list of affirmations our clients with eating disorders have helped develop over the years. Maybe some of these will be helpful to you.

Affirmations

1. I am lovable no matter what my size.

2. My eating disorder is the prison which keeps me from my true self.

3. Food is my medicine.

4. Food is neither good nor bad, but in moderation all foods provide nourishment for my body, mind, and soul.

5. Too much or too little food numbs my feelings and erases my ability to be free and alive.

6. As I feed and care for myself appropriately, I learn to love myself.

7. My body deserves good and compassionate care from me, even if it was not treated so by others.

8. My body will find its normal, healthy weight as I eat normally and healthfully.

9. As I tell myself I am worthy, I treat myself with value, and I learn to believe it.

10. Self-care and self-love is not selfish.

INFERTILITY AND PREGNANCY

Many women with eating disorders want, someday, to have children. They worry that, because of the effects of their disorder, they may not be able to conceive. They worry that they may not be able to nourish the child in utero because they cannot eat enough to sustain their own health. They worry that they may not be able to stop purging. Then, they worry about their ability to feed their infants adequately once they are born.

All of these worries are reasonable. Here are some ways to maximize your chances of conceiving and bearing a healthy child.

Infertility: What are Some Causes?

Although many women with eating disorders do successfully conceive, the following three factors may interfere with ovulation and cause infertility: (a) being underweight, (b) excessive exercise, and (c) chaotic eating. If you are experiencing any of these problems, it is better to seek medical and psychological treatment to correct them than to seek infertility treatment.

A study showed that a high incidence of women attending infertility clinics have weight preoccupation and eating disorders (Goldbloom, 1993). If you are underweight, excessively exercising, or eating chaotically it may not only affect your fertility, but it may affect your growing fetus once you conceive. Therefore, it's better to address these problems in psychotherapy and with the help of a nutritionist and your physician before embarking on a course of infertility treatment. It will benefit you and the health of your unborn child.

Eating disorder behaviors of course are not the only causes of infertility. A thorough work-up by a physician will determine any other possible causes for you.

Pregnancy

AM I READY TO BE PREGNANT?

There is good reason to work on your recovery before becoming pregnant. Studies have shown that many women with eating disorder symptoms at the time of conception had: (a) a worsening of symptoms during pregnancy, (b) gained less weight, and (c) had babies with lower birth weights and lower 5-minute Apgar scores than women whose eating disorder symptoms were in remission at the time of conception.

What this means is that becoming pregnant stresses your body and your psyche. Even when the event is welcomed, many changes occur. Any change, even those that are desired, puts a stress on our coping abilities and requires that we adapt to something new and different.

WILL MY EATING DISORDER WORSEN?

The body's adaptation to pregnancy is dramatic. Even before the body grows in size, hormonal shifts occur. These shifts can cause fatigue and nausea. If you already have problems because you are not eating enough or you are purging, nausea due to morning sickness may present a more serious problem for you than for the non-eating-disordered woman who becomes pregnant. This is because nausea makes it *harder to eat* and *harder not to purge*. Research studies show that women with eating disorders generally do have a more protracted course of *hyperemesis gravidarum*, or nausea and vomiting during pregnancy than do non-eating-disordered women.

Research studies also show that many women with a present or past history of an eating disorder do not divulge this information to their physicians. Doing this, of course, limits your physician's ability to provide you with the optimal course of treatment. If you currently have an eating disorder, a physician may want to treat yours as a high-risk pregnancy. Therefore, it is important that you tell your physician about your symptoms and your history. This will provide you and your unborn baby with better care and a better chance at a positive birth outcome.

WILL PREGNANCY HELP ME RECOVER?

The answer, for some women is "yes"—symptoms decrease, at least during the pregnancy itself. This, however, can be temporary. Recovery requires more than symptom reduction. Pregnancy may move you in the right direction, but recovery means not resuming symptoms once the baby is born. It also means developing the ability to cope with stresses and underlying issues other than through starvation, bingeing, purging, or the adoption of some other harmful means of coping.

For some women with eating disorders who become pregnant, the miracle of a growing life within them suddenly gives them permission to take care of and nurture themselves. Although they do not feel worthy of such nurturing themselves, they would not deprive their growing baby of all that it needs. For many women with eating disorders, there is evidence of a reduction of restrictive eating, binge eating, and purging behaviors during pregnancy. When symptoms are brought under control, the growing fetus has a better chance at survival.

Some women can remain asymptomatic while they breastfeed, as well. They will care for themselves as long as the baby derives its nurturance from their body.

Will My Baby be Affected?

If you are struggling with eating disorder symptoms when you conceive, especially if the symptoms are severe, the answer is probably, "yes." Here are the reasons.

LOW BIRTH WEIGHT AND LOW APGAR SCORES

If a pregnant mother does not gain enough weight during her pregnancy, her growing fetus may not gain enough as well. The normal birth weight is between 5.5 and 10 pounds. But the birth weight of the infant is not all the weight that a mother must gain. The uterine muscle mass must increase tremendously. The breasts become enlarged and the thyroid increases in size and activity. The pregnant woman must also produce an increased blood volume to provide an adequate blood supply to her growing baby. All this weight must be in addition to the weight of her infant. Birth weight is an important index of maturation and chance for survival. A birth weight of less than 5.5 pounds is associated with an increased chance of death in a newborn. The woman who is normal weight before she becomes pregnant should gain 3 to 4 pounds per month of her pregnancy. This means a total average weight gain of 25 to 35 pounds. If you are underweight your obstetrician will likely suggest that you gain more than this amount.

The Apgar score is a system of rating an infant's physical condition 1 minute and 5 minutes after birth. A low score at 1 minute means the infant needs assistance with its breathing. A low score at 5 minutes is an index of the possibility of death. The scoring goes from 0 to 2 on the following indices: (a) heart rate, (b) respiratory effort (or the effort it takes the infant to breathe), (c) muscle tone (does the child respond or remain limp when touched), (d) reflex irritability (does the child respond such as with a cough or sneeze when it's nose is tickled or does it remain unresponsive), and (e) color (is the child blue and pale or completely pink).

There is enhanced technology to increase the survival rate of underweight, premature, and low-Apgar-scoring infants. However, the best defense is a good offense, meaning that your good health will increase the chances of your baby's good health. Get the treatment and support you need to sustain your pregnancy and provide for your future child.

FETAL ABNORMALITIES AND BIRTH COMPLICATIONS

In addition to low birth weights and low Apgar scores, women with eating disorders have a higher rate of miscarriage. They also have higher rates of obstetric complications such as breech presentation and a higher C-section rate. Research studies have also concluded that there is a higher incidence of fetal abnormalities including cleft lip and palate. And, there seem to be more multiple births in those women with eating disorders than in those who are non-eating disordered.

Post-Partum: What About After I Have the Baby?

Although many women do better with their recovery during pregnancy because they wish to care for their unborn child, many do revert to eating disordered behaviors once they give birth. Many embark on weight-loss regimens and restrict their intake. Most worrisome, some restrict the intake of their infants and small children because they are so fearful their children will become fat.

Because it is so critical to the infant's development to have adequate nourishment, it is imperative that your pediatrician, as well as your obstetrician, knows about your history. It is important also to have very clear information about what your infant needs and to have someone review your feeding plan so you feed your infant enough.

Once your baby is born, you will need more, not less support. This is not the time to stop your own therapy. Your therapy is even more important because you will have many more stresses and questions to deal with. You must have help and support to take care of yourself and your child at this time. Your ability to feed yourself and your child adequately will determine yours and the baby's health and the strength of the mother-infant bond.

Although there is not a tremendous amount of research yet on the effects of a mother's eating disorder on her children, the results of two studies (Fahy & Treasure, 1989, and Stein & Fairburn, 1989) of mothers with bulimia nervosa as compared to mothers without eating disorders found the following. Mothers with bulimia nervosa were more likely to: (a) deprive their infants and children of adequate nourishment, (b) neglect their infants while they were binge eating and purging, (c) experience more feeding difficulties with their children, and (d) express greater anxiety about their child's weight and shape.

Motherhood can be wonderful. For women who tend to deprive themselves of love and care, loving and caring for an infant can inspire love and care in the self. Children love their mothers regardless of the mother's size. However, children will thrive physically and emotionally if their mothers are thriving physically and emotionally. Your chances of thriving will be enhanced by continuing in your psychotherapy, consulting a nutritionist for yourself and your baby, making certain your physician and your baby's pediatrician know your history and are actively helping you care for yourself and your baby, and having other loving, supportive family and friends in your life to help you care for yourself and your baby.

MY FIGHT TO FREE MYSELF FROM BULIMIA

Prior to college, I do not think I ever worried about my weight. I had been athletic and active. I was moderately tall and slender, so weight was not an issue for me. When I was in high school I blew out my knee; this was the beginning of seven knee operations which severely limited my sports ability and performance. I remember my brother telling me (prior to going to college) to "watch out for that freshman 15." I laughed at the time and never really thought about it, until I was in the middle of my freshman year and started to gain some weight. My eating habits left something to be desired. I never ate very healthily and with the addition of college food and the freedom, I started to gain a modest amount of weight. I was not exercising much at the time, and that (I believe) was also contributing to the problem. By the end of my freshman year I had gained approximately ten pounds. I felt uncomfortable with this weight gain, and decided to join a weight loss center. Never did I realize that this was the beginning of a battle with an eating disorder that would consume my life. My obsession with food and weight was a gradual, but steady, process. I began weighing myself daily and checking calorie and fat content in everything that I ate. I asked my mother to help me in my quest for weight loss; she participated in what she thought was helping me "eat better"! My new goal was to learn the fat gram and calorie content of every food. Upon returning to college, I continued with my obsession and daily weighing schedule. I was very unhappy with my body and my mind continued to play numerous tricks on me about my weight and need for perfection. I do not remember the first time I binged and purged; I am pretty sure I discovered this method of self-torture on the TV during this sophomore year. When my roommate and I moved into an apartment halfway through our sophomore year, things really started to get out of hand for me. The privacy made it much easier for me to get away with *my little secret* even though we shared a bathroom. I would treasure the time she would go out; I would look at this as my opportunity to be alone with my food! I began to turn down social situations, and found myself clinging to my new best friend . . . Bulimia. What is ironic, however, is that as much as I felt this was my best friend, it was continuing to hurt me and leave me not feeling very good about myself. I wasn't losing weight, despite my desire for weight loss. And as much as I knew that my bulimia wasn't helping me lose weight, I continued to participate in binge–purge behaviors. Slowly, I was digging myself in deeper; I knew this but this knowledge wasn't enough to help me stop!

Things continued to escalate during my sophomore and junior years. I was faced with another knee surgery and being in a cast and on crutches for about two months. This greatly limited my ability to exercise, and gave me more time to binge and purge. When I did go out on weekends, I would get drunk as a way to bury my pain and unhappiness with my body. It never really helped! I had broken up with a boyfriend that I had been with for over five years, in order to "explore" other possibilities. I was very shy and was wanting to date other men, but it was difficult for me as I felt insecure and unattractive. With things truly out of control, I finally told my best friend what I had been doing. Needless to say, she was shocked! I had gained 10–20 pounds and I was miserable with myself and every aspect of my life. I kept telling myself that if only I was thin, everything would be great. My roommate had no idea I had been bingeing and purging, even though we had lived together for 3½ years. I was so desperate and she could sense my unhappiness, but was unsure what was going on with me. She had her own life, and was not sure how to help me. She did help me though; she helped me by recommending that I find a

Continued

therapist and helped me in this quest. Once I was connected with a therapist, she never spied on me, and I never felt watched. I felt very vulnerable giving up my secret to her because I knew that it would make it more difficult for me to binge and purge.

I started seeing a specialist in eating disorders; she looked to me like she was struggling with an eating disorder and NOT in recovery. She was very guarded and did not give me a sense of safety or warmth. Because I wanted to rid myself of this eating disorder that was controlling my life, I continued to work with her (despite my concerns). I met with her for approximately two years, and also attended a support group that she had run. This group was very helpful, as it gave me an opportunity to talk with others experiencing similar struggles.

I remember sharing with my therapist the belief that my father was the problem, and that my mom and I had a great relationship and were the best of friends. Little did I know at the time that my relationship with my mom was part of the problem for me! My mom and step-dad attended several sessions with me, and our focus was on boundaries in our relationship (especially with my mom). It was during this time that I learned that mothers were not supposed to tell their daughters intimate details of their lives. I became very sensitive to boundary issues with my mom, and finally we began to look at these issues. I refused to bring my father into therapy, although my therapist pushed me in this direction. During this time I also began to journal in an effort to express my feelings. At the top of each page, I would document my weight. I guess this was an effort to punish myself on a daily basis. The journaling would help when I would actually follow through with it! Instead, I tended to be rather hit or miss around documenting my feelings, but I never missed a day of charting my weight!

As time went on, I was beginning to become disillusioned with my therapy, and felt that my therapist was struggling with an eating disorder and was not at all honest. After about two years of therapy with her, she referred me to a biofeedback therapist in an effort to address my chronic headaches. I had been somatic all my life, and my headaches were out of control. I agreed to see the biofeedback specialist and bonded with her immediately. She was sincere and down to earth, with little pretense. After seeing her for a few months, I opted to see her exclusively and terminated therapy with my other therapist. I am sure my first therapist served a purpose at that time, however I was ready to move on . . . and did. I saw my second therapist for about four years. I was dedicated to going, felt accepted, cared about, and my therapist was dedicated to working with me.

In addition to my therapy, I was also prescribed an antidepressant medication. In all honesty, I initially agreed to this, as I heard that it helped with weight loss. Well, it did not result in weight loss for me, but it did help me decrease my obsessional thinking. I started to feel much better and realized that I needed to get my priorities straight. I had a goal of getting a Master's degree and becoming a healthy therapist. I had seen what I considered was a person who was not a healthy therapist, and she inspired me to be different! I continued with my job as a mental health technician for seven years, and in 1992 received my Master's degree in marriage and family therapy. I was doing better with my eating disorder, although there were still times that I would struggle and want to revert back. I can recall times that I would drive to the local store, buy my binge foods, drive home and then put all the food down the garbage disposal. A few times I even threw the food out in a dumpster prior to getting home. This behavior was progress for me; I felt as if I had some power over the food, and this feeling empowered me!

In my therapy, I also learned that there was a correlation between these episodes with food and my relationships with men. I learned that I was too dependent on men for happiness and I was trying to break this destructive pattern. However, I was also terrified of being alone. I tried to avoid feelings of loneliness at any cost; this is where the food came to my rescue (or so I thought). I continued to choose men that just were not right for me and inherently I knew it, but I was afraid to leave the situation. I loved the excitement and the thrill and, as such, I found myself in relationships that provided that for me. It was a great escape and diversion for me. This is what I now refer to as the emotional roller coaster that kept me going nonstop. I stayed in a verbally and emotionally abusive relationship because *I* was afraid to hurt *him*! I knew he would not handle it well if I broke up with him, so I tried to convince myself that things were okay. He never raised a hand at me, but he was very passive aggressive and would fight to win; it was very subtle and I often thought I was making it all up. Funny, this was also the feeling I got with my father when I had a complaint about something. I finally got out of that relationship when I met the man who is now my husband. It took me meeting someone else to actually break free from that abusive relationship. The break-up was as bad as I had anticipated, but somehow I survived it with a lot of support. The difficult thing about breaking up with him was that on the outside he was the greatest guy, and everyone loved him. He was not abusive in front of anyone else; as a result, many people thought I was exaggerating (including my mom). But I was able to hold strong with the help of my new boyfriend, and stick to my guns after two years of verbal battery. The first six months with my boyfriend were very shaky, but after that time, things pretty much fell into place.

After dating my new boyfriend for approximately one year, he reported to me that he was going to move to another city to go to work for his father. I was faced with a crucial decision. Do I stay or do I go? I had lived in the same small town my entire life. Could I leave my family? After all, I am the glue that holds us together. If I leave, will my family fall apart? This stayed in my mind, but at the forefront were thoughts telling me that I cannot let my future husband go without me! We were not engaged at the time, but I felt sure we would be, and I wanted to be with him. So, off we went! At this time, my relationship with food was somewhat regulated; I was barely bingeing and purging. I was in a loving and trusting relationship, and I was actually beginning to feel good about myself.

In the summer following my move, I was presented with a wonderful opportunity to work as a therapist, treating those with anorexia nervosa and bulimia. I had intentionally not worked with this population prior to this time, as I felt I wasn't far enough along in my own recovery. The first months of this work proved to be challenging, as I can recall times I would think about "going back" to the eating disorder. I would remind myself that I didn't want to go back there; I wanted to continue my career as a therapist and wanted to hold on to all that I had in my new life! I no longer aspired to be like the people who suffered from this threatening disease; I looked at their disease as a barometer of pain. I saw their amount of pain, not the size of their body. I also became exposed to death as a result of anorexia and bulimia, and it finally became real that people can die from these diseases.

My boyfriend and I are now "husband and wife." We have been married over two years, and life has continued to be somewhat of a roller coaster for me. This time, however, I am riding it differently! Last year, I found out I was pregnant; I was delighted as I was uncertain if I could become pregnant given what I had done to my body. We were both shocked and excited. However, five and one half months into my pregnancy, we learned that our daughter had a fatal heart condition. My husband and I were both devastated. Nothing could ever prepare us for this time in our life. I thought of stopping eating because I thought it would make me feel more in control of my life. But, once again, I had to remember that I did not want to be a martyr and I needed to be healthy for future pregnancies. Almost a year has gone by, and again we are trying to conceive. It has not happened exactly the way I had planned, but I am constantly reminded that I am not the one in charge here. The more I try to control, the less control I seem to have in the long run. The doctors have tried to reassure me that my daughter's heart problem had nothing to do with my eating disorder, but sometimes I still wonder. I have released myself from the guilt and the questions, realizing that they are not healthy for me, my husband, or my future children.

I have learned a great deal about life since being diagnosed with an eating disorder. I would never wish anyone to struggle with an eating disorder, but despite its pain, it has also taught me a great deal. I have learned so much about life and myself. I have found a wonderful man I now call my husband, and I can appreciate him (and our marriage)! I believe this experience will help me be the best wife and mother I can be. If you are reading this and struggling with an eating disorder, please do what my roommate recommended to me: Seek counseling and work on ridding this demon that calls himself your friend. You'll appreciate it more than words can ever fully express!

Jennifer, *age 34*

OSTEOPOROSIS

Osteoporosis is the result of any disease that produces bone loss. The condition becomes apparent when the bone fractures under conditions that would not normally cause damage to the skeleton. The bones that are most frequently impacted are the bones of the spine, however all bones can be affected. Osteoporosis naturally occurs as people age, but it occurs at a faster rate in women, especially once they become menopausal and have ceased their menses which usually ceases permanently between the ages of 35 and 58. Because there is no way to reverse osteoporosis and build bone, the best course of action is to stop further bone loss.

In young women or adolescents, the absence of menses (with the exception of during pregnancy), usually means they are not sustaining an adequate weight to support menstruation. Or it could mean that their eating is too chaotic to support regular menstrual function. The hormones which support menses also support bone growth in adolescents and protect against bone loss in adult women. Therefore, low weight or weight loss below that needed to support regular menses should be corrected. Weight gain and the resumption of regular menstrual function protects bones and allows for bone growth in adolescence.

Osteoporosis also can start due to poor nutrition, lack of exercise, and smoking. Building and protecting bones requires extra vitamin D, calcium, and protein. If you are not getting enough vitamin D from such foods as fortified milk, egg yolks, liver, tuna, salmon and cod liver oil, adding these to your diet is essential. This is the reason milk and milk products are so strongly recommended for children and adolescents. The richest sources of calcium are milk and cheese products and some fish such as sardines, salmon, and oysters. There are lesser amounts in cooked vegetables such as broccoli, spinach, mustard and collard greens, and kale. Getting your vitamin D and calcium from recommend portions of any of these sources is excellent bone protection!

Regular exercise is also important in protecting against bone loss. However, many women with eating disorders not only exercise, but over-exercise. The amount you exercise must be supported by adequate nutrition; in other words, your energy output must not exceed your nutritional input! If you are not eating enough and your weight is too low, no exercise is recommended until you correct this problem. As you regain weight and correct your nutritional deficiencies, a gradual resumption of exercise is the goal. This should be worked out with your physician. If you don't exercise, work with your physician to begin an exercise regimen. It will protect your bones and help you feel better.

Smoking is hazardous to your health for many reasons, among them, that smoking decreases the body's absorption of calcium. Smoking decreases appetite and, thus, reduces weight. Weight gain is recommended for those who are underweight. Adequate nutrition is necessary for recovery from all eating disorders. Smoking interferes with both, and because it reduces absorption of calcium, it also promotes the development of osteoporosis.

SEXUALITY

As with gratification from food, women with eating disorders often believe that they do not deserve gratification sexually. How they avoid or use food appears to be a metaphor for how they avoid or use sex.

Women with anorexia nervosa typically deprive themselves of sexual gratification and sexual experience just as they deprive themselves of food. They have cut off all avenues of bodily pleasure. If they do engage in sexual experiences with their husbands or lovers it is usually as sparingly as possible and generally it is devoid of pleasure.

Women with bulimia nervosa often have more sexual involvement with their partners, but it is often intended to fill the gaping emotional void which they otherwise fill with food. Because of this need to fill an emotional void, some women with bulimia do not choose their partners wisely. Some will stay with partners who are abusive. Some will have indiscriminate sexual liaisons. Sex, like food, in abundance, can temporarily fulfill their emotional needs. Often, as with food, it later feels as if they have eaten "forbidden fruit" and must atone for their "indulgence."

As with food, the woman with anorexia denies and obliterates her needs while the woman with bulimia nervosa has unending, irreconcilable needs.

Women with eating disorders are often unfamiliar with normal sexual needs and appetites. They are often unfamiliar with how their eating disorders may parallel their sexual functioning. Many believe wanting sex, deriving pleasure from sex, and being sexual is as "weak" and unacceptable as wanting, deriving pleasure from, and eating food. Those who do indulge, feel themselves to be unacceptable, morally destitute, and bad. They feel they must "punish" themselves by purging the food or being hurt through sexual encounters.

It is important to discuss your thoughts, feelings, fears, and sexual practices with your therapist. Sometimes there is so much emphasis on food and weight that sex is a forgotten topic in therapy.

For adolescents and young women who are not sexually active, discussing your thoughts, feelings, fears, and questions about sex is also important. You are a whole person, thus, all aspects of your life must become a part of your therapy.

Take a moment before going onto the next chapter to compete the following survey. If you answered "yes" to any of the questions, we strongly encourage you to bring these issues up with your therapist and physician. Discussion of these issues may break the bonds of secrecy and/or shame that keep you sick.

WOMEN'S ISSUES SURVEY

1. Are you shopping around for plastic surgery or other "quick fix" weight-reduction strategies?   Y   N

2. Have you had plastic surgery?   Y   N

3. Are you keeping aspects of your eating disorder (such as what you eat, frequency of bingeing and purging, purging practices, and frequency and intensity of exercise) from your therapist or physician?   Y   N

4. Are you sexually active?   Y   N

5. Are you planning a pregnancy or are you pregnant now?   Y   N

6. Do you have questions, concerns, fears, or worries about your sexuality, sexual practices, or attitude about sex?   Y   N

7. Do you have osteoporosis or are you at risk for developing it because you are low weight, amenorrheic, poorly nourished, a smoker, or sedentary?   Y   N

8. Are you dissatisfied with your body and do you engage in negative self-talk which reaffirms your dissatisfaction?   Y   N

9. Is someone (yourself or another) criticizing, denigrating, or hurting your body now?   Y   N

Men's Issues

Eye of the Beholder

I run aimlessly
on the roads of Andover,
where route 133 runs along the Merrimack River.
I'm a slave,
the sun slapping my back,
burning my skin like a whip.
Stride after stride
I fight the fat
forming in my belly,
in my ass,
sweating all over the nylon shorts.
I stare down
at the double yellow line
leading up the hill. Just seven more miles
until I shed the bagel and yogurt I ate
two days ago.
Flesh and bones
just through my skin,
ribs, vertebrae.
I pretend it doesn't hurt
sitting
at the school desk,
my tail bone scraping the seat
like a nail to an emery board.
Cover stick conceals
the red under my alien eyes,
my cheeks sunken
like the fish face I used to make
when I was little,
when I didn't know my waist size,
when licking cookies and cream ice cream
wasn't punishment.

I'm 5'9, 112 lbs.
Too heavy,
28 inches too wide,
fragile freshman
living on fat-burners,
water,
Acu-Trim,
Senokot laxatives.

I have to lose a few more,
at least a pound a day,
(until my hair clogs the shower's drain,
or the IV needle in my left hand
feeding me
hurts more than what I see in the mirror)
—Jon I.

Jon is an example of the hundreds of thousands of men struggling with eating disorders today. Once considered the illness of upper-middle-class white women, eating disorders now know no ethnic, socio-economic, or gender lines. In actuality, eating disorders were reported in men since the 1700s. Until recently, however, diagnosing men with eating disorders was often questioned and debated due to certain criteria that were specific to women (e.g., amenorrhea, or loss of menses). Now, almost 300 years later, we see less debate around the existence of eating disorders in males, yet men continue to be overlooked and under-treated.

According to recent studies, approximately 1 out of every 10 people struggling with anorexia nervosa and bulimia is male. There are no statistics on the numbers of men who suffer from binge eating disorder. Anecdotal reports by men whom we have treated lead us to believe that men who suffer from eating disorders are less likely to seek treatment for the following reasons: 1) They feel there is a stigma attached to the illness because it is a "female illness," and thus, they hesitate to seek treatment; 2) Physicians seldom ask men about eating disorder symptomatology and, thus, may miss the diagnosis; and 3) Coaches of certain sports (e.g., wrestling) encourage over- or undereating for the good of the sport, thus colluding with men who have lost control of food.

Although eating disorders are far more prevalent in females than males, men are not immune. Eating disorders are not gender specific, yet most of what is written about eating disorders is taken from the feminine perspective. This chapter will focus on eating disorder issues that are specific to men, while the remainder of the workbook will take a more generic or feminine perspective. If you are a male reading this book, we hope you find this chapter helpful in your efforts to recover, especially if shame or denial has kept you from seeking appropriate care.

DIAGNOSIS: HOW IS IT DIFFERENT FOR MEN?

Anorexia Nervosa

Eating disorders have *long* been classified as female disorders; in part, this is because one of the criteria for anorexia nervosa is amenorrhea (absence of menses). According to the DSM-IV (American Psychiatric Association, 1994), in order to be diagnosed with anorexia nervosa one must meet the following criteria:

1. Refusal to maintain body weight at or above a minimally normal weight for age and height (e.g., weight loss leading to a maintenance of body weight less than 85% of that expected; or failure to make expected weight gain during period of growth, leading to body weight less than 85% of that expected).
2. Intense fear of gaining weight or becoming fat, even though underweight.
3. Disturbance in the way in which one's body weight or shape is experienced, undue influences of body weight or shape on self-evaluation, or denial of the seriousness of the current low body weight.
4. In postmenarcheal females, amenorrhea (i.e., the absence of at least three consecutive menstrual periods). A woman is considered to have amenorrhea if her periods occur only following hormone (e.g., estrogen) administration.

Furthermore, there are two specific types of anorexia nervosa; they are:

1. *Restricting type:* During the current episode of anorexia nervosa, the person has not regularly engaged in binge eating or purging behavior (i.e., self-induced vomiting or the misuse of laxatives, diuretics, or enemas).
2. *Binge-eating/purging type:* During the current episode of anorexia nervosa, the person has regularly engaged in binge eating or purging behavior (i.e., self-induced vomiting or the misuse of laxatives, diuretics, or enemas).

Bulimia Nervosa

The criteria for *bulimia* or *bulimia nervosa* are the following:

1. Recurrent episodes of binge eating. An episode of binge eating is characterized by both of the following:
   a. eating, in a discrete period of time (e.g., within any 2-hour period), an amount of food that is definitely larger than most people would eat during a similar period of time and under similar circumstances; and
   b. a sense of having a lack of control over eating during the episode (e.g., a feeling that one cannot stop eating or control what or how much one is eating.
2. Recurrent inappropriate compensatory behavior in order to prevent weight gain, such as self-induced vomiting; misuse of laxatives, diuretics, enemas, or other medications; fasting; or excessive exercise.
3. The binge eating and inappropriate compensatory behaviors both occur, on average, at least twice a week for three months.
4. Body shape and weight unduly influence self-evaluation.
5. The disturbance does not occur exclusively during episodes of anorexia nervosa.

There are two specific types of bulimia nervosa:

1. *Purging type:* During the current episode of bulimia nervosa, the person has regularly engaged in self-induced vomiting or the misuse of laxatives, diuretics, or enemas.
2. *Nonpurging type:* During the current episode of bulimia nervosa after binge eating, the person has used other inappropriate compensatory behaviors, such as fasting or excessive exercise, but has not regularly engaged in self-induced vomiting or the misuse of laxatives, diuretics, or enemas.

As you can see, with the exception of amenorrhea, both women and men can meet the criteria for the diagnosis of an eating disorder. If you believe this is a disorder strictly for women, think again, and ask yourself if you (or someone you know) meets the criteria for an eating disorder.

A third diagnosis is *Eating Disorder, Not Otherwise Specified*. This diagnosis is reserved for those who meet most, but not all, criteria (or some variant of the criteria) for *anorexia nervosa* or *bulimia nervosa*.

At this time, *Binge-Eating Disorder* is an exploratory diagnosis. At present, those with Binge-Eating Disorder would be diagnosed with, Eating Disorder, Not Otherwise Specified.

INCIDENCE: HOW DO MEN STACK UP?

As you have read, approximately 10% of individuals diagnosed with anorexia nervosa and bulimia are males. Of those struggling with anorexia nervosa, 5–10% are reported to be males; 10–15% of those struggling with bulimia are also men. As we reported in the beginning of this chapter, we believe these percentages are low, but reflective of the current research.

The incidence of anorexia nervosa and bulimia in women is reportedly greatest between the ages of 12–30, with the typical age of onset between 12–20. What about men? The age of onset remains unclear in males. It is presumed that there is no significant difference in age of onset between males and females for anorexia nervosa, whereas for bulimia, men apparently have a significantly later age of onset than their female counterparts.

PROFILE: ARE MEN'S "MAKE-UPS" ANY DIFFERENT?

It is assumed that women are "feelers" and that men are "doers." Does this profile suggest that men who are more feeling-oriented like women, would be more likely to develop eating disorders?

Research shows that there are similarities *and* differences between males and females that develop eating disorders. Psychological profiles do tend to be similar. Both sexes struggle with underlying issues of inadequacy, interpersonal ineffectiveness, difficulty with self expression, obsessive-compulsive tendencies, perfectionism, and body image. Both sexes look to achieve weight loss through avoidance of carbohydrates and fats, and purging through laxative use and self-induced vomiting.

Gender-Specific Differences

Both males and females report being influenced by media messages and societal expectations; the difference is that women are encouraged to focus on their weight and men are encouraged to focus on their *shape* or physique in terms of muscle definition.

The gender specific issues that contribute to eating disorders in males are the following: (a) history of being overweight/obese as a child, (b) appearance for professional growth, (c) occupations that reinforce body-image dissatisfaction, and (d) sexuality. These specific differences shape prevention and treatment efforts aimed specifically toward males. We will address each gender-specific issue separately, in order to help you in your own recovery process. Whenever possible, we will also provide you with questions and exercises to help you better assess and understand your unique issues and to assist you on your journey to recovery.

HISTORY OF BEING OVERWEIGHT/OBESE AS A CHILD

As a child, Joshua can remember being teased about his weight. During his early elementary years, he handled the teasing well; however, by the time he was in fifth grade, the taunting by his male peers was much more upsetting to him. This did not stop Joshua from overeating at McDonalds with his friends, or continuing to eat cookies and ice cream as snacks at home. However, when Joshua entered high school, he became increasingly aware of how "awkward" he felt around his peers, and believed that weight loss would help him feel more socially acceptable. To deal with his discomfort, he went on a diet, which progressively led to a diagnosis of anorexia nervosa.

Studies have shown that women experience more societal pressures to be thin than their male counterparts. For example, Anderson and DiDomenico (1992), of the University of Iowa, explored the number of articles on weight loss and shape in 10 popular magazines targeted toward young men and women. What they found was astounding. Women's magazines contained over 10 times more advertisements and articles on weight loss than did men's. As women were being encouraged to slim down, men were receiving messages about the importance of building upper body bulk while slimming the abdominal area. Interestingly, overweight women do not appear to be any more likely to develop eating disorders than their underweight or normal-weight peers, yet women's magazines exhort women, in general, to lose weight. Men, however—like Joshua—are more likely to develop eating disorders due to "real" overweight concerns, yet men's magazines do not focus on weight as much as do women's. It appears that real weight issues predispose many men to eating disorders, whereas body-image distortion and dissatisfaction, regardless of weight pre-onset, predisposes women to the development of eating disorders.

What is also interesting to note in Anderson and DiDomenico's study is that the ratio of body-image articles in women's and men's magazines is similar to the ratio of eating disorders found in women and men. If there is a direct correlation between the two, then we can be sure to find that as the focus on weight and body image in men's magazines increases (due to increasing focus on these issues for men in the culture and in the media in general), so will the incidence of eating disorders in men increase.

Are you ready to explore your childhood weight history and the impact the media has had on you over the years? If you are, please answer the following questions.

MEN'S WEIGHT HISTORY QUESTIONNAIRE

1) How would you describe your weight as a child?

emaciated   thin   average slightly overweight
        overweight   very overweight/obese

2) Were you teased about your weight or other aspects of your appearance? If "yes," please explain:

_____

_____

3) Were there weight issues with anyone else in your family? Please explain:

_____

_____

4) Were there rules about food in your house? (example: having to finish your dinner in order to have dessert) Please explain: _____

_____

_____

Once you have completed this chapter and Chapter 3, What Is Your Relationship with Food?, you should have a better understanding of how your childhood weight and relationship to hunger may have contributed to your struggles with food.

As a valuable way to explore the impact the media has had on you, purchase several popular men's magazines and review them. Then, through words and pictures from these magazines, make a collage depicting how you believe the media is contributing to eating disorders in men today. Have your opinions about your personal appearance changed as you've worked on your collage? As you make the collage, have you become more comfortable or more self-conscious about certain areas of your body? If you could write a letter to some of these magazines, what would you say?

APPEARANCE FOR PROFESSIONAL GROWTH

As you may be well aware, appearance for women is equated with self-esteem and self worth. Women spend billions of dollars each year in their efforts to have that "certain" body and look. What may surprise you, however, is that men are also spending billions of dollars each year trying to achieve their own "certain" look; but they're doing it for very different reasons.

*84% of men surveyed in a recent nationwide study believed
physical attractiveness was important for
power and success on the job.*

*42% felt that improving one thing about their face
would help their career.*

*32% agreed that if they had a more youthful appearance
it would positively impact their job success.*

*22% agreed with the statement
"I use my personal appearance to my advantage
in getting things accomplished on the job."*
Source: www.cosmeticscanada.com

It is astounding, and quite sad, to see the power physical appearance has on us not only emotionally, but professionally as well. Has the statement "It's what's on the inside that counts" gotten lost as we near the beginning of the 21st century? It is understandable that if these statistics reflect what is going on in our workplace today, many men and women are turning to plastic surgery, and potentially developing eating disorders, to maintain their professional status. How ironic it is, though, that those things that appear to be "helping" one's career, are also threatening one's life and happiness, and therefore, one's career! Do you believe your professional growth is in any way linked to physical appearance? Answer the following questions.

Using the scale below, describe how you feel about various parts of your body and your height and weight.

VS = Very satisfied   S = Satisfied   SS = Somewhat satisfied
SD = Somewhat dissatisfied   D = Dissatisfied   VD = Very dissatisfied

Face: _____   Ears: _____   Nose: _____   Eyes: _____   Chin: _____

Mouth: _____   Hair: _____   Hair Line: _____   Hair Color: _____

Eye Color: _____   Arms: _____   Chest: _____   Waist: _____

Buttocks: _____   Thighs: _____   Legs: _____   Height: _____   Weight: _____

Do you believe there is a correlation between the development of your eating disorder and your desire for professional growth? Please explain:

_____
_____
_____
_____
_____

Have you engaged in activities to compensate or overcompensate for your dissatisfaction with your appearance? Please explain:

_____
_____
_____
_____
_____
_____
_____
_____
_____

How willing are you to change your relationship with food, given the pressures you feel about your appearance? Please explain:

_____
_____
_____
_____

If you have completed the first section of this book, you know what behaviors you want to change. Please take this opportunity to review and record those behaviors, and what you need to do to facilitate change.

Behavior Warranting Change   What I Need To Do To Facilitate Change

_____   _____

_____   _____

_____   _____

_____   _____

_____   _____

Writing out this exercise may feel repetitious. However, given your increased understanding of job and appearance pressures, you may now have some ideas about tools and techniques you can use to help you minimize the effect of these pressures on your efforts toward recovery.

OCCUPATIONS THAT REINFORCE BODY-IMAGE DISSATISFACTION

In high school, Kevin was a cross-country "star." Now a physician, he talks openly of his history of vomiting as a way to keep his weight down during cross-country season. Although he believes that purging was always within his control (even today), his eating-disordered weight management techniques continue today. Now he is "sneaking off" during breaks in the hospital to work out at the local gym. To Kevin, this is not a problem, because he is no longer vomiting. Furthermore, he reports the need to work out as a way to allow himself to eat anything he wants without gaining weight. To us, Kevin still continues to struggle with purging; this time he has substituted purging through vomiting with purging through exercise. Kevin believes he is in control, for he is not aware of how this behavior could be interfering with his life. Yet, exercise and body-image issues are controlling him. Until he is willing to face these issues, and challenge himself, or until he experiences a situation where he is faced with not being able to keep up his exercise routine (or an untoward circumstance occurs because he was out of the hospital), he will probably continue to deny his disordered eating behaviors.

When Tom was in high school, he joined the wrestling team. He was very tall and thin, and had a good chance of winning if he could remain in a low weight class. As such, he was encouraged by his coach to "cut weight." He was already at an advantage in that his length and reach would outdistance most others in his weight class. Tom was instructed by his coach to jog in a hot shower wearing a rubber suit, run sprints even on hot days wearing a rubber suit, eat only jello for 2 days before a match, and self-induce vomiting until he could make his weight on the day of the match. Although Tom never developed a formal diagnosis of an eating disorder, 20 years later he continues to struggle with food and weight concerns. Others he knows were not so fortunate. One team member died as a result of these purging and weight-loss practices.

There has been a great deal of research exploring the correlation between athletics and the development of eating disorders in women. As with many other areas of research in eating disorders, there have not been many studies concerning male athletes' risks of developing eating disorders. However, there has been great interest in understanding what similarities exist between the competitive athlete and the individual who develops an eating disorder. As with their female counterparts, there appears to be a significant correlation between the development of eating disorders in men and sports that reinforce body image and physique.

There are particular sports in which performance is directly equated with physique. Examples of these are gymnastics, running, dancing, figure skating, swimming, diving, and jockeying. Many athletes in these sports work diligently at maintaining a particular physique which enhances physical performance and the accumulation of "bonus points" for appearance and attractiveness. Also at risk are wrestlers, who often will "adjust" their body weight in order to compete in a particular weight class. What may begin as an innocent approach to better athletic performance can end in an eating disorder and life-threatening consequences.

The United States Olympic Committee decided to conduct a study to determine whether pressure for athletes to lose weight caused eating disorders in elite athletes (Franseen & McCaan, 1996). Two hundred fifteen elite female athletes only, from four different groups, participated in this study. These groups consisted of *weight class* sports (sports that have different weight categories), *aesthetic* sports (sports in which scoring is based on skills), *endurance* sports (sports in which scoring is based on time and/or distance), and the *precision* group (comprised of athletes who did not participate in sports with an emphasis on body weight). The findings were not surprising, but were rather important for anyone involved in sport.

- More athletes from the *weight class* group than from any other group lost weight specifically for their sport. Despite trying to lose weight more regularly than other athletes, *weight class* athletes did not show more eating disorder behaviors or attitudes than any of the other groups.
- The *aesthetic* group did not show more eating disorder behaviors or attitudes than the other groups studied, however, they vomited and used diet pills more often than the other groups.
- The *endurance* group did not show any behaviors or attitudes similar to females with eating disorders. As a matter of fact, no more than 8% lost weight in an unhealthy way. However, the *endurance group* athletes may also find it easier to lose weight due to the high intensity of their workouts and its effects on weight management.
- The *precision* group did not lose weight specifically for their sport, yet felt tremendous pressure from their coaches to lose weight (even though weight was not a critical factor for success in their sport). The *precision* group also experienced more body image dissatisfaction than any other group of athletes participating in the study. This may be because 37% had a history of weight issues, 57% had family members with weight issues, and weight management is difficult in these sports because their activities do not burn many calories.

Although geared toward women, the results of this study can also be interpreted for men. Elite athletes are more likely to suffer from disordered eating, if not eating disorders. They are more concerned about weight, as weight is a critical factor in their performance. They may also feel pressure from coaches and others, which reinforces these weight issues. For more information on this study, refer to the summer 1996, issue of *Olympic Coach* magazine.

Now add the personality make-up of the serious athlete. This person is motivated, eager to please, perfectionistic, driven, enthusiastic, and determined. These are also characteristics commonly found in those with eating disorders. As you can see, the qualities that make a young man a successful athlete can also contribute to the making of a "successful" anorexic or bulimic. If you consider yourself a serious athlete, go back and read Chapter 7, Your Relationship with Exercise.

YES, MEN STRUGGLE TOO

I remember when Hope was nowhere to be found. My twelve-mile runs on an empty stomach were dismal without her. I used to stare down at the yellow lines leading up the hills of Andover; my only companions being the tedious stomping of my feet, the shallowness of my breath, and an occasional passer by. They never said hello. They looked down and away.

I never understood why people had a hard time looking at me. I thought being skinny was a good thing. I thought that fearing steamed broccoli and baked potatoes with ketchup was healthy. I believed that everyone concerned about my fragility was jealous, especially the girls. I was convinced they were envious of my determination, jealous that they couldn't be as disciplined. They wanted to be 116 pounds. Like me, their best friend, Derek.

Hope disappeared about a year into my relationship with Anorexia. She thought I was being selfish and self-centered, so she said she was going away for a while. I didn't need anyone but Anorexia, so when Hope left me, I figured Anorexia and I were on our way to utter bliss. It was a love affair beyond any other! He was faithful, loyal, powerful, and strong.

Time went on and I got everything I ever wanted and needed in a relationship. Anorexia freed me from all my fears. No longer did I have fears of failure or fears of success. As long as I remained faithful to Anorexia, I would soon be liberated. I'd be emancipated from the constraints of my self that I hated, like my sexuality. I didn't have to hate myself for as long as I was loving Anorexia; he made it seem better.

Family and friends told me that they were concerned about my relationship. They said that Anorexia was all that I cared about. Some even accused him of being abusive and dangerous. I didn't want to believe them, as Anorexia was all that I had. I'd try to get in touch with Hope once in a while for some advice, but she never answered my calls anymore . . .

. . . not until the day I found myself at Beth Israel Hospital answering all sorts of questions about physical trauma. Doctors probed my weary mind and body for answers: Was it a car accident? Did someone kick me in my kidneys? Was I lifting heavy weights? In all of this, it appeared as if they ignored my answers.

No one asked me about Anorexia. After all, men don't usually fall in love with him. I was so scared. How did I get so involved? I felt there was no way out of this relationship. I finally saw what Anorexia was doing to me. The blood in my urine was only the beginning. He could kill me! My body was crying out for help, but I didn't know how to help it. I wanted to be on my own, without Anorexia always by my side.

Hope showed up that day in the hospital. I don't remember who brought her to me. She said that it would be hard, sometimes seemingly impossible to break-up with Anorexia. She said I needed him in a way that I would have to grow to understand and to accept and then to try to change. She said this could take a while. I begged for Hope to stay by my side, no matter how long it would take to leave Anorexia behind. I believed in Hope and Hope believed in me.

The way I looked at Anorexia was never the same. I was no longer monogamous. I saw Bulimia on occasion, too. I didn't really like seeing Bulimia either, but I knew it was a transition that I was making. I allowed myself time and space and realized that the break-up wouldn't happen magically and suddenly. It was going to take time, just like Hope had told me.

Hope sat with me in many sessions of therapy and even in the programs that were specially designed for the kind of relationship I felt trapped in. Hope encouraged me to invite friends and family back into my life. She reminded me that my life was precious and that it had purpose. And that I didn't have to be President of the United States in order to be successful, but that I could be one day if I wanted, even if I was gay.

Today, two years later, I don't see Hope or my therapist everyday like I needed to in the past, but I write to both of them on occasion. They write back and tell me how proud of me they are. They continue to point out to me how I really relieved myself from one of the most painful, destructive relationships I'll ever encounter in my life.

I am lucky to be as strong as I am today. Everyone says that my face glows, my hair shines, and my eyes glimmer in a way they never did before. When I see Anorexia passing on the street, I am able to say "hello." Sometimes he even stops me in my path and begs for me to take him back. But I know he isn't good for me, not if I want to be an inspiration for others who fell for a wrong lover as I did.

For others in a relationship like mine was with Anorexia, I would like to tell you to think about the amount of energy you are handing over to the mercy of Anorexia, Bulimia, or Binge Eating and see if you can hold onto a handful of Hope. Soon a handful will turn into a cup, and a cup will turn into a bowl, a bowl to a plate, and a plate to a meal! This meal will be one that you can begin to enjoy as energy, or nurturance, or love that you deserve! You can then share it with family and friends, and of course . . . with Hope!

Derek, age 24

SEXUALITY

Good Enough

Here in our house
you make your mind up
in the clouds
and I want to bring you down
to my level,
where growing up is hard
enough
without having a daddy
I know is embarrassed
that I can't hit home runs
or shoot three pointers.
It's hard
enough
knowing myself
that I am different
from the other boys
who laugh at me
when I'd rather play jacks or hop scotch
with the girls on the playground.
I want to tell you
that I'm sorry
for being
an A student,
a good friend,
a good son
that many parents wish for.
I'm yours,
but not enough
for you,
the man I am supposed to love
as some hero,
like Hercules, or Superman.
You are no super man.
You are not my hero,
because heroes don't make exceptions
when they save people,
and it's clear
I'm not man enough for you
to save.

                                        Jon I.

Is there a correlation between eating disorders and homosexuality in men? This appears to be *the* question! Studies appear to conflict tremendously in this area. Here's what we know.

It has been hypothesized that there *is* a correlation between eating disorders and male homosexuality. Homosexual males are more likely to experience body image and appearance pressures than their heterosexual male counterparts. This results in greater body-image dissatisfaction, disordered eating, and in some cases, eating disorders. The following is a representative sample of the research found on the topic of eating disorders, sexual orientation, and males.

Herzog and colleagues (1984) found greater sexual isolation, inactivity, and conflicted homosexuality in men with eating disorders than in women with anorexia nervosa.

Yager and associates (1988) found that homosexual male college students had higher incidences of bulimic behaviors and fear of weight gain, than did their male heterosexual counterparts.

Silberstein and colleagues (1989) studied 71 homosexual and 71 heterosexual male college students and found similar results to those presented by Siever.

Carlat and Carmago compiled data from a 1991 research study and concluded that there is a higher prevalence of homosexuality in bulimic males than their female counterparts, and that homosexuality is a risk factor for bulimia in males.

Siever (1994), in a study of 59 homosexual college men, and 62 heterosexual college men, found that homosexual men experienced greater body dissatisfaction, and felt appearance to be more central to their sense of self, than did the heterosexual men studied.

In a study done at Massachusetts General Hospital, Carlat, Carmago, and Herzog (1997) concluded that homosexuality/bisexuality appears to be a consideration in the development of eating disorders, (particularly bulimia) in males.

There is also research that minimizes the correlation between male sexual orientation, and eating disorders.

In a 1995 interview, Arnold Anderson, professor of psychiatry at the University of Iowa and specialist on eating disorders in males, reported that only approximately 21% of males struggling with eating disorders are homosexual (Knowlkon, 1995; cited on www.mhsource.com).

Small sample sizes limit our ability to draw definite conclusions, however, it does appear that homosexuality in males may be a risk factor for the development of eating disorders. Because eating disorders suppress/repress sexual desire because testosterone is gradually reduced, some men may misinterpret their low desire as homosexuality. This is a complex issue that further research alone may clarify. If you are uncertain about your sexual identity, it may be contributing to your difficulty in seeking treatment and overcoming your eating disorder.

WHAT ABOUT FEELINGS?

Are grown men "supposed" to cry? As much as the answer to this question is more of a "yes" than it used to be, there are still strong sanctions against boys and men showing feelings of sadness, depression or other emotions that may depict weakness.

I can recall an occasion where my friend's son fell off a chair and landed head first on the kitchen floor. As he began to cry, my friend picked him up and consoled him by telling him that it did not hurt and that there was no need for him to cry. If this accident had happened to her daughter, I believe her manner of consoling would have been very different! (Laura Goodman)

As we know, eating disorders are maladaptive yet creative ways of coping. Eating disorders help suppress (stuff down) or repress (block from consciousness) feelings. Men have been encouraged to suppress feelings of sadness. It is not "macho" to cry.

Yet, sadness is a normal human emotion, which knows no gender bounds. This culturally sanctioned suppression and/or repression of feelings makes it difficult for men to seek support and treatment. Statistics indicate that women struggle with depression at significantly higher rates than their male counterparts, yet it is difficult to assess the validity of the current statistics, when we know that women are much more likely to request support and treatment than men.

Men are supposed to be *strong;* but what does this mean? Men are given such conflicting messages today. On the one hand, they are discouraged from showing feelings of sadness, for it depicts "weakness"; yet, at the same time, men are supposed to be "sensitive," and express how they feel. This can lead to feelings of confusion in the most self assured man. For the man whose identity is shaky this message can be destructive.

What Do You Feel?

Below you will find a list of feelings. Put a ✓ next to the feelings you are aware you feel. Put a ? next to those feelings you are not sure you feel. And put a * next to the feelings you believe you have been told (directly or indirectly) *not* to feel.

aggressive _____	angry _____	anxious _____
arrogant _____	bored _____	cautious _____
cold _____	confused _____	confident _____
curious _____	demure _____	determined _____
disappointed _____	disgusted _____	enraged _____
envious _____	exhausted _____	frightened _____
frustrated _____	grief stricken _____	guilty _____
happy _____	horrified _____	hurt _____
indifferent _____	innocent _____	interested _____
jealous _____	lonely _____	loving _____
self loathing _____	mischievous _____	miserable _____
negative _____	optimistic _____	paranoid _____
pessimistic _____	puzzled _____	regretful _____
relieved _____	sad _____	surprised _____
suspicious _____	sympathetic _____	

other (please describe): _____

_____

COMMUNICATION

You have identified the feelings you are aware you feel, those that you are uncertain you feel, and those that you have been encouraged not to feel. It is possible your eating disorder has either "expressed" your feelings metaphorically or prohibited expression of your feelings. Your next step is to learn to acknowledge and express feelings directly and verbally. How you express yourself is likely to contribute to the kinds of responses you receive, and how satisfied you will be with the outcome. Below are four major styles of communication; try to find the one that describes your style most appropriately.

Passive: Holding back your true feelings (suppression), and portraying that things are okay, when they really are not. *Example: A man reassures a woman it is okay with him that she has canceled the date at the last minute, when in actuality, he is quite upset.*

Passive-Aggressive: Holding back your verbal expressions around an event, yet expressing them through an action. *Example: A man tells a woman it is okay with him that she has canceled the date at the last minute, but then because of his anger, doesn't return her next phone call when she asks to reschedule.*

Aggressive: Expressing your feelings in an combative manner, whether it be verbally or physically. *Example: A man tells a woman that she is an insensitive person, when she chose to cancel their date at the last minute.*

Assertive: Expressing your feelings in a way that will result in discussion, versus defensiveness. *Example: A man tells a woman, "I felt hurt when you abruptly canceled our date."*

Your style of communicating may vary depending on who you are talking to. In the space below, list 8 people with whom you speak often. Next to their names, record your most frequent style of communication.

Name	Style of Communication
1) _____	_____
2) _____	_____
3) _____	_____
4) _____	_____
5) _____	_____
6) _____	_____
7) _____	_____
8) _____	_____

Congratulations. You are beginning your journey toward healthy self-expression! To take this exercise one step further, in the spaces below, give an example of a time you used passive, passive-aggressive, and aggressive communication. Under each example of an ineffective communication style, change each response to an assertive response. Assertiveness is key to healthy expression and good health and happiness!

(Hint: An assertive response can look like this . . . "I feel _____, when you do _____.")

Passive: _____
_____
Assertive response: _____
_____

Passive-Aggressive: _____
_____
Assertive response: _____
_____

Aggressive: _____
_____
Assertive response: _____
_____

Practice assertive forms of expression. This may feel difficult and awkward in the beginning, but in the long run you may find it will enhance your esteem and your relationships. How you communicate with yourself, as well as how you communicate with others, has a tremendous effect on your health and happiness. Negative self-talk is destructive. As much as you may feel you hate various parts of your body, it is critical that you do not allow yourself to go down the path of verbal self-destruction. Remember the adage "sticks and stones may break my bones, but names can never hurt me"? Well, guess what? Names can hurt a person emotionally; they may not leave physical scars, but the emotional scars last much longer than any bruise from a stick or stone! The next step is to stop all verbal self-destruction. One way of doing this is through *affirmations*, or asserting positive self-statements. Reciting affirmations on a daily basis is a way to nurture yourself through positive self-talk. For example, if you are having a day in which you are feeling particularly fat, you may come up with an affirmation in which you tell yourself something like the following:

> When I am *feeling fat* I am feeling badly about something (and that something is not just my weight). When someone I care about feels badly I don't call him or her names (e.g., "fat"). I try to understand, comfort, and assist this person. I am learning to understand, comfort, and assist myself as I would a good friend or close family member.

Affirmations

In order to avoid society's trap of food and weight obsession, you must find a way to fight its message. Make a list of affirmations that address your particular struggle, below. Once you have completed this list we recommend that you write each affirmation on an index card and place the cards in places that you regularly see (e.g., your mirror, the chest in the bathroom, the dashboard of your car, etc). Words can hurt . . . it is our hope that you will use the power of words to heal!

Example: *My body is a gift. I can walk, talk, hear, see, and work long hours at a demanding job. I treat my body with respect and care. It deserves no less.*

_____

_____

_____

_____

_____

_____

_____

_____

_____

_____

_____

_____

_____

Men, like women, can engage in negative self-talk, which contributes to the development and maintenance of eating disorders. Reducing negative self-talk and increasing positive talk or affirmations (what we call cognitive restructuring), is an essential ingredient in the recovery process for men and women. Asking for help is difficult for many of us; society makes it even more difficult for men. If you can identify with the issues in this chapter consider seeking out someone you trust to help guide you in the direction of health and happiness. Swallow your pride; feed your heart . . . and your soul! You deserve it.

MEN'S ISSUES SURVEY

1) Were you overweight as a child?   Y   N

2) Do you participate in a career that reinforces appearance?   Y   N

3) Do you have difficulty expressing feelings?   Y   N

4) Do you have questions, concerns, fears, or worries about your sexuality, sexual practices, or attitude about sex?   Y   N

5) Do you struggle with fueling your body as it needs, or purging through vomiting, exercise, or restriction?   Y   N

6) Are you unhappy with parts of your body? Have you considered plastic surgery, or have you had plastic surgery?   Y   N

7) Are you dissatisfied with your body and do you engage in negative self-talk which reinforces this dissatisfaction?   Y   N

Substance Abuse and Eating Disorders

Do you use food as a way to "numb" yourself?

Are there other substances that you use to help "numb" yourself?

Do you use laxatives, diuretics, or diet pills for a longer period of time than recommended, or use more than recommended?

Do you find yourself looking for external objects to help you tolerate emotional pain?

Have you found yourself trying to decrease the frequency of use without avail?

Is there a family history of substance abuse in your immediate or extended family?

If you answered "yes" to any of the questions above, it is imperative that you continue with this chapter. We are going to look at substance use and abuse as it pertains to eating disorders. Although substance abuse most often refers to alcohol and illicit drug use, substance abuse also refers to the use of prescription and over-the-counter medications for weight control. We are going to discuss the use of alcohol, illicit drugs, and other prescription and non-prescription medications that may play a critical role in the development of an eating disorder. Even if you believe you do not have a problem with substance use and/or abuse, we still encourage you to read this chapter.

First, let's look at how the *Diagnostic and Statistical Manual of Mental Disorders* (DSM-IV; American Psychiatric Association, 1994) defines Substance Dependence. According to the DSM-IV, the presence of at least three of the following symptoms, for at least one month, constitutes Substance Dependence.

1. The person uses more of the substance or uses it for a longer period of time than recommended.
2. The person recognizes excessive use of the substance and may have tried to reduce it but has been unable to do so.
3. Much of the person's time is spent in efforts to obtain the substance or recovery from its effects.
4. The person is intoxicated or suffering from withdrawal symptoms at times when responsibilities need to be fulfilled, such as school or work.
5. Many activities are given up or reduced in frequency because of the use of the substance.
6. Problems in health, social relationships, and psychological functioning occur.
7. Tolerance develops, requiring larger doses (at least 50% increase) of the substance to produce the desired effect.
8. Withdrawal symptoms develop when the person stops ingesting substances or reduces the amount.
9. The person uses the substance to relieve withdrawal symptoms. For example, one may drink alcohol early in the morning because one feels withdrawal symptoms coming on.

In order for there to be a classification of substance *abuse*, one of the following must exist:

1. Continued use despite knowledge of having a persistent or recurrent social, occupational, psychological, or physical problem that is caused or exacerbated by the use of the substance.
2. Recurrent use in a situation in which use is physically hazardous. For example, driving while intoxicated.

THE CYCLICAL ROAD TO ADDICTION

Now that you understand the definitions of substance dependence and abuse, we'd like to take you through a journey down the cyclical road to addiction. Let's start at *Emotional Hunger Way*. Here at *Emotional Hunger Way*, a feeling of unmet emotional needs is experienced. This emptiness may be from a sense of loss of others' love, or a struggle with one's own sense of self (self-esteem). The directions at *Emotional Hunger Way* lead the individual to *Low Self-Esteem Drive*. Here, the individual experiences feelings of low self-worth and loneliness. In order to feel worthwhile and fulfilled, something we all wish to feel, the cyclical road to addiction leads many to *Addiction Alley*. This is the place where substances are used to mask feelings of unworthiness and loneliness. The body feels rejuvenated and fulfilled, though only temporarily. The individual believes she is getting off *Addiction Alley*, and is heading to *Happiness Hill*. But slowly the "heart" breaks down, and the feelings of unworthiness and loneliness are now coupled with shame and guilt. As a result, instead of taking a turn toward *Happiness Hill*, the individual finds herself back at *Emotional Hunger Way*.

Now, the individual is feeling a greater sense of unworthiness and loneliness, as a result of the guilt and shame brought about through the misuse of a substance. Again, she finds herself heading toward *Low Self-Esteem Drive*. In order to relieve herself of the feelings, she again turns down *Addiction Alley*, resulting in the downward cycle of addiction.

To avoid addiction one must avoid *Low Self-Esteem Drive.* In other words, in order to fight addiction, it is important that you take an inventory of what you find yourself "hungry" for, and work toward fulfilling those hungers with the recommended nourishment. Feeling "hungry" for sleep, for example, requires rest, not sedatives, stimulants, or food.

Before moving on, let's take a moment to learn to H.A.L.T.

Hungry: When you feel hungry for food, EAT.
Angry: When you feel angry, EXPRESS IT.
Lonely: When you feel lonely, CALL or REACH OUT to someone.
Tired: When you are tired, SLEEP.

Twelve-step programs for addictions refer to the acronym H.A.L.T. as the foundation for healthy living. H.A.L.T. stands as a reminder never to get too Hungry, Angry, Lonely, or Tired. We must all H.A.L.T. in order to live a healthy life. If we don't, we will find the wrong nourishment.

MY STRUGGLE TO ESCAPE BULIMIA

"Getting treatment for my eating disorder has only led me to getting treatment for what caused the eating disorder in the first place."

When I was first offered the opportunity to write about my experiences with recovery, I was so excited. I thought I'd have so much to share—so much to write about. Yet it's taken me months to even begin to write. In a way I guess that's due to a trait that contributed to my eating disorder . . . perfectionism . . . "all-or-nothing thinking." I wanted what I wrote to be perfect, concise, and moving. Yet when it comes down to it, I'm afraid to write my story because that means remembering the many painful years of sickness. I have thought a lot about when it started, and why it started. For some reason, those two questions that cause my mind to go blank. I think it's the fact that I don't know *perfectly*, and will never know *perfectly;* this bothers me! All I do know is that it *did* start and it continued in many shapes and forms for several years.

I believe the best thing that ever came out of the many years of treatment happened during one of the initial visits with my current therapist. I had seen another therapist for a little over a year before going to college; a relapse at college caused me to re-enter treatment and find a new therapist. Before this particular appointment, I can recall eating and throwing up during the entire car ride from my college apartment to the therapist's office. I had been doing this for weeks, unable to attend classes or concentrate. I felt scared and powerless; the stupid eating disorder had found me again. This time I felt that it would destroy me. I knew if I couldn't stop, I would not be able to finish school and achieve the goals I had set for myself. I saw the life that I had fantasized about being stuffed down and thrown up and out!

I made it to all my appointments with my therapist, and within a few sessions with her, I learned that I needed to stop eating and throwing up before we could work on any *issues.* She had faith in my abilities to stop these behaviors; her faith helped me stop beating myself up with food and vomiting. Once I began to realize that recovery was a realistic option, I began to make an effort to stop vomiting. At first I had to address it in small steps, and take it one minute at a time. I took the approach similar to those struggling with alcohol; unfortunately, this approach for an eating disorder is much more difficult, as abstinence is not an option! We **need** food; we don't *need* alcohol. In the past, my perfectionistic tendencies hindered my recovery. I was unable to allow myself to consider recovery as a process, but instead had unrealistic demands that I was unable to keep, and would then beat myself up for. When I finally attempted to accept the fact that I may not stop *perfectly,* recovery became much easier. I was able to nurture and care for myself enough to develop ways to combat the desire to turn to binge purge behaviors. Instead, I began to journal whenever thoughts of throwing up would enter my head. I became less spontaneous in my actions and took the time to sit with myself and try to get in touch with what it was that I was really feeling. In doing so, I was able to recognize a lot of the underlying emotions that I had been stuffing down and throwing up! I practiced "H.A.L.T.", a method I found very helpful. When I would become anxious because I was having a difficult time determining what it was I *really* needed, I'd ask myself if I was Hungry-Angry-Lonely-Tired. I didn't always know the answer, but stopping and checking became very helpful as a part of my recovery process.

Continued

I believe the hardest, and yet most meaningful parts of my recovery began when the eating disordered behaviors were under control. It was then that I began to see and feel the pain I had been trying to escape from. It was that pain that had kept me hidden for so long. This pain did cause me to relapse on occasion, but I learned something with each relapse I experienced. This helped me see the benefit of a slip, rather than only viewing it as a failure (as I did in the past)! With each experience, came a stronger belief in my abilities to cope effectively. With this added belief came hope . . . this time, however, it was no longer my therapist's hope for me. I owned this feeling of hope!

When I think back on those years that the eating disorder consumed my life, it's not so much the food, weight, exercise, and throwing up that I remember. It's how I felt during those years that is so hard to think about. I know now, after years of therapy and growth, that the eating disorder behaviors were only symptoms for how I was feeling inside. One of the biggest and best lessons I have learned through my recovery is that I am not perfect and I cannot control the path of events that make up my life. This helped me become realistic with my recovery and myself.

Recovery has not been the way I imagined it to be when I first began fighting to escape this all-consuming eating disorder. I had believed at one time, especially way back when I barely understood what was happening to me, that I'd see a therapist to learn how to stop eating compulsively and lose weight. I hated how much weight I had gained from those continuous episodes of binge eating and assumed that my therapist's goal was to help me lose it. This false assumption, I feel (looking back in hindsight), was reinforced by my first therapist. I can remember her smiling with pride while telling me I had lost weight prior to my high school graduation. My current therapist helped me to see that if I am solely focusing on food and weight, I am not recovering. Recovery means *also* addressing the *purpose* the eating disorder served, and *finding more appropriate coping mechanisms.* For me, recovery meant finding out who I am and learning how to take care of myself (instead of believing that taking care of myself meant taking care of everyone else).

I have been thinking a great deal about recovery and my life since I've come out of the disorder. There are so many pieces, so many experiences, people, and emotions that surface during these thoughts. Today I am a therapist; it has been about ten years since I was first diagnosed with an eating disorder. So often I feel I 'should' understand everything about *why* I got sick. But recovery has taught me that I need to erase the 'shoulds' from my life, and become more comfortable letting go of trying to have control over events in my life over which I have no control. I have found this incredible peace inside of me that I once feared would never be possible. I was talking with a close friend of mine recently, discussing suicide! This discussion brought me back to a memory of one of my lowest points; I can recall feeling as if I would never be capable of escaping from the demon of the eating disorder that was consuming me. I can recall being with my mother after breakfast and talking with her about how I couldn't stop all the obsessive thoughts about what I had just eaten. I remember sitting there telling her, "I just want it all to go away."

Although it is difficult for me to say *perfectly* when or how I have recovered, I do know some of the important aspects that led to my recovery: medication, weekly therapy, family therapy, talking, behavior modification to deal with exercise and other purging behaviors, meetings with a nutritionist, agreeing not to know my weight when I go to the doctor, not buying "beauty" magazines, eating foods that make me feel good, and eating foods just because they are yummy, getting enough sleep, learning to listen to *my* needs, learning to pamper myself, and treat myself on a daily basis, writing, yoga, friends, family, art.

I don't want to make it sound as if it was that easy. Years of therapy helped me take the steps in recovery. I was lucky to find a therapist who specialized in eating disorders. Her style worked for me. It felt good to know someone could sit with me . . . and tolerate me . . . when I had such difficulty sitting and tolerating myself.

My mom used to cry, asking where her daughter went. I can proudly say to her, and all of you, " I am back!"

Lori, *age 27*

ALCOHOL ABUSE

Let's begin by testing your Alcohol IQ. You can find the answers at the end of this chapter.

1)	Alcohol is a stimulant.	T	F
2)	Alcohol is less dangerous than marijuana.	T	F
3)	A 12-ounce can of beer contains more alcohol than an ounce of alcohol.	T	F
4)	Drinking several cups of coffee can help enable the drinker to "sober up."	T	F
5)	Alcohol can cause sleep disturbances.	T	F
6)	It is the amount of alcohol in the bloodstream that determines intoxication, rather than the mix of alcohol.	T	F
7)	An impaired judgement happens only after the physical symptoms of intoxication.	T	F
8)	Individuals with a family history of alcoholism are more likely to develop alcoholism.	T	F
9)	Alcohol is not physically addictive.	T	F
10)	Excessive intake of alcohol affects white blood cells, which in turn can cause disease and increased risk of cancer.	T	F

Alcoholism is a chronic disease in which a person becomes dependent upon and addictively misuses alcohol in order to achieve a particular emotional state. It has been found that genetics, psychosocial factors, and environmental factors influence its development. In other words, a family history of addiction, a particular psychological make-up, and outside stressors (e.g., relationships, work, etc.), all contribute to the disease of alcoholism. As with eating disorders, alcoholism is a progressive disease that can be fatal. It is characterized by symptoms such as: (a) a strong desire to drink despite its negative consequences (e.g., relational difficulties, decreased job performance); (b) increased consumption of alcohol in order to feel the desired effects; (c) changes in behavior, mood, relationships, eating and sleep patterns; (d) distortions in thinking; (e) feeling the "need" for alcohol in order to cope and/or feel good; and, (f) very often, denial. As stated above, alcoholism is progressive; it develops over time, and with its development comes increased severity of symptoms and complications.

How can you tell if you have a problem with alcohol? A simple self-test was developed by Dr. John Ewing; let's see if you are in the alcohol "CAGE."

Have you ever thought you needed to *Cut down* on your drinking?

Have others ever *Annoyed* you by criticizing or commenting on your drinking?

Have you ever felt *Guilty* about your drinking?

Have you ever had an *Eye opener* . . . that is, taking a drink first thing in the morning in order to steady your nerves or get rid of a hangover?

Answering "yes" to any of the above suggests a possible chronic misuse of alcohol. If there is more than one "yes," it is quite likely a problem exists. Treatment for alcoholism and eating disorders will be addressed at the end of this chapter.

Here are some statistics on alcohol and alcoholism:

- Fourteen million people in the United States abuse alcohol. That is the equivalent of one out of every 13 adults.
- Young adults between the ages of 18–29 have the highest incidents of alcohol-related problems. The lowest rate of alcohol abuse occurs among adults 65 and older.
- More men struggle with alcohol-related problems than women.
- Alcohol contributes to 100,000 deaths annually, making it the third leading cause of death in the US, after tobacco and poor diet and lack of exercise.
- About 43% of US adults—76 million people—have been exposed to alcoholism in the family. That is, they grew up with, married, or were a blood relative of someone who abused alcohol or was a problem drinker.
- 64% of high school seniors report that they have been drunk; more than 31% say that they have had five or more drinks in a row during the last two weeks.
- People who begin drinking before age 15 are four times more likely to develop alcoholism than those who begin at age 21.

DRUG ABUSE AND ADDICTION

Similar to alcoholism, drug addiction is a chronic disease in which a person becomes dependent upon and addictively misuses drugs in order to achieve a particular emotional state. The definition of drug abuse is the use of any drug for a purpose other than that for which it was intended. Drug dependence occurs when an individual needs to continue taking a drug in order to maintain a desired effect and/or prevent symptoms of withdrawal. As with alcoholism, drug addiction also has as its foundation genetic, psychosocial, and environmental factors. That is, the person's family history, personality make-up, and stressors can lead to the misuse of drugs. As with alcoholism and eating disorders, drug addiction is a progressive disease that can be fatal. It may start out as an "innocent" experimentation with drugs, and quickly cycle down to physical and psychological dependence. Drug addiction is not restricted to "illegal" drugs; it can include the abuse of prescription and over-the-counter medications. If you use *any* medications or drugs, it is important that you complete the following exercises. Not all drug use is misuse; at the same time, it is possible to overlook a situation of misuse. If, at the end of these exercises, you feel you may have a problem with drug use, we strongly encourage you to share your concerns with your therapist and/or physician.

Before we explore your *Substance Abuse I.Q.*, take a moment to answer the following questions:

1) Do you take any prescription medications?   Yes   No
   If so, list medications, and frequency.

   _____

   _____

   _____

2) Do you take any illicit drugs?   Yes   No
   If so, list drugs and frequency.

   _____

   _____

   _____

3) Do you ever find yourself taking drugs to improve your mood?   Yes   No
4) Do you ever find yourself taking drugs in order to help you avoid your feelings?   Yes   No
5) Do you ever find yourself taking drugs first thing in the morning, as a "pick me up"?   Yes   No
6) Have you ever found yourself not being able to afford personal needs because you used your money to purchase drugs?   Yes   No
7) Have you ever found yourself borrowing and/or stealing money in order to buy drugs?   Yes   No
8) Has your job/school performance suffered as a result of drug use?   Yes   No
9) Have you ever found yourself missing work/school because of drugs?   Yes   No
10) Do you lie about your use of drugs to your family and friends?   Yes   No

11) Has a friend ever confronted you about your drug use?	Yes	No
12) Have you ever lost friends due to your drug use?	Yes	No
13) Have you ever tried to stop your drug use, only to return?	Yes	No
14) Do you feel more socially secure when using drugs?	Yes	No
15) Have you ever felt guilty about your use of drugs?	Yes	No
16) Have you ever wondered if you have a problem with drug use?	Yes	No
17) Have you ever blacked out as a result of drug use?	Yes	No
18) Have you ever become physically ill as a result of drug use?	Yes	No
19) Have you ever found yourself becoming physically ill from not using drugs?	Yes	No
20) Have you ever wondered if you are addicted to drugs?	Yes	No

If you answered "yes" to question 20, in all likelihood you addictively misuse drugs. If you have answered "yes" to more than 1 of the questions it is important that you work on decreasing your drug use. There is nothing to be ashamed of! As with eating disorders, drug use is a maladaptive approach to coping; treatment will help you learn more appropriate coping mechanisms and foster self-care.

The following questionnaire is designed to help you test your knowledge of the various drugs, their effects, and signs of misuse. The answers to these questions are at the end of this chapter.

Substance Abuse I.Q.

1) Narcotics are:
   a) Drugs used to increase alertness
   b) Drugs used to dull the senses, relieve pain, and induce sleep
   c) Drugs used to relieve anxiety and tension
   d) All of the above

2) Examples of stimulant drugs are:
   a) Cocaine
   b) Crack
   c) Ice
   d) All of the above
   e) None of the above

3) Another word for marijuana is:
   a) Rock
   b) Methamphetamine
   c) Reefer
   d) Opium

4) Steroids do all of the following, but:
   a) Increase physical endurance
   b) Increase muscle strength
   c) Increase sex drive
   d) Enhance athletic performance
5) Inhalants may cause:
   a) Loss of muscle control
   b) Brain damage
   c) Slurred speech
   d) None of the above
   e) All of the above

Below you will find two lists. The list on the left categorizes the *types* of substance. On the right, you will find examples of those *particular* substances. We ask that you match the particular substance to its type. For example, you would match glue to inhalant.

Inhalants	LSD
Depressants	Heroin
Cannabis	Amphetamine
Steroids	Toluene vapors
Stimulants	Marijuana
Narcotics	Ethyl alcohol
Hallucinogens	Diazepam
Alcohol	Dianabol

Before we close this section on drug abuse, let's explore some of the commonly held myths about drug addiction.

1. **Myth:** It is easy to identify a drug abuser because he or she is always high.
   Reality: It is not how often one uses the drug, it is the lack of control over the drug when used. That is, a drug abuser can be someone who uses once a year. The problem is that when the person is using, he or she won't stop using until it is gone.
2. **Myth:** Alcohol isn't as dangerous as other drugs, because if it was it wouldn't be legal.
   Reality: Alcohol is the #1 substance of abuse due to its availability. In addition to this, it has been found that alcohol is the catalyst for further substance use, which in turn can be lethal.
3. **Myth:** Drug abuse is a young person's problem.
   Reality: Drug abuse is quite common among the elderly. Suicide rates from drug abuse among those over 60 years of age are higher than any other age bracket.
4. **Myth:** Using legal drugs is different than using illegal drugs.
   Reality: A drug is a drug! Regardless of whether or not a drug is legal, if one is using a drug to achieve a particular emotional state, one is abusing that drug.

LAXATIVE ABUSE

Of all the substances available, the substance most commonly abused by people with eating disorders is laxatives. The (faulty) belief that laxatives will help with weight loss, and or prevent weight gain can lead to abuse. As with the substances mentioned above, the abuse of laxatives can also be fatal.

First and foremost, laxatives are an ineffective means of weight loss. They do not prevent the absorption of calories, but rather they affect the emptying of the large intestine which occurs *after* the calories have already been absorbed by the small bowel. There have never been any findings that laxatives help eliminate fat. The weight loss that *may* occur following laxative use is strictly that of water weight. Once you eat or drink again your body will extract all the moisture from these substances and you will experience *rebound water retention; not only have you lost no weight, but also you may feel as if you've gained weight because your body is retaining fluid.* The way to stop this cycle is to stop using laxatives. Unfortunately, people with eating disorders often become so panicked by rebound water retention (which they believe is weight from *fat*), that they use more laxatives, which leads to laxative abuse.

Laxative Use Questions

If you find yourself using laxatives more frequently than recommended, you are abusing laxatives. The answers to the questions below will help determine whether or not you abuse laxatives.

1) Have you ever used laxatives?	Yes	No
2) If yes, how often do you use laxatives, and how many laxatives do you use per episode?		
3) Have you ever used laxatives as a means of determining what you were going to eat?	Yes	No
4) Have you found yourself needing to increase the number of laxatives used in order to achieve your desired effect?	Yes	No
5) Do you experience episodes of constipation following episodes of laxative use?	Yes	No
6) Have you tried to decrease your use of laxatives without much success?	Yes	No
7) Have you concealed your use of laxatives from others?	Yes	No
8) Have you ever stolen laxatives or related products in order to maintain your use?	Yes	No

If you have answered "Yes" on questions 3–8, it is important that you disclose your use of laxatives to your therapist and physician. Laxative abuse can be fatal; it is also progressive and can cause major health complications.

The following are the complications that can result from the abuse of laxatives:

Electrolyte imbalances: Purging, whether through use of laxatives, vomiting, or diuretic abuse, can result in a depletion of potassium, chloride, and sodium. These three elements, called "electrolytes," are essential for metabolic processes, and nerve and muscle cell functioning. A depletion of these chemicals can result in weakness, tiredness, depression, constipation, cardiac arrythymias, and death.

Edema: Abuse of laxatives can result in periods of dehydration, which in turn can produce excessive water retention, called *edema*. Edema is experienced as swelling of the joints (primarily the fingers, ankles, and knees) and face. It generally occurs immediately after laxative abuse has ceased and can cause profound physical and psychological distress. Cessation of laxative abuse (or other purging behaviors) will gradually reduce the edema. However, for people with eating disorders, the bloating associated with fluid retention can panic a person into believing she is "fat" and propel her back to purging before her body has had an opportunity to achieve balance. Education about laxative abuse and withdrawal is an important component in relapse prevention.

Constipation: Laxative abuse can result in constipation, as the function of the colon is impaired. The body learns to respond to the cues of the laxatives, and loses its ability to adequately function on its own. As with edema, the individual can experience both physical and psychological complications, as the feeling of being constipated can also leave the individual feeling "fat."

Cardiac Irregularities: As stated above, the abuse of laxatives can result in electrolyte imbalances, which in turn can cause arrhythmias and sudden death.

Kidney Dysfunction: As with cardiac irregularities, electrolyte imbalances can also result in kidney dysfunction and, in severe cases, kidney failure.

Here are some suggestions to help you stop your laxative abuse. However, as with withdrawal of any substance of abuse, we *strongly* recommend that you consult your physician to determine what plan is best for you.

How To Stop Laxative Abuse

1. In most cases it is recommended that you discontinue laxative use right away. Some physicians recommend a gradual tapering off; however, there have been few studies showing that this increased the likelihood of recovery. If bowel functioning appears impaired as a result of this discontinuation, it is recommended that you speak with your physician.
2. Increase your fiber intake. Added dietary fiber can serve as a catalyst to normal bowel functioning.
3. Meet with your physician regularly during this process, as medical complications can arise. Physiological and psychological support can help fight off relapse!

DIURETICS

Diuretics are medications that help rid the body of excess water. They are commonly used by women before and during their menstrual periods, and for those who experience high blood pressure. Unfortunately, they are also used, and abused, by millions of individuals in their quest for thinness. Diuretics can be found "over the counter" or by prescription. It has been found that prescription diuretics are much more potent, and can have serious adverse effects, such as weakness, constipation, nausea, abdominal pain, and heart irregularities. As with laxatives, the misuse of diuretics can result in electrolyte imbalances and edema. Treatment for diuretic abuse is similar to that of laxative abuse (see How to Stop Laxative Abuse, above).

1) Have you ever used diuretics?   Yes   No

2) If yes, how often do you use diuretics, and how many diuretics do you use per episode?

_____

3) Have you found yourself needing to increase the number of diuretics used in order
   to achieve your desired effect?   Yes   No

4) Do you experience episodes of edema (water retention) following episodes of diuretic use?   Yes   No

5) Have you tried to decrease your use of diuretics without much success?   Yes   No

6) Have you concealed your use of diuretics to others?   Yes   No

7) Have you ever stolen diuretics or related products in order to maintain your use?   Yes   No

We *strongly* recommended that you disclose your usage to your physician and therapist.

DIET PILLS

Second to laxative abuse, diet pills are the #2 most abused substance by those with eating disorders. Even knowing that the main ingredient in diet pills, phenolpropanolamine, can be toxic, individuals with eating disorders continue to take them (even at higher dosages than recommended). As with the abuse of other substances, the misuse of diet pills can result in complications ranging from nervousness to seizures and death. The treatment for the misuse of diet pills is similar to that for laxative and diuretic abuse. Fortunately, it appears that stopping diet pill abuse is not as difficult as stopping laxative and diuretic abuse. It may be because diet pills do not provide *immediate* gratification (i.e., perceived weight loss).

1) Have you ever taken diet pills?   Yes   No

2) If yes, how often do you take diet pills, and how many diet pills do you take per day?

_____

3) Have you ever taken more diet pills than is recommended?   Yes   No

4) Have you found yourself needing to increase the number of diet pills used
   in order to achieve your desired effect?   Yes   No

5) Have you found diet pills help you with weight loss?   Yes   No

6) Have you tried to decrease your use of diet pills without success?   Yes   No

7) Have you concealed your use of diet pills from others?   Yes   No

8) Have you ever stolen diet pills in order to maintain your use?   Yes   No

IPECAC ABUSE

Ipecac syrup is a substance found in most medicine cabinets. It is a first-aid tonic given to those who have ingested toxic substances. Parents often keep a bottle handy in case children accidentally swallow a dangerous substance. Some with eating disorders use ipecac syrup to induce vomiting. Abuse of ipecac syrup can be fatal. It can cause serious heart irregularities and death. We *strongly* recommended that if you use, or have ever used, ipecac syrup that you stop immediately and tell your physician. It is critical that you have a thorough examination to make sure that no damage to your heart has occurred. Fortunately, if the syrup usage has not caused heart damage, a full recovery is possible as long as ipecac use is terminated.

1) Have you ever used ipecac syrup to aid you in vomiting?   Yes   No

2) If "yes", how often have you used ipecac syrup over :

The past week: _____

The past month: _____

The past six months: _____

The past year: _____

3) Have you ever experienced changes in your heartbeat after using ipecac syrup?   Yes   No

If "yes," please explain: _____

_____

_____

_____

_____

_____

If you have answered "yes" to either question 1 or 3, please contact your physician immediately.

We have identified six common substances abused by those with eating disorders: alcohol, drugs (both illicit and prescription), laxatives, diuretics, diet pills, and ipecac syrup. Summarize your usage in the space below by circling all substances that you use with feelings of guilt, shame, and/or difficulty stopping despite your knowledge of their negative consequences.

Alcohol   Illicit drugs   Prescription drugs

Laxatives   Diuretics   Diet Pills   Ipecac

Now, let's explore what you *gain* through your use of these substances. In the spaces below, list the substances you circled followed by their perceived benefits to you. The "benefit" is the purpose the substance serves for you.

Substance: _____

   Benefits: _____
_____
_____
_____
_____

       * _____
_____
_____
_____
_____

Substance: _____

   Benefits: _____
_____
_____
_____
_____

       * _____
_____
_____
_____
_____

Substance: _____

   Benefits: _____
_____
_____
_____

       * _____
_____
_____
_____
_____

Substance: _____

Benefits: _____
_____
_____
_____
_____

* _____
_____
_____
_____
_____

Substance: _____

Benefits: _____
_____
_____
_____
_____

* _____
_____
_____
_____
_____

Substance: _____

Benefits: _____
_____
_____
_____

* _____
_____
_____
_____
_____

You will notice that there is an asterisk (*) following each explanation of benefits. At this time, we would like you to revisit your recorded substances, and next to the asterisk list reasons for terminating the substance use.

Before continuing, please refer back to Chapter 3. Here you will find an explanation of the Stages of Change. In the space below, please record what stage you believe you are in regarding your substance use.

Remember, your stage of change will determine your readiness for "letting go" of a behavior or attitude.

You may wish to return to the chapter on stages of change before continuing, in order to remind yourself of the approach to recovery based on your stage of change. Before ending this chapter on substance abuse, take this opportunity to identify coping strategies that you will use to prepare yourself for recovery from substance abuse. These strategies may be similar or different from those you chose regarding your eating disorder. Now, take a moment to complete the following sentences.

1) When I begin to think about using, I will:

_____   _____
_____   _____
_____   _____
_____   _____

2) If I feel negative feelings as a result of my decision to abstain, I will remind myself of the following reasons why I made a good decision:

_____
_____
_____
_____
_____
_____
_____
_____

3) I will nurture myself following my healthy decision to abstain by:

_____   _____
_____   _____
_____   _____
_____   _____

Congratulations! Recovering from an eating disorder is a difficult feat. Having multiple addictions make recovery that much more challenging. We applaud you for identifying substances you (maladaptively) use to cope. We hope that this chapter has helped you understand the harm you are causing yourself, and given you the confidence to take the steps to recover.

ALCOHOL TRUE AND FALSE ANSWERS

1) False	2) False	3) True	4) False	5) True
6) True	7) False	8) True	9) False	10) True

SUBSTANCE ABUSE I.Q. ANSWERS

1) B	2) D	3) C	4) C	5) E

MATCHING (SUBSTANCE ABUSE)

Inhalants—Toluene vapors
Depressants—Diazepam
Cannabis—Marijuana
Steroids—Dianabol
Stimulant—Amphetamine
Narcotics—Heroin
Hallucinogen—LSD
Alcohol—Ethyl alcohol

Trauma and Abuse

As you know, we believe that eating disorders are creative yet maladaptive ways of coping with difficult feelings. Certain situations in life can cause difficult feelings; for example, the loss of a loved one can leave you sitting with tremendously painful feelings. Eating disorders can develop to help you tolerate such pain. This chapter is going to explore particular painful events that can result in the development of an eating disorder. In this chapter we will talk about *trauma* and *abuse* (physical, sexual, and emotional) and their implication in the development of an eating disorder. This section may help you understand whether you have been abused, identify the abuse's impact, and explore ways you might have used your eating disorder as a protection. This acknowledgement and understanding will help you develop a healthier, more nurturing response.

We hope this exploration will help you see that *you* may be perpetuating the abuse you received, through restrictive eating, binge eating, purging, or other self-harming behaviors.

The goal of all trauma and abuse work is to help you love and nurture yourself the way you should have been loved and nurtured.

PHYSICAL ABUSE

Abuse, whether physical, sexual, or emotional, is about power and control. The perpetrator wields power and control at the expense of his or her victims. Its impact is tremendous; for after any bruises or scars fade, the emotional scars last and, if not addressed, grow and fester. Although physical abuse leaves more apparent marks, it is quite common for the victim to find ways to disguise the cause of the bruises, scrapes, or cuts by telling stories of being accident-prone or bruising easily.

The following are some examples of *physical* abuse:

slapping	choking	punching	pushing	grabbing with force
biting	kicking	assaulting with an object		twisting arm
beating	throwing of objects		cornering one against one's will	
shaking	burning	shoving	bruising	cutting

If you have experienced any of these or something similar, then you have been physically abused. There is no excuse for physical abuse. No matter what you may have done to upset someone else, there is absolutely no excuse for someone to express anger through physical violence. Many individuals who have been physically abused deny that it is abuse, for they feel responsible for having upset the perpetrator. Furthermore, it is not uncommon for the perpetrator to later express feelings of sorrow and love, which further confuses the victim. If you believe or *feel* you have been abused, continue the journey set forth in this chapter. If it doesn't feel safe enough to take this journey alone, ask a friend, loved one, or therapist to go through this chapter with you. Many journeys are better taken with a companion.

SEXUAL ABUSE

The impact of sexual abuse is traumatic, yet its scars and bruises are more internal than external. Not all sexual abuse involves sexual contact. Pornography shown to children, for example, is a form of sexual abuse where no physical contact occurs. Some examples of sexual abuse are:

being touched in private areas of the body against one's will
being fondled or kissed in an uncomfortable manner
being raped or penetrated in some other way
being forced to perform or receive oral sex
being forced to look at or touch another's genitalia
being forced to watch or participate in pornography
being subjected to unnecessary and invasive medical treatments of a sexual nature
being forced to engage in sexual torture

If you have experienced any of the incidents, or incidents like these, you have been sexually abused. As with physical abuse, there is *no excuse* for such events! It does not matter how pretty/handsome you are, how much you may flirt, or how you dress. None of these are reasons for another person to violate you. Most perpetrators know their victims. As with physical abuse, this leaves the victim with feelings of confusion, anger, guilt, and shame.

EMOTIONAL ABUSE

Many of us learned the adage *"sticks and stones may break my bones, but names will never hurt me."* It is a common comeback for young children when they're teased. Unfortunately, this adage is not completely truthful. Names may not physically hurt us, as sticks and stones may; but names leave us with emotional scars that never completely heal. They just fade. Emotional abuse strips us of any positive sense of self, which has a direct impact on our self-esteem. So often, we talk of the child with a low self esteem and look to the parents to see why this is the case. What we fail to realize is that despite love at home, if an individual is being emotionally abused, her sense of self is undermined or shattered. If you have experienced any of the situations below, you are a victim of emotional abuse:

being called derogatory names
being teased
being neglected, overlooked, not provided for emotionally
being put down
being made to believe you are crazy
being told how to feel and/or think
having someone play mind games
being belittled
being insulted
being criticized
being rejected

These are only some examples of emotional abuse. As with other forms of abuse, no one deserves to be a victim of such treatment. The impact of any abuse is intense and profound.

EXPLORING YOUR HISTORY OF ABUSE

Look at your own particular history of abuse. This can be a difficult task to do, for it is going to make your experiences more "real." It is going to fight the natural response of denial, yet breaking through denial is also the beginning of recovery.

In the columns below, list the people who you feel have abused you. In the column next to each name, record the types of abuse you received. If you believe you have experienced abuse at the hands of certain individuals, but have no direct memories, list them as well and place a ✓ in the column under the question mark.

Name	?	Type of abuse (physical, sexual, emotional)

Take a deep breath! You have just taken a big step in your journey to recovery. At times, this may feel very difficult and bring up uncomfortable feelings. You may need to return to previous chapters in order to remind yourself how to initiate self-care during these difficult feeling states. You may need to do this work only in the presence of your therapist. However you do it, know that these feeling states, as tumultuous and painful as they might be, will pass, and you will become even stronger in your recovery.

TRAUMA

Trauma is a painful emotional or behavioral state resulting from emotional stress or physical injury, such as the forms of abuse discussed here. Studies show that there is a strong correlation between eating disorders and abuse (Bulik, 1989; Vanderlinden & Vandereycken, 1993). But why?

Remember, eating disorders are faulty coping mechanisms. Trauma is an experience which leaves many individuals searching for ways to cope with untenable, unbearable pain. They are desperate for coping mechanisms that can bring protection, escape, denial, or the numbing of feelings. If individuals can make the memories disappear, or fade, then they won't experience the painful feelings that are so terrifying for them. In addition, many trauma victims suffer alone. Guilt, shame, fear of abandonment, blame, or retribution silences many victims. The pain of abuse is overwhelming; suffering alone is unbearable. An eating disorder may anesthetize or occlude the pain for a moment. Sadly, it is only a moment; and, ultimately, it perpetuates the cycle of abuse.

The Siren song of the eating disorder promises escape and peace, but like the abuser, it is a charlatan. It is the abuser in disguise. How does the eating disorder "help"? Bulimia and binge eating, for example, can help the victim of trauma "stuff down" feelings. Food becomes her "drug of choice" numbing intolerable feelings. Purging helps the victim release or expel feelings she cannot "digest." Denial of food supports her wish to "disappear." If she disappears, there will be no more abuse. For those who have been sexually abused, food restriction or overeating erects a visual barrier to continued abuse.

Will her emaciated or obese appearance obliterate any sexual appeal, effectively keeping her safe from further victimization? Regardless of the nature of the trauma, eating disorders provide the trauma victim with one aspect of control in her life. For those with a history of emotional or physical abuse, food can become the victim's "best friend." It "tells" her it will never talk back; it will never hurt her. It will never abandon her. Being able to control what goes in and comes out of her body can be a way of coping with the total lack of control she experienced when she was traumatized.

HOW HAS FOOD HELPED YOU SURVIVE?

Up until now, we have been referring to the individual who has experienced trauma as the victim. From this point on, we are going to replace "victim" with *survivor*! You have found creative ways to keep yourself functioning while under the most horrific of circumstances. Empowerment is a part of recovery. It is important that while you explore the painful feelings associated with the trauma, you applaud yourself for the fight you underwent in order to survive!

In the space below, describe the role you believe food has played in your efforts to survive. What would it be like to let go of this security? What are the pros, and what are the cons? As we have said many times, it is not only important to understand the benefits of change, but the losses and fears you will face as well. Do not underestimate the role your eating disorder has played in your survival; and, thus, the fear it is likely to evoke as you begin to let it go.

How my eating disorder has helped me survive

You have just taken an important step in your journey. Identifying the ways in which food has helped you face intolerable feelings is the beginning step toward breaking free of the abusive impact of the eating disorder and the abuser. Below is a list of feelings and behaviors that survivors often experience as a direct result of trauma. Please check all those that apply:

depression_____   crying episodes _____   anxiety _____

nightmares_____   flashbacks _____   panic attacks _____

feelings of re-experiencing the trauma _____

hopelessness _____   helplessness _____   guilt _____

shame _____   numbness _____   confusion _____

anger _____   rage _____   fear _____

isolation _____   sexual issues _____

feeling dirty _____   feeling crazy _____   self doubt _____

feeling disconnected from one's body _____   difficulty with relationships _____

suicidal thoughts _____   self destructive behaviors _____

other (please explain): _____

The feelings and behaviors that you have checked are the feelings and behaviors that your eating disorder is helping you avoid. These can be rather intense and terrifying to experience. Letting go of the eating disorder in and of itself is not enough to protect you from the possible flooding of feelings or the urge to behave in other self-destructive ways. You will need to practice finding alternative, more nurturing, ways to protect yourself while experiencing these emotions.

In the spaces on the next page, make a list of the feelings and behaviors you have checked. Below these, list alternative coping mechanisms that you can begin to practice.

Example: Feeling or behavior: <u>anger</u>

Things I can do: <u>punch a pillow</u>

        write my feelings <u>on paper</u>

        <u>take a walk, paint, listen to music</u>

Feeling or behavior: _____

Things I can do: _____

_____

_____

_____

_____

Feeling or behavior: _____

Things I can do: _____

_____

_____

_____

_____

Feeling or behavior: _____

Things I can do: _____

_____

_____

_____

_____

Feeling or behavior: _____

Things I can do: _____

_____

_____

_____

_____

Feeling or behavior: _____

Things I can do: _____

_____

_____

_____

_____

Feeling or behavior: _____

Things I can do: _____

_____

_____

_____

_____

_____

Feeling or behavior: _____

Things I can do: _____

_____

_____

_____

_____

Feeling or behavior: _____

Things I can do: _____

_____

_____

_____

_____

It is important to know that having an eating disorder is not a conscious choice. An expression of feelings and an effort at coping through food is often unconscious in creation and maintenance. The eating disorder works effectively to protect many trauma survivors from intolerable pain. This is important to understand. It is not going to be *easy* to feel the same immediate benefits from writing about your feelings as throwing them up in the toilet. But, on paper, you and trusted others can review and address your feelings over and over again until you feel affirmed, acknowledged, and blessed with greater peace. In the toilet, no one sees your feelings. They are indecipherable; they are gone; and the relief is fleeting, at best.

This work is very difficult, but keep practicing. It took time for you to develop this coping mechanism; it is going to take time, and practice, to learn new, more-adaptive methods of coping.

MY STRUGGLE WITH AN EATING DISORDER AND SEXUAL ABUSE

My name is Laura; I am forty years old, and the youngest of four girls. I have always been a perfectionist; everything I embarked on had to be done perfectly. Weight has always been an issue for me. Growing up, I was a competitive swimmer and cheerleader. Both sports required a thin body type in order to enhance performance. In order for me to perform at my peak, I made sure I was "in shape." To me, being in shape meant working out . . . a lot! "Weigh-ins" during my college years as a cheerleader only reinforced my self-consciousness with weight. This alone, however, did not contribute to my eating disorder.

When my eating disorder began, so too did turbulence in my marriage and memories of childhood sexual abuse. I was terrified of being alone, and focusing on food served as a distraction. This was not a conscious happening. In fact, to me it felt as if my eating disorder was a direct result of wanting to lose weight. I can recall wanting to lose ten pounds before going back to my college homecoming. I went on an innocent diet, and lost 25 pounds in four months. My wish to lose ten had quickly turned to twenty five, as the monster of the eating disorder had taken over. I was unable to stop losing weight; I was preoccupied and obsessed with food and weight, and would find myself achieving a "high" when I would step on the scale four to five times a day and see the weight loss. My use of exercise quickly turned into misuse; it was now my punishment for eating. I was unable to see that the one thing I loved so much was slowly killing me. It cost me almost everything I had. I had now lost my marriage and felt I was in jeopardy of losing my children.

I knew finding a good therapist was critical in order for me to save my children. I knew that my therapy needed to focus less on food and weight, and more on the underlying issues. I knew that eating disorders are not about food; they are about issues in your life that are out of control. For me, my marriage was failing and I was experiencing flashbacks from my history of sexual abuse. I needed to find a therapist that could help me with these issues, while helping me let go of my destructive coping mechanism . . . my eating disorder.

Today I am at a normal weight. I consider myself *in recovery*, for I believe recovery is a process. I have struggled with it for eleven years; it is not going to go away overnight. I have learned new ways of coping with stress. I now communicate my feelings instead of bingeing and purging them. I have also learned that I am a worthwhile person. I deserve to eat; I deserve to live. You do, too. You are not alone.

Laura, *age 40*

As bizarre as this may sound, *surviving* trauma (not the trauma itself) has its benefits. Your ability to survive is a testament to your fortitude and character. For example, one trauma survivor told me about the compassion she has for children of abuse, and how she believes her own experience has helped her understand children in ways that others (who have not been abused) cannot. She believes this is a "benefit" that she can bestow on others because she survived. Another survivor talks of her startle response and how it protects her from situations of danger. She believes she would not have such a response, had she not been abused. She is thankful for this response, for she believes it helps her see danger before it happens.

Your next step is to consider any positive impact surviving your trauma may have on you today. This can be a difficult task to do, for it can sound as if you are grateful for the trauma. We know that is not the case. But you are a survivor; it is important for you to see the skills and traits that have contributed to your ability to survive.

In the space below, list *all* of your positive attributes. When you have finished with this, please put an asterisk (*) next to the traits you believe are the direct result of your trauma history. Place a check mark (✓) next to the traits you believe are more innate (part of your personality from birth). Please note that a trait can have both a * and a ✓ next to it.

Here is a list of feelings to help you:

sensitive	compassionate	empathetic	sympathetic	caring
cautious	determined	driven	dedicated	devoted
	focused	structured	aware of surroundings	

_____   _____   _____
_____   _____   _____
_____   _____   _____
_____   _____   _____
_____   _____   _____
_____   _____   _____
_____   _____   _____
_____   _____   _____
_____   _____   _____

Our goal is to help you accentuate positives, while acknowledging your past. You cannot take away the trauma; however, you can put it in a place where it will no longer interfere with your goals and dreams. The traumatic events cannot go away, but their impact can!

You should now have an understanding of what we mean by physical, sexual, and emotional trauma. You have given consideration to both the negative impact of the trauma and the many positive qualities and attributes you possess that contributed to your survival. We hope you understand how the eating disorder initially protected you from unbearable feelings. We hope you now see how the eating disorder, despite its promise of protection, became your abuser in disguise.

If you cannot acknowledge any positive feelings about your ability to survive, we suggest you complete the following exercise.

This exercise is intended to help fan the embers of compassion you have for yourself. Those who have been abused often have tremendous difficulty feeling compassion for themselves although they are capable of feeling it for others. We hope this exercise will help you feel the compassion you deserve! Using a childhood photo of yourself will greatly enhance this possibility. It can be difficult to look through photographs from years when you were abused; if you anticipate experiencing painful feelings while looking for a photo, consider doing it with a loved one or therapist. Remember, you need not travel this road alone.

Place Picture Here

The next step of this exercise can be a painful one. You may feel strong feelings. Please do this with a therapist or trusted other, or make a safety plan for yourself. Before you begin, outline things you can do for yourself, as well as people you can call, if painful feelings arise. Keep this list close to you, as you progress with this work.

Things I can do for myself if painful feelings arise:

1) _____

2) _____

3) _____

4) _____

5) _____

People I can call if painful feelings arise:

1) _____

2) _____

3) _____

4) _____

5) _____

In the space below, please write a letter to *that person* in the picture. Pay close attention to the age of the person. What were the circumstances like at this time in his or her life? Who were his or her friends? Teachers? Did he or she have particular interests or hobbies? How did he or she perceive the world and his/her surroundings. What type of support did this person receive? What type of love was available? If the trauma took place during childhood, consider closely the developmental stage of a child that age. If you have difficulty with this, you may want to "people watch" and see if you can find a young child that represents the age you were when the trauma occurred. This may help you understand perceptions of the world through the eyes of a child.

_____
_____
_____
_____
_____
_____
_____
_____
_____
_____
_____
_____
_____
_____
_____
_____
_____
_____
_____
_____
_____
_____
_____
_____
_____
_____
_____

You are so very courageous! It is much easier to remain in a state of self-loathing than it is to risk self-love. Before you continue, take a moment to reflect on the exercise above.

What did you learn about yourself through this exercise?

_____

_____

_____

_____

_____

Are any of the feelings that you are currently experiencing similar to those you experienced before this exercise? If so, which feelings?

_____

_____

_____

_____

_____

Are any of the feelings that you are currently experiencing different from those you experienced before this exercise? If "yes," how are they different?

_____

_____

_____

_____

_____

Did you glean any insights from this exercise that you want to remember (and call upon) as you continue with your journey? If so, what are they:

_____

_____

_____

_____

Finally, if you could talk to this child, would you have questions for him or her? If "yes," what are the questions?

_____

_____

_____

_____

The questions you have listed are questions for you to to reflect upon as you take this journey to recovery. Now, let's take the next step.

Part of recovering from an eating disorder is placing feelings where they belong. For example, recovery from anorexia may be moving the anger that you feel toward yourself (as expressed through your eating disorder), and placing it where it belongs. There are conflicting theories as to whether one needs to confront one's perpetrator as a part of recovery. We do not believe direct confrontation is necessary for recovery. Many people recover from trauma without ever having had an opportunity for confrontation. We do believe, however, that being given an opportunity to express feelings about the perpetrator and the abuse is critical for recovery.

In the space below, write a letter to your perpetrator(s). We hope that you will write from the heart; do not "edit" your thoughts. This letter is for your purposes only unless you choose to share it with a trusted other. You do not need to share it with anyone, nor do you need to send it to your perpetrator. What you do need, however, is the opportunity to let go of the painful feelings that may have contributed to the development of your eating disorder.

To_____,

_____
_____
_____
_____
_____
_____
_____
_____
_____
_____
_____
_____
_____
_____
_____
_____
_____
_____
_____
_____
_____
_____
_____
_____
_____
_____
_____
_____
_____

_____,
_____

It is okay to cry! It is okay to scream! It is okay to be angry! Just, *please* be constructive with these feelings. If you have experienced abuse and trauma, you may have survived the trauma by suppressing these painful feelings and expressing them toward your self. If you have removed yourself from these abusive relationships, you have now created a safe environment for expressing these feelings. It will be okay; you have already survived the worst! Your recovery may be emotionally painful; however, as long as you continue to practice self care and self expression, you will be safe in your recovery. If you continue to be in contact with someone who is abusive, it is critical that you tell a trusted person in your life. If you have no such support person, go to a therapist in a local clinic or hospital, tell your doctor, or tell your counselor at school and work toward removing yourself from the abuse and toward safety and health. We understand that it is easy for us to say this, and difficult for you to do. The first step will, in all likelihood, be the most difficult. Using your supports, and continuing with your efforts at self-care, will galvanize you in this process.

Special Circumstances: Obsessive-Compulsive Disorder, Depression, and Diabetes

In this chapter we are going to focus our attention on mental health and medical diagnoses that complicate eating disorders. In some situations, they may be one of the causes of the eating disorder; in others, they may reinforce the thoughts and behaviors of the eating disorder. We will discuss: obsessive-compulsive disorder, obsessive-compulsive personality traits, depression, and diabetes.

OBSESSIVE-COMPULSIVE DISORDER

Obsessive-compulsive disorder (OCD) is an anxiety-based disorder in which individuals experience recurrent and intrusive thoughts (obsessions) which, in turn, bring about anxiety. In an effort to alleviate these feelings of anxiety, compulsions to engage in repetitive acts occur. These compulsive behaviors, though equally disruptive, work to temporarily diminish anxiety. As the anxieties return, so do the obsessive thoughts and compulsive behaviors, causing tremendous distress to the individual. The more the individual is aware of the obsessive-compulsive tendencies, the more she must allow for time for them to ride through their course. As with the "eating disordered voice," intellect or reasoning is not enough to stop the obsessive thoughts and compulsive acts. The ultimate results of obsessive-compulsive disorder are: (a) emotional exhaustion, (b) loss of time (due to repetitive acts), (c) low self-esteem, (d) depression, (e) frustration, and more.

OCD can be mild to severe; and its impact on the individual can be experienced as mildly frustrating to overwhelming and debilitating.

Before we give you a more detailed definition of OCD, let's take a look at some examples of how OCD may present itself in the life of someone with an eating disorder.

> Elizabeth is a 21-year-old college senior, battling a two year struggle with anorexia nervosa. She is very concerned with her appearance, and finds herself in front of the mirror for up to 30 minutes every day, searching for that "perfect" outfit. Shamefully, she acknowledges how, on occasion, she has been late to class because of this quest.
>
> As we talked, Elizabeth began to describe her closet. She spoke of the "order" of her blouses, pants, skirts, and dresses, and how none of the hangers could touch one another. She giggles as she talks of the good natured ribbing she receives from her roommates. In actuality, she is embarrassed with how rigid she is with her closet, and other aspects of her life.
>
> When asked to describe her dorm room, she spoke of how everything has a "place," and how she finds herself feeling agitated when her roommates' side of the room is not as neat and clean as her side is.
>
> What we gradually learned is that Elizabeth's rituals with food, weight, body image, and dressing are symptoms of obsessive-compulsive disorder.

> Lindsay is an 18-year-old high school senior, with anorexia nervosa and bulimia. She speaks openly of her rituals with food, eating the green items first, followed by a sip of water before continuing on to her next item. She will *never* allow any food items to touch one another, and if they do, she must throw the food away, and serve herself again. She must eat her dinner no later than 7 p.m., and must have her meals no closer than 4 hours apart.
>
> In exploring her history further, we learn of a family history of addiction, depression, anxiety, and obsessive-compulsive disorder. In fact, her mother struggles with her own experience with OCD, but it does not "debilitate" her in any way. As such, neither Lindsay nor her mom looked at Lindsay's food rituals as anything other than issues related to her eating disorder. Yet, when Lindsay was given a trial of medication to help with OCD symptoms, she experienced a dramatic decrease in food rituals, as well as other rituals which were unrelated to her eating disorder.

The DSM-IV in its description of Obsessive-Compulsive Disorder defines obsessions and compulsions in the following way:

Obsessions
1. Recurrent and persistent thoughts, impulses, or images that are experienced, at some time during the disturbance, as intrusive and inappropriate and that cause marked anxiety or distress.
2. The thoughts, impulses, or images are not simply excessive worries about real life problems.
3. The person attempts to ignore or suppress such thoughts, impulses, or images, or to neutralize them with some other thought or action.
4. The person recognizes that the obsessional thoughts, impulses, or images are a product of his or her own mind.

Compulsions
1. Repetitive behaviors or mental acts that the person feels driven to perform in response to an obsession, or according to rules that must be applied rigidly.
2. The behaviors or mental acts are aimed at preventing or reducing distress or preventing some dreaded event or situation; however, these behaviors or mental acts are not connected in a realistic way with what they are designed to neutralize or prevent or are clearly excessive.

You have learned about obsessive-compulsive disorder, and seen examples of how it might appear in those who have eating disorders. Now assess your own obsessive-compulsive tendencies:

1) Do you ever find yourself worrying excessively that you may experience harm?   Yes   No

2) Do you ever find yourself worrying excessively that someone you love may experience harm?   Yes   No

3) Do you find yourself excessively concerned about becoming contaminated or getting germs?   Yes   No

4) Do you ever find yourself needing to repeat tasks in order to do them perfectly?   Yes   No

5) Do you ever find yourself counting or needing to do something in a particular numerical sequence?   Yes   No

6) Do you ever find yourself riddled with anxiety until you achieve a particular order in a task (e.g., having your clothing hanging a particular way in your closet)?   Yes   No

7) Do you ever find yourself compelled to repeat a task despite your knowledge that you already successfully completed it (e.g., washing the stove, closing the door, etc.)?   Yes   No

8) Do you ever find yourself repeating thoughts in your head and worrying that if you do not continually repeat them harm might befall someone or something?   Yes   No

9) Do you ever find yourself checking and rechecking a task?   Yes   No

10) Do you ever find yourself hoarding objects?   Yes   No

11) Do you ever find yourself endlessly rearranging objects in order to achieve a particular outcome of perfection?   Yes   No

12) Does anyone in your family struggle with anxiety disorders, or has anyone in your family ever been diagnosed with an anxiety disorder?   Yes   No

13) Does anyone in your family struggle with obsessive-compulsive symptoms, or has anyone in your family ever been diagnosed with obsessive-compulsive disorder?   Yes   No

If you have answered "yes" to more than four questions, it is likely that you may have obsessive-compulsive disorder. We know that even for those without a history of OCD, eating disorders often take on obsessive-compulsive qualities.

To take one step further in your exploration, please take a moment to answer the following questions:

1. Do you ever find yourself being rigid with regard to order, organization, or schedules?
2. Do you find yourself needing to make lists in order to track what you need to get accomplished?
3. Are you a perfectionist?
4. Do you find yourself unable to complete a task or project because it has not met your standards of excellence?
5. Do you find yourself being so committed to your work that you find yourself neglecting friends and/or leisure activities (for reasons *other* than economic)?
6. Do you find yourself being overly conscientious and inflexible about matters of ethics and morality (unrelated to issues of religion)?
7. Do you find it difficult to part with objects even when they have no sentimental value?
8. Are you reluctant to delegate tasks to others due to your frustrations that their approach may not be exactly the same as yours?
9. Do you find yourself struggling to part with money?
10. Would you describe yourself as strong-willed, rigid, or stubborn?

If you have answered "yes" to four or more of the above questions, you may have an *obsessive-compulsive personality*. Though similar to OCD, its major difference is that it is *personality-based*; that is, it is an innate collection of personality traits. For many, this style of organization and focus results in personal and/or professional success! In others, it can cause distress, as the individual's inflexibility can interfere with accomplishments and relationships, and result in feelings of depression and anxiety.

Not all individuals with obsessive-compulsive personalities have OCD. However, individuals with this personality type may very well possess obsessive-compulsive traits. In our experience, most individuals struggling with eating disorders have an obsessive-compulsive personality style. They may not meet diagnostic criteria for OCD, but they may exhibit their personality style through their rigid control of food, weight, and their thinking.

In the space below, please list any intrusive, recurring thoughts that cause you anxiety. Put a check mark (✓) by the ones that seem related to your eating disorder.

_____
_____
_____
_____
_____
_____
_____
_____
_____
_____
_____

Now that you have identified some of these thoughts (obsessions) that cause anxiety and reinforce the eating disorder, let's identify some of the behaviors (compulsions) that help decrease your anxiety (but may also reinforce your eating disorder). Here is an example: "If I eat a food that touches another food, I feel anxious and out-of-control" (obsessive thought). "Therefore, I only eat foods that are pure" (i.e., foods that do not touch other foods; compulsive behavior). "Because it is difficult to find/be served foods that are *guaranteed* not to have touched other foods, I eat less and less and drop more and more weight until I am emaciated." In the space below, list any obsessive thoughts and compulsive behaviors (also known as *rituals*), you have with food, weight, body image, and exercise:

_____
_____
_____
_____
_____
_____
_____
_____
_____

Next is the hard part. We'll begin with the compulsions (behaviors), for they are easier to address and conquer than obsessions (thoughts). Do you remember learning about cognitive restructuring? This is when we asked you to question your automatic thoughts and put rational thoughts in their places. Here's what we want you to do: Taking one behavior at a time, develop some strategies and "healthy" reasons to challenge your eating disordered behaviors. Please note that it is likely that as you decrease your compulsive behaviors, your obsessive thoughts may increase. The key to success will be *positive self-talk* and affirmations, which will fight and conquer those intrusive, destructive thoughts as you work toward behavior change.

In the spaces below, begin by listing those behaviors (compulsions) you want to change. Following each behavior, record "healthy" reasons for making a change. Once all compulsive behaviors and "healthy" reasons are recorded, you will see a space for affirmations (positive self-talk). In a different colored ink, please list affirmations (positive self-talk) and make them stand out so that you will remember them while practicing for change.

Example:

Behavior: If I eat one bite of a "forbidden" food (e.g., chocolate), I have already "blown it" so I eat chocolate until I feel sick because I know I'm going to throw it up anyway.

Reason to change: I love chocolate. I'd love to be able to have it once in a while like other people do. I know my constant binge eating and vomiting are bad for my health. My dentist has told me my dental problems are directly related to my vomiting. I want to change this behavior.

Positive Self-talk/Affirmation: I eat chocolate sometimes. No foods are "bad" or "forbidden." Whatever I eat, my task is to keep it down. Vomiting hurts me.

Behavior: _____

Reasons For Change: _____

_____

_____

_____

_____

Positive Self-talk/Affirmation: _____

Behavior: _____

Reasons For Change: _____

_____

_____

_____

_____

Positive Self-talk/Affirmation: _____

Behavior: _____

Reasons For Change: _____

_____

_____

_____

_____

Positive Self-talk/Affirmation: _____

Behavior: _____

Reasons For Change: _____ .

_____

_____

_____

_____

_____

Positive Self-talk/Affirmation: _____

Behavior: _____

Reasons For Change: _____

_____

_____

_____

_____

_____

Positive Self-talk/Affirmation: _____

POSITIVE SELF-TALK/AFFIRMATIONS

1) _____

2) _____

3) _____

4) _____

5) _____

6) _____

7) _____

8) _____

9) _____

10) _____

11) _____

12) _____

13) _____

14) _____

15) _____

16) _____

17) _____

18) _____

19) _____

20) _____

If you have answered "yes" to many of the questions related to obsessive-compulsive disorder, please tell your therapist and/or physician know about this. Obsessive-compulsive disorder is more common than you may think. The thoughts and behaviors are distressing, intrusive, and senseless, but with the appropriate treatments, many people who suffer from OCD can experience great relief. The primary treatments for OCD are cognitive-behavioral therapy, medication, or both in combination. You do not have to be ruled by your thoughts and behaviors. You are searching to be *in control*, and you can be with appropriate treatment.

MY EATING DISORDER: A DESPERATE ATTEMPT FOR CONTROL

You wouldn't know from looking at me that I have an eating disorder. I am not extremely skinny; as a matter of fact I look like an average college student. Yet, I have been struggling for close to six years now with an eating disorder. As far back as I can remember, I have been on a diet, or exercising to lose weight. I was always the fat kid on the playground. No matter how much weight I lost on diets, on the inside I always felt as if I was still that fat kid!

Like others with eating disorders, I, too, chose to take care of everyone but myself. I always needed "order" in my life; things had to be "just so." I now see that this is "obsessive-compulsive behavior." At the time, I thought it was me being rigid and needing to be in control.

I began running my freshman year of high school. I believed that exercise could help me lose weight, and felt that running was a healthy way to exercise. I was not compulsive with my running as I was with other things in my life. That is, I wasn't compulsive initially! I continued to run as a sophomore, yet in addition to running, I now began to watch my fat intake. *Unfortunately* during this time, I learned a *trick* that would help me get rid of the fattening foods I ate. I say "unfortunately" because this is where it all began to happen. I was beginning to feel successful in my attempts at weight loss; the attention I received from others helped to increase these feelings of success. Finally, I was getting noticed for something other than being fat!

The attention kept me in my destructive behaviors, and although I continued to relish the attention, I began to notice that my behaviors were no longer feeling as if they were a choice. I began to realize that I had become *unable* to eat normally; my eating disorder had taken over, and now "it" was in control! I found myself using my eating disorder as a way of rewarding myself and punishing myself. If something went wrong, I would focus on what I needed to do in order to lose weight. If something went right, I would reward myself with food, and then get rid of it. It had become much easier for me to focus on food and weight; after all, I felt successful with this. I became accustomed to what I could expect from eating or restricting; I couldn't say the same about what I could expect from feelings of stress.

When my freshman year of college approached, instead of gaining the "Freshman 15," I lost it. Once again, however, it didn't last. My body was not meant to be that thin, no matter how badly I tried. My friends would comment on how bizarre they saw my relationship with food to be. They had no idea of the internal battle that was playing out in my head; I continued to look average on the outside, even though there was a disease taking over every aspect of my life.

My days were filled with thoughts of what I could and could not eat. I religiously kept a food journal, recording what I ate and analyzing over and over whether or not it was okay. It was an awful way to live, but it was "in control." My intellect and logic had no power over this disease. Life for me had become a series of deprivations or bingeing and purging.

This past year, I developed a stress fracture from calcium deficiency due to my eating disorder. I thought that this would be the scare I needed; I thought that realizing that I may never be able to run again would cause me to change my ways. It wasn't so easy.

What I did learn, instead, was how much this eating disorder had control over me. I realized how comfortable it made me, and how terrified I was to let go of it. It had become my best friend. I received counseling, and began to fully understand the battle of recovery. It was going to be an uphill battle with every bite I put in my mouth. With counseling, I am now doing better. I hold on to a statement I once read about the actress Tracy Gold; I, too, want to be able to eat cake at my wedding someday!

Jacqui, age 22

DEPRESSION

As you have just learned, those who suffer from OCD or have obsessive-compulsive traits often feel depressed over their efforts to control their thinking and behaviors. Depression can also manifest itself as obsessive-compulsive disorder as the individual unconsciously attempts to find "control" over the intolerable feelings of depression. Furthermore, sometimes people aren't sure whether they are experiencing anxiety or depression or both. Depression and anxiety can look and feel the same to the person who is racked by excessive worry, irritability, and fatigue (to name a few). In this section, we are going to explain more about depression. In particular, we'll tell you about the various types of depression, their unique characteristics, how each is experienced, and the relationship between depression and eating disorders. At the end of this section, we hope you'll be able to identify whether you are suffering from depression.

DEPRESSION SELF-REPORT QUIZ

Over the past two weeks, have you experienced any of the following:

1)	Depressed mood for most of the day?	Yes	No
2)	Change in appetite or weight?	Yes	No
3)	Change in sleep (either more or less)?	Yes	No
4)	Fatigue or loss of energy?	Yes	No
5)	Loss of interest or pleasure in activities?	Yes	No
6)	Feelings of worthlessness and/or hopelessness?	Yes	No
7)	Difficulty concentrating or a decreased attention span?	Yes	No
8)	Self-destructive thoughts or behaviors?	Yes	No

If you answered "yes" to questions 1 and/or 5, and answered "yes" to a total of 5 of the 8 questions, you are most likely struggling with depression.

You are not alone. Research indicates that approximately 17 million Americans are diagnosed with depression every year. This is the equivalent of 1 out of every 10 Americans. Furthermore, statistics show that one out of every four women and one out of every ten men are diagnosed with depression. Recognizing and treating your depression will support your recovery efforts.

Depression can mask the bluest of skies and leave them looking dark and dreary. It can make you dislike everyone and everything you once adored. It can tell you all is hopeless, when the world is at your fingertips! Some people are better able to describe or express their depression through the artistic mediums. We suggest that you try this.

In the box below, using colored pencils, crayons, or markers, draw what your depression looks like to you. Your drawing maybe abstract, symbolic, or realistic as long as it is an unedited expression of what is inside you. The goal of this exercise is to put it "out there" and gradually relieve you of the burden of keeping it inside. This exercise can also help you to better understand what might be causing your depression so you and those whom you have entrusted with your care can better understand how to treat it.

Think about your depression; visualize what it would look like, and put it "out there" on this paper. If the expressive or artistic mediums help you experience some relief from your depressive feelings you may see a concurrent reduction in your purging, restricting, or overeating behaviors.

My Depression

Once you have completed your drawing, answer the following questions.

1) How did you feel while drawing your depression?

_____

_____

_____

_____

_____

2) When you look at your drawing, what do you see?

_____

_____

_____

_____

_____

3) If you were to give a title to your artwork, what would it be?

_____

4) If you were to rid yourself of your depression, what would your drawing look like?

Please draw that picture in the space below.

My Life Without Depression

Types of Depression

Now that you have a better understanding of your depression and what it looks like to you, read on so you know what the different types of depression are. This might help you more clearly identify the type of depression from which you are suffering.

ADJUSTMENT DISORDER WITH DEPRESSED MOOD

This form of depression is in response to a particular stressor that has occurred within the past three months. The stressor has caused you feelings of depression that have been difficult to "shake." However, unlike a major depressive episode, this depression is temporary.

SEASONAL AFFECTIVE DISORDER (SAD)

This form of depression generally occurs during the months between November and March. Studies have linked this form of depression to a lack of sunlight during these months. As with other forms of depression, individuals with seasonal affective disorder experience: lethargy, decreased pleasure, difficulty concentrating, decreased motivation, hopelessness, sleep and appetite disturbances, social withdrawal, and anxiety. What separates seasonal affective disorder from other forms of depression is the recurring pattern of increased depression during the fall/winter seasons.

DYSTHYMIC DISORDER

This depression is a mild to moderate form of depression. It is different from a major depression in that its major feature is a depression that lasts for at least two years. Clinically, in order to be diagnosed with dysthymic disorder, you must have two of the following (in addition to a depressed state for two years):

1. poor appetite or overeating
2. insomnia (inability to sleep) or hypersomnia (sleeping too much)
3. low energy or fatigue
4. low self-esteem
5. poor concentration or difficulty making decisions
6. feelings of hopelessness

Although people with depression do not necessarily experience feelings of depression every hour of every day, those with dysthymic disorder have not experienced relief from feelings of depression for more than two months at a time.

BIPOLAR DISORDER

Bipolar disorder, also known as manic depression, is a more severe form of depression in which the individual alternates between feelings of depression and mania. Usually, in-between is a relatively "normal" emotional state. The depressive state is characterized by the symptoms listed for dysthymic depression, above. Characteristics of mania are:

1. exaggerated self confidence and heightened mood
2. decreased need for sleep without feelings of fatigue
3. excessive irritability and/or aggressive behavior

4. racing thoughts, shift of movement from subject to subject
5. impulsiveness
6. inflated sense of self importance or self esteem
7. increased talkativeness, rapid rate of speech
8. poor judgement
9. easily distracted
10. reckless and destructive behavior (e.g., driving fast, over-spending)

The characteristics of mania are considered to be maladaptive because they cause impairment in academic, occupational, interpersonal, social, and emotional functioning. In its most severe forms, those experiencing manic episodes can die as a consequence of their own reckless or destructive behavior.

Depression Self-Assessment

Answer the following questions:

1) Could you personally relate to any of the symptoms of the various types of depression? _____

2) If "yes," which form(s) of depression did you relate to and how do you experience this depression?

_____
_____
_____
_____
_____

3) Do you believe you have ever experienced episodes of depression in the past? If "yes," please explain:

_____
_____
_____
_____
_____

4) Do you believe anyone in your biological family has had bouts of depression? If "yes," please list who they are and what you have seen or heard to indicate that they may have suffered from depression:

_____
_____
_____
_____
_____

Now that you have a clearer understanding of the various forms of depression, let's take a moment to look at its possible causes. The following are some of the factors contributing toward depression.

GENETICS

Studies have found depression can run in families. Numerous studies have supported this finding. As such, it is important that if you suffer from feelings of depression, you learn as much as you can about your biological family history of depression. However, it is also important to keep in mind that a family history of depression must also take into consideration the shared environmental factors that may contribute to depression. It is not enough to consider the genetic predisposition to depression as proof of causation.

BIOCHEMISTRY

Biochemistry refers to the biological make-up of a person. It has been found that certain brain chemical deficiencies (serotonin and norepinephrine) may result in episodes of depression. In technical terms, it has been found that depression may result from disruptions in, or malabsorbtion of, the substances that regulate the brain's nerve cells (neurons).

The neurons fire from one to another, transmitting nerve impulses. Neurotransmitters are the chemicals that help with this transfer; the disruption of neurotransmitters inhibits the firing of the next neuron in its chain, resulting in depression.

ENVIRONMENTAL FACTORS

Trauma, loss, stress, and neglect are only a few of the environmental factors that can precipitate a depression. What researchers have found is that environmental factors such as these affect biochemical balances and the neurophysiology of the brain , leading to depression in some individuals. It is important to understand that not everyone who has experienced trauma, loss, stress, or neglect will become clinically depressed. However, these factors may contribute to depression in certain predisposed individuals.

PERSONALITY FACTORS

Individuals who posses certain personality traits may find themselves more susceptible to feelings of depression. For example, those individuals who have low self esteem, bouts of anxiety, feelings of hopelessness, or overall pessimism are more likely to develop depression than those that do not possess such traits.

FOOD

In the past few years, researchers have been attempting to draw a link between what you eat and how you feel. In particular, there has been a focus on certain foods and links to depression. Researcher Judith Wurtman, Ph.D., has found that carbohydrates affect levels of neurotransmitters, which appear to correlate with feelings of depression. Although these theories have been met with much skepticism, the high correlation of depressive disorders and eating disorders requires that we carefully consider these findings. If, as Wurtman's research indicates, eating or *retaining* inadequate amounts of carbohydrate foods decreases neurotransmitter function, then depressive symptomatology may be caused, at least in part, by low carbohydrate intake.

EATING DISORDERS

What you will not find in any of the textbooks on depression is that eating disorders can contribute to and may even cause depression. Remember at the beginning of this chapter we asked you which came first . . . ? It is quite possible that you were depressed and your eating disorder helped you cope with feelings of depression. It is also quite possible that your eating disorder has so contributed to your poor nutrition that your depressive feelings are the result of the eating disorder.

The physical toll of restriction, bingeing, and purging can affect brain chemicals. In addition, the emotional turmoil you may be experiencing as a result of your obsessive thoughts about food and weight and your compulsive behaviors to control your food intake and weight may be contributing to your depressed state. It is true that depression can be one possible cause of an eating disorder, but we believe that eating disorders can cause depression as well.

We know you are reading this book because you are struggling with an eating disorder. If after reading this segment on depression you believe you are struggling with depression as well, it is important that you share this information with your therapist and physician.

Which do you think came first . . . your eating disorder or your depression? Please explain:

_____

_____

_____

_____

_____

Depression can be treated. Studies have found that 80–90% of those treated for depression find substantial relief through a variety of treatments. These treatments include: psychotherapy, medication, diet, and light therapy (for those suffering from a seasonal depression). There is hope. Please speak with your physician and therapist and see what options are available to you.

DIABETES

Diabetes mellitus is a condition in which the body does not produce enough insulin, or does not use the insulin produced correctly. The body needs insulin in order to convert food to energy. Without insulin, sugar builds up in the bloodstream, and can cause serious damage to the body. Approximately 16 million people in the United States have diabetes. Some of these 16 million individuals may not even be aware that they are diabetic. This is very concerning because untreated or poorly controlled diabetes can lead to serious health problems: including blindness, amputation, kidney failure, heart attack, stroke, and death. Poorly controlled diabetes is currently the sixth cause of death in the United States.

There are two types of diabetes: Type I and Type II. In Type I diabetes, the pancreas does not produce insulin. Those struggling with this type of diabetes rely on insulin injections for treatment. Another term for Type I diabetes is "juvenile onset diabetes." In Type II diabetes, the body is resistant to insulin, or uses the insulin ineffectively. For those with Type II diabetes, control of insulin can be achieved through oral medication and diet.

Regardless of whether the individual has Type I or Type II diabetes, those who have these illnesses must follow prescribed diets and carefully manage their exercise and weight. This constant focus on food and weight can precipitate the development of an eating disorder. Chronic binge eating and obesity can precipitate the development of Type II diabetes. When an individual is diagnosed with diabetes, her life as she knows it will change. She will no longer be able to eat as freely as those around her. She will need to pay constant attention to what she is eating, when she is eating, and what happens to her when she eats. She will need to make sure her weight is within appropriate limits and she will need to distinguish between "safe," "unsafe," and "potential" foods. She may also find herself under the scope of protective parents or other loved ones, concerned about her health and making sure she is making healthy choices and taking care of herself. She is a prime candidate for a potential eating disorder. Let's take a moment to look at Keri.

> Keri is 13 years old. An active child who loved sports and the arts, her life changed a couple of years ago. At this time she was diagnosed with an illness that had food as its focus. What she used to be able to eat so innocently, she now struggled to consume. She would find herself paying attention to calorie content, fat content, and sugar content. She was envious of those around her, as they indulged in chocolate and other "forbidden" foods. She had rules she had to follow regarding when, why, and what she would eat at any given time. Her parents watched over her closely to make sure she was eating, and eating the appropriate foods at that. Her weight began to drop, but not to a place that was dangerous. Tension ran high in Keri's household, and Keri's food issues affected the entire family.

In reading this, it may sound as if Keri was struggling with an eating disorder. In actuality, Keri was diagnosed with Type I diabetes. Through this example you can see the similarities between eating disorders and diabetes. These similarities can mask struggles with eating disorders in those individuals diagnosed with diabetes. Let's explore this a little more closely.

As you are aware, individuals struggling with eating disorders are *preoccupied* with weight, food, and diet. So, too, are people with diabetes. Individuals with diabetes may develop an eating disorder as a result of becoming overly rigid with their food, diet, and weight in order to maintain health. In addition to this, those with both an eating disorder *and* diabetes may use their diabetes as an excuse to maintain their eating-disordered behaviors.

Control is another common theme for those struggling with diabetes and eating disorders. It is not uncommon for those diagnosed with diabetes to feel out of control of their bodies. This is especially profound for those who must rely on insulin. Under- or overdosing of insulin can lead to emotional dyscontrol. A change in blood sugar can lead to sudden feelings of anxiety, depression, or agitation. As we have explained earlier in this book, eating disorders may become a means of coping with a life which feels out of control. It becomes a coping mechanism for those feeling out of control over some aspect(s) of their lives. For those with eating disorders and diabetes, focusing on food, weight, and diet, can be a way to "regain" control of their lives.

For those diagnosed with diabetes and eating disorders, "safe," "unsafe," and "potential" foods become the language of eating. Both have *forbidden* foods that can result in emotional and/or physical distress. The timing of foods eaten, amount of food eaten, and types of food eaten also play a role in wellness (or illness).

Finally, those diagnosed with juvenile onset diabetes or an eating disorder often have parents who were, or will become, overprotective. The seriousness and potential life-threatening consequences of these illnesses lead many parents to become over-involved concerning the eating and weight of their children, leading some children to rebel. It is difficult for parents to balance their need to protect their children with their children's need to learn to be the masters of their own bodies.

You have learned how diabetes can precipitate the development of an eating disorder. Now lets look at the ways in which an eating disorder can lead to diabetes.

> Joanne is a 42-year-old mother of 3 young children. She has been married for 12 years, and reports a history of binge eating since the birth of her first child, 9 years ago. She was overweight as a child, and acknowledges episodes of overeating. She never saw the overeating as a problem; it did not interfere in relationships, or other aspects of her life.
>
> After the birth of her first child, Joanne found herself using food to comfort herself through times of loneliness and emptiness. She had gone from being a successful businesswoman, working many hours, to being a stay-at-home mom with little intellectual stimulation. She was envi-

ous of her husband, who was able to continue to build his career, and felt guilty about these feelings of envy. She was ashamed of the feelings of resentment she was having toward her son, and didn't feel that she could share such shameful feelings with anyone. As a result, she began to eat.

The food became her best friend. It took away feelings of loneliness, and left her feeling fulfilled. She felt "hugged" by the pressure placed on her stomach by the fullness she experienced through overeating. Her husband began to express concern over her 40-pound weight gain in 6 months. But this concern didn't stop her from overeating. In fact, she began to gain weight at an increasingly rapid rate. Joanne was struggling with binge eating disorder.

Nine years later, Joanne continues to struggle. Two years ago, Joanne was diagnosed with Type II diabetes. She has met with numerous physicians concerning her diabetes, and they have encouraged her to moderate her diet and lose weight. Yet, Joanne continues to eat and gain weight. Her physicians and husband are extremely frustrated and concerned with her, so much so that her husband has considered leaving her (and his three children). Joanne is aware of what she is doing to her body, her family, and her marriage, yet she has not stopped her behaviors. She is suffering from an eating disorder.

Joanne's eating disorder precipitated her diabetes. Treating the diabetes without acknowledging the eating disorder made those who should have cared for her—her husband and doctor—treat her as if she were at fault for having an illness she could not control. It led Joanne to believe that she was a failure.

Joanne can listen to everything her physicians tell her. She understands the potential loss of her marriage and life as she knows it; but without diagnosing and treating the eating disorder she may lose it all . . . her health, her husband, and her life.

1) Have you been diagnosed with diabetes?   Yes   No

2) If "Yes," when were you diagnosed, and how is it being treated?

_____

_____

_____

_____

_____

3) When do you believe you first began to struggle with disordered eating? _____

4) Do you believe your eating disorder resulted from diabetes? If "yes," please explain.

_____

_____

_____

_____

_____

5) Has your eating disorder resulted in diabetes? If "yes," please explain.

_____

_____

_____

_____

_____

6) Do you ever misuse insulin in an attempt to lose weight? _____
   (If you answered "yes" to this question, it is critical that you share this information with your doctor. Under- or overdosing with insulin can have life-threatening consequences).

7) Why do you want to recover from your eating disorder? How will recovery benefit you?

_____
_____
_____
_____
_____

If you are struggling with both diabetes and an eating disorder, remember, both are treatable, and you can recover from your eating disorder. Before we end this section, here are some helpful tips for recovery.

1. Pay attention to your body; learn the signs that tell you have high and/or low blood sugar.
2. Take any prescribed medication as directed.
3. Tell your physician about your eating disorder.
4. Meet with a nutritionist to help you manage your diabetes and your eating disorder.
5. Explore and address body image issues.
6. Explore underlying feelings of anger, sadness, anxiety, and fear.
7. Develop strategies to help you relax and express yourself.
8. And most of all, LOVE and RESPECT yourself!

CONCLUSION

In conclusion, we hope that by covering these mental health and medical diagnoses, we may positively impact your recovery. We realize these are not the only medical and mental health issues which may complicate your recovery, but they are some of the most commonly seen comorbidities (additional medical and mental health diagnoses) for people with eating disorders.

If you are faced with other special circumstances, discuss them with your physician and therapist. Seeking and accepting help from knowledgeable, caring professionals concerning any circumstance affecting your physical or emotional health will aid in your recovery. Weave a net of care around yourself. It will make your journey to recovery less lonely and arduous, and it will lead you more directly to your destination . . . *Recovery*.

The Treatment Team

The struggle with an eating disorder is a lonely battle. It alienates you from family and friends. It tells you that all you need in order to feel good is more food, less food, or no food. The *voice* of the eating disorder is so powerful that it convinces intelligent, rational men and women that their irrational thoughts about the body and the self are real.

Mesmerized by the power of the eating disorder's voice, many drown in its Siren song of deception while entrusting it to save them from peril. Others, though aware of its deception, are powerless to fight it.

Recovery from an eating disorder means recognizing that the eating disorder voice is the voice of a charlatan. It promises to "protect" you and consistently be there for you. It does not tell you that while it "protects" you from hurt, fear, anger, or the control of others, it is enslaving you. It owns you, your voice, and your very life. Freeing yourself from the Siren song of the eating disorder, however, means risking vulnerability, and opening yourself to feelings of powerlessness in your quest for help. It means when you are frightened, angry, feeling controlled by others, empty, sad, and bereft you will not have the eating disorder to turn to. You will need to turn to other, more nurturing and adaptive coping strategies. This is hard to do but you will spend time in this workbook learning more adaptive strategies for coping and you will have opportunities to practice them. The goal of this chapter is to empower you in your recovery from an illness over which you feel powerless. You may have been alone as your eating disorder developed. You should not be alone in your recovery. This chapter will help you develop your "recovery team" and explain what you can expect from each player.

THE PHYSICIAN

If you believe you are struggling with an eating disorder, you should first contact your physician. A physical exam and appropriate blood work is necessary to determine your level of health or illness.

Once your physician has determined your medical needs, he or she can make appropriate referrals for treatment. In order for your physician to do this, however, he or she must have an understanding of eating disorders. This understanding must go beyond medical awareness and include an understanding of the psychological components of the illness. In addition to this, you should feel safe talking with him or her about your fears, questions, and other feelings. Below is a list of questions you should ask yourself in order to make sure your physician is the right one for you.

1) Do I feel that I can tell my physician something in confidence?   Yes   No

2) Can I trust that my physician will take my concerns seriously?   Yes   No

3) Do I feel my physician will take the time necessary to make an appropriate
   diagnosis and recommendations?   Yes   No

4) Do I feel that my physician will listen to me and not judge me?   Yes   No

5) Can I trust that my physician will not break my confidence by telling my parents
   (if under 18) and loved ones information about me without my permission?   Yes   No
   Laws of confidentiality bind physicians. These laws must be respected unless
   there are concerns of immediate, imminent danger. It is recommended that physicians
   speak with patients about confidentiality rights before safety issues arise.

6) (If male) Can I trust that my physician is educated enough to understand eating
   disorders occur in males as well?   Yes   No

7) Can I trust that my physician will take my eating disorder seriously even
   if I'm not severely underweight?   Yes   No

If you have answered "Yes" to most of these questions, you have chosen a knowledgeable physician whom you trust. If you've not yet done so, call this physician and set up an appointment for a complete exam. If you have answered most of these questions with a "No," we suggest that you contact a local hospital or eating disorder organization for a referral to a specialist in your area. If you have health insurance, your insurance company may also have access to lists of specialists in your area.

What You Can Expect

It is not uncommon for individuals struggling with eating disorders to feel ashamed of their symptoms, particularly if they include binge eating or purging. This shame is most often magnified during the first visit with a physician. The added feelings of fear (of the unknown) or fear that the physician will take the symptom away (especially for those who are low weight and eating restrictively) can cause such emotional distress that you may find yourself wishing to avoid or cancel the appointment. Scared or worried as you may be, please don't avoid or cancel appointments with your physician. Allow yourself to receive the care you deserve!

When seeing a new physician, if you think it might make you more comfortable, we suggest that you request not changing into a "johnny" until after you've spoken with the physician. Although this may sound trivial some clients have told us that it decreased their feelings of vulnerability in a new and scary situation. Many physicians ask nurses or other personnel to weigh their patients and take their vital signs before they meet you. If you think it would make you more comfortable to meet and speak with the physician before you have these procedures done, request this.

If you are concerned about how this new physician may respond to you when you share your concerns with him/her, we suggest that you tell the physician this prior to disclosing any information. Sharing how you feel with the physician can help create a safe atmosphere by allowing your physician to hear your vulnerability. Finally, we recommend that you come prepared with a list of questions for your physician and make sure you do not leave the exam room until all your questions have been answered. These questions can be asked before and/or after your physical examination.

Next comes the physical exam. Below is a list of common tests administered to those struggling with an eating disorder. They are in no particular order, and are not all repeated with every follow up appointment. You may want to check with your physician to make sure all the necessary tests are performed.

The Physical Exam

Temperature: Lowered body temperature reflects dehydration, lowered blood pressure, and insufficient body fat which reduces the body's ability to insulate itself from the extremes of heat and cold.

Blood Pressure:
Low Blood Pressure (Hypotention) reflects lowered body temperature, dehydration, and malnutrition. This tends to occur in those struggling with anorexia nervosa.
Orthostatic Hypotention refers to a sudden drop in blood pressure upon standing or sitting up.
High Blood Pressure (Hypertension) refers to blood pressure that is greater than 140 over 90. This tends to occur in those struggling with binge eating.

Heart Rate: A lowered heart rate reflects malnutrition, dehydration, and a low blood pressure. All are common symptoms associated with anorexia nervosa.

Weight: A measurement of one's weight helps determine medical stability and measures significant changes that can put pressure on the heart.

Lanugo: A soft downy hair that appears on the face, arms, and back as a response to starvation and malnutrition. It is the body's mechanism to keep itself warm as body temperature decreases.

Edema: The swelling of joints, abdomen, and feet as a result of excess water accumulation. This is the body's way to adapt to the dehydration caused by purging through the use of vomiting, laxatives, or diuretics.

Swollen Face: Often referred to as "chipmunk cheeks," a swollen face is a common symptom seen in those who frequently vomit.

Bruised Fingers: As with the swollen face, bruised fingers can be a sign of self-induced vomiting.

Bruised Skin: Frequent bruising can be a result of vitamin deficiencies, extreme weight loss, and low blood pressure.

Cold Hands and Feet: Poor circulation can result from starvation and malnutrition.

The Blood Tests

Complete Blood Count (CBC): A CBC will check for anemia, infection, and immune system functionality. This is determined by counting white blood cells, red blood cells, and platelets.

Electrolytes: Needed to maintain healthy body function, electrolytes are a combination of minerals (potassium, sodium, and magnesium) the body needs to maintain physiological balance. Electrolyte imbalance can result in kidney failure, heart attack, and possible death.

Blood Glucose (Blood Sugar): Malnutrition and dehydration can result in a disturbance in blood sugar, which can result in hypoglycemia and diabetes, and can be dangerous.

Cholesterol: Important to maintain a healthy heart, it is important to make sure the ratio of "good" to "bad" cholesterol is within normal limits. High "bad" cholesterol (LDL) and low "good" cholesterol (HDL) can lead to a heart attack and possible death.

B12 and Folic Acid: Important in the assessment of depression and anxiety, a lack of B12 and Folic Acid can lead to difficulties with the body's ability to absorb nutrients. This, in turn, can lead to difficulties with metabolizing protein, carbohydrates, and fat.

Thyroid Function: Because the thyroid gland controls the body's metabolism, it is important that this test take place initially to rule in/out difficulties with weight gain or loss due to abnormalities in thyroid function. People with an overactive thyroid may have difficulty gaining weight; those with an underactive thyroid may have difficulty losing weight.

Liver Function: Although not needed often, elevated liver enzymes can reflect liver disease, gallbladder disease, or if the patient has had a heart attack.

Kidney Function: As with the liver function test, this test is not needed often. It is performed to assess kidney function, an important test for those struggling with eating disorders, or taking certain medications.

The Urine Tests

Complete Urinalysis: Helps to assess the function of the kidneys, urine sugar, and ketone levels. Also helps with diagnosis of a variety of systemic diseases and urinary tract disorders.

Ketones: Starvation and malnutrition can cause ketones (substances that are formed during the digestion of fat) to accumulate in the blood. The formation of ketones indicates that the body is burning itself for fuel. This accumulation of ketones in the blood can cause coma or death.

Other Tests

Echocardiogram or Electrocardiogram: Helps with the identification of causes of heart irregularities.

Bone Density: Helps identify osteoporosis (bone loss) caused by calcium and vitamin D deficiencies and/or hormonal imbalances (amenorrhea).

Infertility Testing (for those wishing to become pregnant): Important for those women having difficulty getting pregnant. Eating disorders can lead to high-risk pregnancy, problems with fetal development, and birth defects.

Final Questions

In completion of your exam, your physician may ask you questions about your personal history with food, exercise, medications, family relations, depression, anxiety, substance abuse, trauma, and other psychological issues. This can feel uncomfortable for those who consider their physician to be the monitor of *medical* issues; but if your physician is aware of these he/she will be better able to offer a thorough diagnosis and recommend the most appropriate treatments for you.

Please take the risk and answer your physician's questions honestly. Only "good" will come from it! Remember if you want the physician to be a player on your "recovery" team he has to know all the "plays." If you don't answer his/her questions honestly, it may, at times, feel like he/she is playing for the "other team." Without all the information, he/she won't know the best and most appropriate ways to help you.

It is not uncommon to feel anxious before a visit to the doctor. This anxiety can, at times, cause you to lose focus and forget what you wanted to ask. In the space below, please list the questions you want to ask your doctor. (example: *What is your policy around weight? Will I be able to know my weight? What is your experience with eating disorders?*)

1)_____
_____

2)_____
_____

3)_____
_____

4)_____
_____

5)_____
_____

6)_____
_____

THE THERAPIST

Once you have contacted your physician, the next step is to find a therapist. There are many questions to consider before beginning such a search. In the space below, please answer the following 3 questions. Your answers will help you search for the best therapist for your needs.

1) Do you have health insurance? If "Yes," do you wish to use your health insurance benefits for psychotherapy?

_____

2) Do you have a preference for a male or female therapist? If so, which do you prefer, and why?

_____

_____

3) Are you interested in receiving treatment within a particular geographic location? If so, please list those communities you are considering: _____

_____

Okay, now that you have identified some of your concrete needs, the next step is to begin your search. Education is key; the better educated you are as a consumer, the more likely you are to find what you need for recovery. Before you explore what to look for, let's quickly take a moment to differentiate between the different types of therapists and therapies.

Categories of Therapists

Psychologist: A individual with a doctorate degree in clinical or counseling psychology. The letters after the psychologist's name are either **Ph.D., Ed.D.,** or **Psy.D.**

Social Worker: A person with a Master's degree in social work, which focuses on social issues. There are a variety of foci of social work. Those working in the field of psychotherapy usually have a training in clinical social work. The letters **MSW** represent a Master's-level social worker. **CSW** represents a Clinical Social Worker.

Mental Health Counselor: A person with a Master's degree in counseling, psychology, or related fields. This person may also have a specialty in marriage and family counseling. A professional mental health counselor will have either **LMHC, LFMT, CAC,** or **CMHC** representing his or her degree.

Psychiatrist: A person who has completed medical school, and has a specialty area in mental health. In addition to psychotherapy, a psychiatrist can prescribe medication. Psychiatrists have the initials **MD** representing their education and specialty.

Clinical Nurse: A person with a Master's degree in nursing, with a specialty in clinical psychology. In many states now, a clinical nurse can prescribe medication as well as provide psychotherapy services. Clinical nurses have the initials **CN, RS** respresenting their degree.

Therapeutic Approaches

Below is a list of common psychotherapies for the treatment of eating disorders. No one technique is better than another. Rather, different approaches may be more effective for different individuals. In addition to this, a combination of therapies and techniques may be used within one treatment setting.

COGNITIVE-BEHAVIORAL THERAPY

The theory behind cognitive-behavioral therapy is that problems result from one's illogical thinking about oneself, one's world, and one's future. The goal of cognitive-behavioral therapy is to help one learn about oneself through unbiased tasks that allow one to disconfirm one's false beliefs. In therapy, the client and therapist will identify the individual's thoughts. The client will be encouraged to "risk" challenging these illogical thoughts in hopes that logic will ensue, and behaviors will begin to change. The change in behavior will also be a result of working with the therapist to challenge current behaviors and, again, risk change.

PSYCHODYNAMIC PSYCHOTHERAPY

Psychodynamic psychotherapy stems from Psychoanalysis, which is a long-term intensive therapeutic approach originated by Dr. Sigmund Freud that focuses on uncovering repressed memories, thoughts, fears, and conflicts that stemmed from one's early childhood, and overcoming one's resistances to living freely in the present. Its premise is that this work results in greater interpersonal understanding, and that resolution of early childhood conflicts via the patient's verbal free association will result in freedom from "neuroses." Unlike cognitive-behavioral therapy, which focuses primarily on the present, psychodynamic psychotherapy explores the impact of the past.

INTERPERSONAL THERAPY

Interpersonal therapy focuses on the need to help individuals identify and resolve current interpersonal struggles. Unlike psychodynamic psychotherapy, interpersonal therapy is generally considered short-term therapy. Its premise is that interpersonal difficulties contribute to the onset and maintenance of many symptoms, including eating disorders.

FEMINIST THERAPY

Feminist therapy focuses on the psychology of women and its impact on issues such as eating disorders. Particular issues, such as empowerment, identity, trauma and abuse, role conflict, and assertiveness are addressed; treatment is interactive and explorative, emphasizing the importance of interpersonal relationships and experiences in women.

FAMILY THERAPY

Family therapy is a form of interpersonal therapy focusing on the family. In relationship to eating disorders, family therapists look at the role that dysfunctional family relations have on the development and maintenance of eating disorders. Family therapy is critical in conjunction with individual psychotherapy for those under 18 and living at home. It is desirable for all struggling with eating disorders, despite age and living situation.

GROUP THERAPY

Group therapy is a form of therapy which brings people together in a group, usually of no more than 8 people, to discuss, explore, learn, and support one another in their efforts to cope with a similar difficulty or illness. Group therapy often offers members a sense of belongingness and support because each group member has a unique understanding of the issue which brings them together. Group therapy can be the only therapy or an adjunctive therapy to any of the therapies listed above.

PHARMACOTHERAPY

Pharmacotherapy refers to treatment through the use of medication. It is recommended that medication therapy *never* be the sole form of therapy, but rather considered in conjunction with individual psychotherapy and nutritional counseling.

Although the therapeutic approaches described have their own distinct character, therapists may use a combination of theories and techniques in their practice. Above is only a sampling of those theories that have been found to be most useful in the treatment of eating disorders. When interviewing a potential therapist, if you hear that he or she uses several therapies and techniques, please remember that this is common (and practical). The use of several therapies and techniques is an indication that the therapist understands that he or she must work with you to modify your hurtful or self-defeating behaviors and thoughts; assist you in understanding and expressing your feelings; help you learn to better cope with, or change, your life circumstances; and appreciate how your history may have contributed to the development of your eating disorder. You and your therapist need the tools to work flexibly, creatively, and effectively. Although you have an eating disorder, you are unique and your treatment should fit your unique needs.

What To Look For

1. Licensure: The therapist you choose should be licensed in your state. This person should be credentialed as a licensed psychologist, social worker, mental health counselor, psychiatrist, or clinical nurse.
2. Specialty/Expertise: It is important that you find a clinician that specializes in the treatment of eating disorders. Participation in local/national eating disorder organizations, as well as continuing education in eating disorders is just as important as years of practice in this field with this population.
3. Experience: As stated above, experience with this population is also important.
4. Team Approach: It is equally important that you find a clinician who is willing to work collaboratively with your physician, nutritionist, psychiatrist, family therapist, and all other treatment providers.
5. Compassion: It is critical that you find a therapist that has compassion for you and your struggles with your eating disorder. You deserve to feel respected and understood.

Once you believe you have found a therapist that fulfills the above criteria, the next step is to determine whether his or her style of treatment is compatible with your needs. For example, if you feel it is important to be able to contact your therapist outside of the therapy hour, will your therapist be willing to have such contact? Below is a list of questions you may wish to ask the therapist, to help clarify what you expect from therapy.

1. Do you have an answering service?
2. If "yes," what are your policies around what constitutes an emergency, and when may I contact you outside of the therapeutic hour?
3. If "no," what is your policy around emergencies? What do I do if I feel I need to talk to you outside of the therapeutic hour?
4. What is your policy around collateral contacts with other treatment providers?
5. What is your cancellation policy?

6. What do you do to maintain confidentiality in the office?
7. Do you work with treatment contracts?
8. What is your policy around hospitalization?
9. What is your treatment approach?
10. Do you weigh your clients? (It is *not* recommended that your therapist be in charge of monitoring your weight. This is something you and your physician should monitor.)

We recommend that you seek personal recommendations when looking for a therapist. Such recommendations can come from physicians, friends, coworkers, family, your insurance company, local hospitals or eating disorder organizations. We do not recommend that you do a "blind" search for a therapist by contacting names in your local phone book. Your life is too important! You deserve the best treatment available.

What To Expect

We recommend that you arrive a few minutes before your scheduled appointment. Fill out the necessary paperwork ahead of time by arriving early so it won't take up your therapy time. The office should maintain an atmosphere of confidentiality. Full names should not be heard, nor should you be referred to by your full name if there are others in the waiting area. Once you have entered your therapist's office, he or she should try to make you comfortable, while initially reviewing your intake information. Generally, therapists explain what to expect from this first session. The therapist should explain the laws of confidentiality, educate you concerning your insurance coverage (if you are billing your insurance company), and explain how he or she works. Then the therapist will begin to ask you about your concerns, what brings you to therapy, and explore your history with food, relationships, and other potential problem areas while leaving time to inquire about your physical health, psychological health, and family history. In this interview, he or she may ask you what your goals are for psychotherapy.

All of this information will help the therapist understand your readiness for change (see chapter on Hunger to review this information) and determine a suggested course of treatment. The therapist should save some time at the end of the session for you to ask questions and discuss what might happen next. You may want to ask some of the questions above, if you do not have that information yet. Depending on how much information you and the therapist were able to cover by the end of the first session, your therapist might ask you to return so he or she might complete an assessment, or he or she may have enough information to make necessary recommendations. Anxiety and fear during the first session can sometimes distort your feelings about the therapist or the session. We recommend that you consider meeting with your therapist for a few visits before deciding if he or she is the right therapist for you.

If after a few visits you don't feel connected or understood, you may want to share this with the therapist and explore your options. Negative feelings about the therapist or the therapy may be valid indications that this is not the right fit for you. However, we recommend that you discuss your feelings about the therapist or therapy with the therapist as well as with trusted others to explore whether your desire to see someone else is the best move for you, or if you might encounter the same issues with someone else. Sometimes negative feelings about the therapist or therapy are representations of your feelings about yourself, your relationships, or your world and not indications that the therapist or therapy is wrong for you.

MY RECOVERY PROCESS: FROM LONELINESS TO CONNECTION

It is difficult to nail down the factors that have carried me through the process of recovering from anorexia nervosa. Two or three years ago, on my fourth admission to the hospital, depressed and disappointed that I was an inpatient again, I remember a nurse on the eating disorders unit drawing me a graphical representation of her understanding of recovery. She pointed out that although the general trend was in a positive direction, there were many valleys and plateaus along the way. She felt it was important for me to understand that my recovery would not be linear; I had a difficult time believing her (but I saved the drawing anyway).

When I returned to college, after being out for a year, I did not think that my life could ever again be normal. The "anorexic" label pasted on my forehead clearly spelled out that I was a lost cause. My last serious therapeutic relationship had ended when I refused the intense treatment strategy that the therapist proposed. However, at the urging of my friends and family, I found a new therapist and began yet another course of outpatient therapy. I had little hope; treatment failure seemed imminent.

Much to my surprise, this time was different. Within a few weeks of our first session, I realized that for the first time in my six years in therapy, I was in a therapeutic relationship where I was valued. I finally felt comfortable sharing the scariest parts of my life. Uncomfortable situations that were common in my past therapies, such as snack time with the therapist, were never forced upon me. Therapy was individualized; we worked together as a team to find the best solutions for me. At the time, I lived alone. Activities involving food (in particular, eating) were completely under my control. Feeling guilty about my needs, shopping and cooking were frequently difficult. In therapy, we discovered a new solution. I needed to eat with people.

I set up meals with my closest friends: lunches on Tuesday with Merlin, and Wednesday with Molly, and dinner on Thursday with Theresa. It gave me three times each week when I knew that I would eat with supportive friends. Frequently, I brought my own meal—foods that I felt safe with—and they would bring their meals or buy them at the food court. I laid down the rules ahead of time to ensure that I would always feel comfortable. Initially, I told them that they could not comment on what or how much I was eating. Also, I expected them to eat, too. As I got stronger, the rules changed. I began to ask them to tell me if what I was eating was ridiculously small or devoid of calories; I promised not to get angry. We began to eat out in restaurants that I would select. I would tell them beforehand not to let me wimp out and order a dressing-less salad. My friends stuck by me; they played by the rules and helped save my life. Although I sometimes felt foolish needing this structure, this was not silly to them.

Sometimes I wonder where my life would now be had I not had such fabulous friends, an empathic therapist, a loving mother, an involved minister, a caring choir director, and numerous others. The support network that surrounded me in my despair frequently pulled me from the isolation and loneliness that was "Anorexia." I think recovery without them would have been impossible.

Ultimately, all of the decisions that were made regarding my treatment, and that led to my recovery, were made by me. Letting me make the decisions and rebuild my own life on the infrastructure provided by my support network allowed me to become a woman of great strength. In the past, I depended on others to fulfill my needs. I now rely on others as they rely on me. Together we form an interdependent web.

Amanda, age 22

THE NUTRITIONIST

Some symptoms of an eating disorder are psychological and some are the result of medical or nutritional problems which appear to be psychological problems. By this we mean that your nutritional status may affect your mood, your attitude, your behavior, and your thinking. Psychological interventions may help you deal with these difficulties, but they will not cure the underlying problem if the cause is due to nutritional deficiencies. Nutritional rehabilitation is needed. Malnutrition affects brain function which, in turn, can weaken the vulnerable person's resistance to the "voice" of the eating disorder. Although "re-feeding" the body does not necessarily counter the voice of the eating disorder, research indicates that when the body is adequately nourished, preoccupation with thoughts of food and weight tend to decrease.

The role of the nutritionist is to develop a plan with each client to correct nutritional deficiencies, allay fears about food, and educate each client on the importance of proper nutrition. For many individuals struggling with eating disorders, the nutritionist is the "least threatening" person on the treatment team. This is because the nutritionist does not take on a role that is challenging in any way, but rather represents herself or himself as an expert on dietary needs. The advice given by a nutritionist is scientific; that is, it is concrete and can be proven. For those struggling with feelings of "control," the concept of concrete intervention can be reassuring.

Psychotherapy, on the other hand, is much more abstract in nature. It is a process for which benefits cannot be immediately proven. It can cause individuals and families to search for answers. With the nutritionist, there are answers. The difficulty is in accepting and following the prescribed nutritional plan.

Many individuals struggling with eating disorders think that they don't need to meet with a nutritionist. They feel they are well educated on nutrition. Take the following quiz to quickly test your nutrition knowledge. The answers are at the end of the quiz.

Nutrition Quiz

1. 1 gram of fat contains how many calories?
2. What is a calorie?
3. How many calories equal 1 pound?
4. If Josephine's body requires 1,800 calories a day to maintain her weight, how many calories would she need to ingest in order to gain 1 pound the next day?
5. What is the average caloric intake needed for adolescent girls?
6. What are the physical and psychological consequences of excessive dieting?
7. Why is it that many people that struggle with bulimia are of average or above average weight?

Nutrition Answers

1. 9 calories
2. a unit of energy
3. 3,500 calories
4. 5,300 calories
5. The amount varies depending on activity level and size.
6. Impaired judgement, decreased concentration, increased depression and anxiety, increased obsessive-compulsiveness, muscle atrophy, fatigue, decreased motivation, and other symptoms associated with excessive restriction and dieting.
7. Purging through vomiting, laxatives, and diuretics does not result in permanent weight loss.

What To Expect

There are two types of nutritionists: nutrition educators and nutrition counselors. The role of nutrition educators is to provide education on the importance of diet and nutritional needs. These professionals tend to be well-versed on many illnesses affected by diet. Nutrition counselors, on the other hand, have a strong educational background in psychology and the psychological impact of food. You are more apt to find nutritional educators in hospitals, whereas nutrition counselors are more apt to be found in a private practice setting or connected with a psychological or medical practice. Whenever possible, you should search for a nutrition counselor who has an expertise in eating disorders.

The referral to a nutritionist should be made early in treatment. It is usually made in connection with the referral to the individual therapist, or made shortly thereafter by your physician or therapist. Like all the other visits, during your visit with the nutritionist you will be asked questions about your history. But this time the questions will be about your history with food and weight. The nutritionist will want to explore your current intake; behaviors, fears, and anxieties associated with food; weight history; body image; hunger; family history of dieting, food issues, illnesses; and your understanding of nutrition.

Once your history has been taken, he or she may want to weigh you and keep record of your weight. If your physician is monitoring your weight, you don't need to have this repeated in your nutritionist's office. Different scales can yield different results, which can exacerbate anxiety. Furthermore, frequent weigh-ins by numerous providers can serve as a distraction to the issues at hand, and instead reinforce the focus on numbers (something we are trying to minimize).

Finally, you can expect your nutritionist to ask you to set goals. It is recommended that you clarify both short-term and long-term goals. Short-term goals are those that are short in duration. That is, these are goals that are smaller, and more immediate. Long-term goals, on the other hand, are those that you hope to achieve over time as you make progress with your short-term goals. Your nutritionist may very likely work with you to develop short-term goals to focus on between nutrition visits. The hope is that in meeting the short-term goals, the long-term goals will be reached as well . . . leading to recovery.

Initially, we recommend that nutritional counseling take place on a weekly basis. The beginning meetings will help build a trusting relationship, educate you on nutrition, and focus on helping you and the nutritionist develop a treatment plan and strategies that meet your needs. As your eating behaviors "normalize" and you work toward maintaining your weight goals, you may decrease the frequency of your nutritional visits. From that point on, the role of the nutritionist will be to help you maintain your *lifestyle change* of healthy eating and self care.

In the space below, please make a list of questions you have for your nutritionist.

1)_____

   _____

2)_____

   _____

3)_____

   _____

4)_____

   _____

5)_____

   _____

Now that you know what questions you wish to ask, you need to decide what information is important for you to share with the nutritionist.

We recommend you begin with your recent food history. The following worksheet will help you track several days' worth of meals and snacks. In the space provided, record your intake over the past three days, including liquids (such as water, diet sodas, and alcohol) and condiments (such as salad dressing, mustard, etc.). Also, write how much and what kind of exercise you engaged in on those days. If you did not exercise, write "no exercise."

Recent Food History

Breakfast: _____

_____

Snack: _____

_____

Lunch: _____

_____

Snack: _____

_____

Dinner: _____

_____

Exercise: _____

Breakfast: _____

_____

Snack: _____

_____

Lunch: _____

_____

Snack: _____

_____

Dinner: _____

_____

Exercise: _____

Breakfast: _____

_____

Snack: _____

_____

Lunch: _____

_____

Snack: _____

_____

Dinner: _____

_____

Exercise: _____

Some clients have told us it was helpful to write down their food and weight fears as well as behaviors and attitudes they wished to change.

Behaviors Warranting Change

_____

_____

_____

_____

_____

_____

_____

_____

_____

Fears

_____

_____

_____

_____

_____

Family Medical Hisotry

Finally, it may be important for you to know your family medical history. Please answer the following:

1) Is there a history of overweight/obesity in your family? If so, whom?

_____

_____

2) Is there a history of diabetes in your family? If so, whom?

_____

_____

3) Is there a history of high cholesterol in your family? If so, whom?

_____

_____

4) Is there a history of eating disorders in your family (anorexia nervosa, bulimia, binge eating)? If so, whom?

_____

_____

5) Is there a history of high blood pressure in your family? If so, whom?

_____

_____

6) Is there a history of heart disease in your family? If so, whom?

_____

_____

7) Is there a history of addictions in your family? If so, whom?

_____

_____

8) Is there a history of dieting in your family? If so, whom?

_____

_____

9) Are there cultural issues with food? If so, please explain.

_____

_____

_____

_____

THE PHARMACOLOGIST

It has been found that medication can be an effective treatment for eating disorders *in conjunction* with psychotherapy, medical monitoring, and nutrition counseling. The role of the pharmacologist is to prescribe the appropriate medication; this person is usually a psychiatrist, or clinical nurse specialist, but it can also be the primary care physician. Before we explore what to expect in a visit to the pharmacologist, let's explore why such a referral may be necessary.

First of all, it's important to remind yourself that eating disorders are *symptoms*. For treatment to be effective, it is important to address the symptoms. But more importantly, it is critical that there be resolution to the underlying issues. As with the saying, "Which came first the chicken or the egg?", it can be difficult to assess whether the eating disorder caused the depression, anxiety, and/or obsessive-compulsive tendencies, or whether depression, anxiety, and/or obsessive-compulsive disorder was one of the factors in the development of your eating disorder. Regardless, what we do know is that depression, anxiety disorders, and obsessive-compulsive disorder have their roots in physiology. That is, there is research evidence to support that depression, anxiety and obsessive-compulsive disorder are associated with brain chemistry. For example, we know that a low serotonin level in the brain can cause both depression and obsessive-compulsive disorder.

Medications can remedy disturbances in brain chemistry that may precipitate depression, anxiety and obsessive-compulsive disorder, therefore, improving a person's ability to cope with feelings and behaviors that may have hindered recovery. Medication alone is not a complete treatment; however, used in conjunction with psychotherapy it may offer significant aid in the treatment of symptoms commonly experienced by those with eating disorders.

Not everyone diagnosed with an eating disorder will require medication as a part of her treatment. However, if it is recommended by the pharmacologist, we strongly urge you to consider it as an aid in your recovery.

Recovery from an eating disorder can be arduous. If a medication trial is recommended in an effort to treat symptoms that may be impairing your ability to cope with other difficult feelings, thoughts, and behaviors, you deserve that support. We know that many people with eating disorders don't feel comfortable taking medication. In order to help you with this decision, let's take a moment to challenge four myths that many of our clients have told us contributed to their ambivalence about taking medication:

Myth #1: *Taking medication will cause you to gain weight.* Medication does not cause you to "not care" about what you eat. It will not cause you to become "free" with food, nor will it cause you to become fat. What medication can do, if it is effective, is "take the edge off" the intensity of your feelings in order to help you better cope on *your journey to recovery*. It will diminish the feelings of depression, and in certain dosages, help decrease obsessive thinking, compulsive behavior, and anxiety.

Myth #2: *Taking medication means you are mentally ill.* Starvation can cause brain chemical disturbances that lead to depression and obsessive-compulsive rituals. Re-feeding can aid in a return to "normal" brain chemical make-up, but for those with eating disorders, "re-feeding" onself adequately is often too difficult. Medication can help with this re-feeding process, by decreasing obsessive-compulsive rituals, feelings of depression, and anxiety that make re-feeding difficult.

Myth #3: *You can do this by yourself; you do not need medication.* Not everyone diagnosed with an eating disorder may be referred for a trial of medication. However, if you are having difficulty implementing change, medication can help you better cope with the feelings, thoughts, and behaviors that are keeping you "stuck."

Myth #4: *You will feel different if you take medication.* Most antidepressant medications are mood altering, but not mind altering. That is, you will not be able to *feel* the change. Instead, what you will notice, if antidepressant medication is helpful, is that you are not finding it as difficult to make necessary changes or sit with certain feelings. Anti-anxiety medications, if recommended, can be *felt* shortly after ingestion; a person can feel a change within approximately 45 minutes, and can feel its effects for approximately 4–8 hours, depending on the medication. Antidepressants have a longer life span, and do not have the same immediate effects as anti-anxiety medications.

What To Expect

If you are meeting with a pharmacologist for a medication consultation, you can expect to have an experience similar to the one you had with your therapist in the initial evaluation. We recommend that you arrive a few minutes early to fill out any necessary paperwork. When you finish the paperwork, you will meet with the pharmacologist for approximately 45–50 minutes. The focus of this meeting will be on your current emotional and physical well-being. In addition to this, the pharmacologist will want to know as much about your family, medical, and psychological history as possible. You may be asked to fill in one (or more) self-report questionnaires on depression, anxiety, or eating. At the end of this assessment, if the pharmacologist feels that medication could be helpful he or she will make this recommendation. He or she will explain how the medication works and will give you a list of potential side effects. You will be told how to take the medication and be given some time to ask questions. The pharmacologist may start you with a sample, or may write a prescription for you to fill at your pharmacy. In general, pharmacologists begin any medication with a low dose, and increase the dosage once it is seen that you can tolerate the medication without any major side effects or complications. Usually the pharmacologist recommends that you return for a follow-up appointment within two weeks of beginning the medication. Follow-up visits thereafter are determined by the pharmacologist, and usually range from once every one to three months. These visits are usually about 15 minutes in length.

To help you prepare for your appointment with the pharmacologist, please answer the following questions:

1) Have you ever been on medication for psychological issues? If so, what medications:

_____

_____

_____

_____

_____

2) If you answered "Yes" to question 1, did you have any adverse reactions to any medications prescribed? If "Yes," please list those medications, and the adverse reactions that you experienced.

_____

_____

_____

_____

_____

3) Are you currently taking any medications? If "Yes," please list:

_____

_____

_____

_____

_____

4) Are any family members taking medication for psychological issues? If so, please list those members, and their medications:

Name: _____ Medication: _____

Name: _____ Medication: _____

Name: _____ Medication: _____

Name: _____ Medication: _____

Name: _____ Medication: _____

The four questions above should help you and your pharmacologist explore medication options. The following are questions you may want to ask the pharmacologist at the end of her assessment. The empty spaces at the end are for additional questions that may occur to you to ask.

1. Why have you chosen "this" medication (if the pharmacologist recommended a medication)?
2. Why did you not recommend a medication (if appropriate)?
3. What are potential side effects?
4. How long do you anticipate I will be on this medication?
5. Do you know what dosage you are looking to have me on?
6. Are there certain over-the-counter or prescription medications that I will not be able to take along with this medication?
7. How will I know that this medication is effective?
8. _____
9. _____
10. _____

You now have what it takes to create your own treatment "recovery" team. You are now an educated consumer. An effective treatment team is one that works together. It is important for you to feel safe, trusting, and valued as a member of the team. Even though you are the "patient," you have a voice! You should be empowered to use this voice. The team may not agree with all you have to say, but you should feel heard. We hope this chapter will help you to choose the right professionals for your treatment team. You deserve their support.

Media Madness

Media influence may not cause eating disorders per se, but they sure do contribute to the development of eating disorders! Every day we are exposed to hundreds of direct and indirect messages focusing on appearance. These messages range from the numerous ads on TV for diets and diet products, to the more subtle messages from toys, such as the Barbie and Ken dolls.

Adults may very well be able to differentiate a sales pitch from reality to determine the validity of advertisements and television. Children and adolescents, however, do not necessarily have this ability, and as such are likely to base their self-worth on how well they conform to media images.

Did you know

- 1 out of every 3.8 TV commercials contains some form of "attractiveness" message.
- Women's magazines have more than ten times the number of advertisements on body image and weight loss than their male counterparts.
- Adolescent girls use the media as their main source of information on female health.
- In a review of teen magazine articles focusing on fitness and exercise, 74% encouraged girls to exercise more to become more attractive and 51% emphasized exercise for purposes of weight loss. Rarely was exercise encouraged for health.

Adults may read the cover of a magazine and see the sensationalism. Young people, however, may see the same article and study it to learn what they must do in order to achieve *happiness*. The adolescent's wish to achieve a body as ideal as that of the female models in magazines can contribute to the development of an eating disorder. Not every adolescent reading magazines is going to develop an eating disorder in order to achieve the media body ideal, however, the insecure adolescent in search of identity, acceptance, love, and esteem may be seduced by the *eating disorder/media promise* that that body in the magazine could be hers if she would just lose weight. Furthermore, she believes that if that body were hers, her life would be better.

THERE IS NO MAGIC

I was 17 years old, and about to graduate from high school and go to college 200 miles away. I was terrified—terrified of making new friends, being away from my family, and of being responsible for myself. I had spent most of my senior year trying to figure out how I could feel good about myself. I would wonder how I would be capable of handling all of the challenges that college would be presenting me. One answer always prevailed . . . lose weight! After all, everyone knew that all thin people have friends. Thin people get dates. Thin people are happy. If I could be thin then I wouldn't have to worry about anything; my questions would be answered!

I developed what therapists often call "magical thinking." That is, I began to diet, believing that weight loss was the answer to my questions. I wanted to go to college feeling good; I was afraid of the "freshman 15" and wanted to do whatever I could to prevent the weight gain from happening to me. So, I started to diet. I had certain foods that became "good" to me, and would spend a great deal of time trying to decide what to eat and what not to eat. I had placed an added pressure on myself by requesting that I lose a significant amount of weight in a relatively short period of time. In order to accomplish this goal, I felt the only option was to continuously cut back on what I was eating. So cut back I did! I began to feel guilty every time I ate; I felt I should have been strong enough to resist eating, and when I wasn't I would emotionally self-destruct. "If only I were stronger" or "if only I had more willpower" were only two of the many negative statements I would make to myself. In hindsight, I wonder if these statements were my unconscious way to help myself continue with my restriction. Well, whatever it was, something was beginning to *work!* I found myself able to eat less and less, and my weight was beginning to drop more. What I also began to notice more was that my mood was becoming contingent upon my weight and the foods I'd eaten. Whenever I ate I would become upset with myself; I would feel miserable, guilty, and angry. When I didn't eat, I could feel strong, in control, and powerful. After all, what is more powerful than being able to overcome your natural human needs?

It bothered me a little bit that I was so tired that I could barely walk up stairs, and that it took me fifteen minutes to get out of bed in the morning in order not to pass out. It bothered me some that I couldn't spend much time with friends or family that summer. It's amazing how many social activities are planned around food! It bothered me a little that it took up so much time trying to figure out what I would and would not allow myself to eat. As such, it also bothered me that I had to lie in order to avoid situations in which there was food. Although all these things bothered me, they did not feel as if they were going to bother me as much as it would have bothered me if I had been eating more regularly. Avoiding food became the easier way of living . . . despite its difficulty!

If you are reading this, you probably have an eating disorder and/or know someone who does. Let me tell you my experience with my eating disorder. Although in the beginning it feels great, those great feelings soon turn into disappointment, despair, and fear. The fear is intense; it feels more intense than any fear there is because what you are afraid of is your own body. You can't escape it; you can't get it away from you. It is fighting you because it doesn't want you to be sick. Yet nothing you do is good enough. It's sheer terror—like you are fighting an uphill battle and every time you are about to reach the one thing that you feel will make you better, happiness slips further and further away. Imagine spending years of your life trapped by something hurtful that surrounds you every single day. Everywhere I turned there was food. There were magazines urging me to lose weight. Everyone around me was constantly talking about food, weight, and body image. I can recall people asking me what my diet secret was . . . how did I manage to stay so disciplined to get to the gym every day—or twice or three times a day—and how did I resist those delicious foods? They looked up to me as having "willpower," despite my unhealthy bony body. It didn't appear to matter that I had trouble getting through the day without feeling like I was going to pass out, or that I hadn't had my period in six months and was risking permanent infertility. What mattered was my "willpower" and my unhealthy bony body!

No one knew how obsessed I was with food; I gave off the presentation that I was indifferent to food, and that I could pass it up and not give it a second thought. Yet in my head an amazingly loud battle was taking place. *I thought of food every waking moment*, and on occasion even dreamt about food. I had no escape from my thoughts. Even after I had recognized my obsession, I still couldn't get away from it because it is a part of life, and as such I was surrounded by it. The hardest part of recovery had been to separate myself from my (negative) thoughts and focus instead on what was healthy for me.

Recovery has been an immense feeling of freedom. It wasn't easy; it took many years and lots of steps forward and backward. But most importantly, it took me wanting to get better more than wanting to hold onto my eating disorder. This was a gradual process; despite what anyone may say to you, it does not happen quickly or with a steady uphill climb. Expect lots of curves, detours, and slick oil patches that send you backward. Recovery involves a great nutritionist, therapist, physician, medication, and other supportive environments. But even with these, it won't happen if you do not want it to happen. Recovery happens when you are *ready* for change. Recovery happens when your eating disorder is no longer serving its purpose in survival. For me, recovery came when I realized that I was sick of my life revolving around my eating disorder. I no longer wanted to live my life in order to please it. Recovering from my eating disorder was the hardest feat I have had to face, but also the greatest that I have ever done. Having an eating disorder was paralyzing; recovery was terrifying, but being recovered is the greatest feeling I will ever know!

Naomi, *age 29*

Adults can fall victim to media messages as well. Whether you are that innocent adolescent in search of self or the adult in search of youth, you may be falling victim to the myriad *eating disorder/ media messages* filling every women's, men's, beauty, fashion, entertainment, and teen magazine. It is a Herculean task to maintain perspective when confronted with the plethora of media messages that say you are not good enough as you are. In this chapter we hope to teach you how to challenge media messages. We hope to help you question whether you wish to support media messages which undermine yours and others' self esteem, worth, and health.

Let's begin by taking a journey back in time. As a young child, what kinds of toys do you remember playing with? Did you play with dolls or action figures? If so, what types did you play with (baby dolls, Barbie, G.I. Joe, Ken, The Incredible Hulk, etc.)? What were the physical characteristics of your dolls or figures? Did any of them have any birthmarks or disfigurements? What did you do with your doll(s)? Did you ever change their appearance, or cut their hair? Do you recall wanting to look like one of your dolls/figures? Did you ever want to be one of your dolls/figures? Now travel back in time and in the space below write about the fantasies you developed with your doll/figure. Use the questions above as jumping-off points for your writing.

_____

_____

_____

_____

_____

_____

_____

_____

_____

_____

_____

_____

_____

_____

_____

_____

_____

_____

_____

_____

_____

_____

_____

_____

_____

_____

_____

_____

You may believe that the dolls that you played with a long time ago had no bearing on the development of your eating disorder, and, you may be correct. But let's take a brief moment to explore the impact of fashion dolls on children. On the positive side, dolls help with creativity. They provide a playmate for the lonely child. They can help a youngster with social skills, conflict resolution, and self-expression. On a more negative note, fashion dolls can increase a child's insecurity by misrepresenting the human body. Girls look at fashion dolls and compare themselves in negative ways.

For example, the Asian child may become aware of differences between herself and her Caucasian doll, and reject herself because she is different from her doll. Likewise, the overweight child may look at the unrealistic waist of a fashion doll, and begin to go to drastic measures in an attempt to look like that doll.

Did you know that by the time a girl is six years old, she has determined what she must look like in order to be loved? This is *frightening*! Six-year-olds live in a world of make believe; toys that reinforce creativity surround them; there is a tremendous amount of *fiction*! If these young children are not taught to love the body they have in all its uniqueness, they risk rejecting it and themselves. They may not actively reject their bodies until puberty approaches; however, the risk grows through the childhood years as they see and hear that they do not meet the body ideal of their dolls or the media. The risk may not come for another 6 years or so, but nonetheless, they are at risk. What is more frightening is that we are finding that girls are developing eating disorders at much earlier ages; we do not have the time to "deprogram" these young girls. Preventive *education* is essential.

Here are a few interesting statistics:

- If fashion dolls were human, they would not have enough room in their body cavity to hold their vital organs.
- If fashion dolls were human, they would not have enough body fat to menstruate.
- Fashion dolls are inaccurately proportioned; for example, they have the foot size of a toddler with the breasts of a woman and legs longer than most women!
- The average measurements of a fashion doll, if human, would be approximately 44-18-40!

Earlier in this chapter we addressed the impact that teen magazines and television have on adolescents (adolescent girls in particular). Adolescence is a time of vulnerability, insecurity, and confusion. Often the adolescent feels as if she is treated as a child, while being given adult responsibilities. Searching for an identity, adolescents often turn to magazines, television, and their peers. Unfortunately, these magazines and television shows too often reinforce an adolescent's insecurity. To reduce insecurity adolescents attempt to emulate media images. Confused and insecure, adolescents also succumb to peer pressure. So eager to fit in and be accepted, they attempt to be what the media and powerful peers tell them to be. If that means altering their appearance, they will do it. To not fit in, to be an outcast or an outsider, is the most dreaded fate of most adolescents. To be thin, like the mass media images, is the first step toward fitting in, reducing insecurity, and confusion.

Let's look at the media's potential impact on you:

As a teen, what kind of magazines did you read? If you are a teen, what magazines do you currently read?

_____

_____

_____

What television shows did you watch as a teen? If you are a teen, what television shows do you watch now?

_____

_____

_____

Now, think about these magazines and television shows. What messages do you think they gave you about your appearance, happiness, and popularity? If you are a teen, what impact do magazines and television shows have on your appearance, happiness, and popularity now?

_____

_____

_____

_____

_____

Our society's obsession with thinness, has caused us to support a multi-billion dollar diet industry. The industry's focus is money, as there is little scientific support for many of the claims that are made. The diet industry and the media collude to promise that thinness is both attainable for all and necessary for happiness. The media and the diet industry have contributed to the epidemic of eating disorders.

To see if our claims are accurate, collect between 3 and 5 fashion, teen, women's, men's, sports, health and wellness, or entertainment magazines. List the magazines you have gathered in the space below:

_____

_____

_____

With scissors cut out any words, pictures, and articles that reinforce society's message that a thin appearance is important. Now take what you have cut out and make a collage on the following page. Then return to these magazines and cut out messages that reinforce size acceptance, whatever your size. Make this collage on the next page.

What can you learn from these collages?

1) Were the ads, stories, and pictures equally balanced between encouraging thinness and encouraging size acceptance? Please explain.

_____
_____
_____
_____
_____

2) Were there any common themes that you came across? If "yes" please explain.

_____
_____
_____
_____
_____

3) Do you feel that these magazines encourage you to feel good about and appreciate yourself at your present size? Please explain.

_____
_____
_____
_____
_____

If you found yourself feeling more self-critical, discouraged, or angry because you do not match the media ideal, you are not alone. Surprisingly, many people continue to read magazines that make them feel badly about themselves. You don't have to do this anymore! If you want to show the media that you do not support their messages, please consider doing the following:

- Write a letter to the editor of your favorite magazines requesting healthy media messages, and pointing out messages that encourage eating disorders and discourage self-acceptance.
- Make note of companies that consistently portray negative messages and write them a letter requesting healthier messages. Let them know you will refuse to purchase their products unless you see a change in their messages.
- Write a letter to companies that portray positive messages. Thank them for their messages and request that they continue their positive media campaigns.
- Do not buy products from companies that participate in negative advertising.
- Start petitions against magazines and companies that encourage the development of eating disorders and discourage size acceptance. Mail the completed petitions to the companies and/or magazines.
- Log onto companies' and magazines' websites and note your disagreement with their advertising and messages. Encourage them to support size acceptance and discourage messages and images that support the development of eating disorders.

None of us is strong enough on our own to force a change toward size acceptance. Together, though, we can have an impact. Your voice matters. If you want to be heard, stop supporting the industries that encourage you and so many others to reject and abuse your bodies. Support those magazines and industries that encourage us to accept, appreciate, and care for the bodies we have.

Here are a few other thoughts . . .

1. Don't comment on anyone else's size (whether you consider it complimentary or not). (Example: "Oh, Marge, you look so good! Have you lost weight?" The next time you see Marge, if you make no comments should she think that she doesn't look good because she is the same weight or has gained weight?)

2. Don't make derogatory comments about your body. It conveys disrespect for yourself and, if you are a parent, teaches your children—especially your daughters—to disrespect their bodies. (Example: "My thighs are so fat! No I can't put on a bathing suit and take you and your brother to the beach!" Should the daughter think that if her mother's thighs are too fat to put on a bathing suit and go to the beach, perhaps her thighs are that fat too? If she doesn't think this yet, she will be watching for signs of fat thighs so she too can deny herself the pleasure of the beach.)

3. Don't go along with others who ridicule or criticize the bodies of people they know or see. Be assertive and let others know such ridicule is hurtful, prejudicial, and unacceptable.(Example: If a friend says, "Look at that rear end! How does she dare wear shorts in public?" you might say something like, "I wonder how it might be for her to hear such hurtful comments from people who don't know her or her circumstances? She has as much right as you and I to wear shorts without ridicule or prejudice.")

4. Do tell others that you love and respect them for who they are, not for how they look. (Example: "You sang so beautifully at the concert" or "I appreciate how hard you tried to help me while I wasn't feeling well" rather than, "Oh, you looked so beautiful during your performance" or "Now that you've lost weight, you're so much more helpful.")

5. Comment on qualities of character and behavior, not appearance or size, when complimenting or critiquing others. (Example: "It really upsets me when you don't clean the counters and do the dishes after you make a snack for yourself. It makes more work for me" or "I so appreciate it when you clean the counters and do the dishes after you make a snack for yourself. It feels so good to walk into a clean kitchen after a long day at work.")

Media and our society encourage criticism of self and others. Do not fall captive to this sad cultural pastime. Find, watch, and read materials that encourage people to celebrate their uniqueness and care for the bodies they have. Be an advocate for size acceptance. Who knows, maybe you can make a difference!

For Families, Friends, and Loved Ones

Eating disorders are not individual struggles; they affect loved ones as well. Whenever possible, recovery should include any family and friends that are actively involved in your life. *This chapter is written for your loved ones*, yet we have included it in this workbook for *you!* We are not asking *you* to help *them*, as this is so often the role those with eating disorders feel they must play. Rather, we are asking that you share this with them so they may help *you* in *your* recovery! Throughout the book, you have read personal stories from people who have recovered from eating disorders; in this chapter you will hear from three mothers of young women who have recovered or are in recovery. We hope that sharing these stories with those who care about you will help them understand you better and support you in your efforts toward recovery.

We have broken this chapter into four sections. The first section will give you *information* about eating disorders. The second section will help *those who suspect someone they love has an eating disorder*. The third section will be for *those who are actively supporting someone in recovery*. The fourth section has a list of "Do's & Don'ts" which we hope will help loved ones better understand how to provide support for a loved one in recovery.

THE FIGHT OF OUR LIVES: A MOTHER'S STORY

My daughter struggled with an eating disorder for three years. It was all-consuming! Everything we did centered on Stephanie. When she was in a hospital, we planned our work schedule and eating schedule around visiting hours. When she was at home, our plans were based on her needs, whether it was when she ate or when she had a doctor's appointment. She had no life, and neither did we!

The worst part of the disorder was what it did to our family dynamics. All spontaneity was lost; we now all walked on eggshells. The family no longer knew what it was like to have fun. Holiday celebrations became dreaded and took on a morbid undertone. There were holidays that we could not face, so we ran away. We went on mini-vacations, but as the cliché goes, "You cannot run away from your problems."

My biggest fear was that my daughter would never again lead a normal life. I feared that she would deteriorate to the point of no return—she would never be able to work, complete college, date, or marry. I saw her existing, but not living!

My daughter was bright, articulate, beautiful, popular, and athletic. This is a difficult image to sustain. I think people's expectations of Stephanie, and Stephanie's expectations of herself became too hard for her to manage. She didn't know how to tell the world that she could no longer live up to these expectations! In an attempt to avoid disappointing anyone, she began to control the one thing she could . . . what she ate!

I thought being supportive would be easy, but it wasn't. There is a thin line between being controlling and helpful support. Our family therapist became our guide. He helped us formulate workable strategies. We let Stephanie know that we were not giving up on her, and that we would try anything to help her survive. For an entire summer, we were attached to Stephanie's hip.

My recommendation to those families who have a child struggling with an eating disorder is to remember your role. You are not her doctor or therapist; you are her parent. Your job is to keep her safe. This means making sure there is a team of professionals in place who can monitor her medical well-being and her mental health. Show your love and support by becoming her advocate. Stand up to a strong professional and act as a buffer in disputes with insurance companies or managed care professionals. Let her know you understand how much she is suffering. DON'T GIVE UP!

A variety of activities were helpful to me during my daughter's treatment and recovery. The treatment and recovery process is a long and painful one. In order to help my daughter, I had to take care of myself. I saw a therapist and participated with my family in family therapy. Having someone to talk openly and honestly to was a major support. It was also reassuring to know that survival was obtainable.

I needed quiet time for myself and I set aside time each day to read. I know exercise was necessary for my well-being, so I tried to take a walk or use my treadmill every day. It helped clear my head.

Keep in mind that it takes as long to recover as it does to get to the lowest point in the eating disorder. Recovery will be difficult for everyone, but worth it! Your lost child will return as the happy, healthy individual that you remember!

Maxine

EDUCATION

Before you can begin to support your loved one's recovery, it is important that you understand eating disorders. You may never be able to understand why your loved one starves herself, why he feels the need to run after eating a typical meal, or why she eats long after she is physically full. You can, however, educate yourself on what constitutes an eating disorder, and what purpose (though maladaptive) it serves for your loved one. We hope this information will help you become an active supporter. First, some definitions.

Anorexia Nervosa

Anorexia nervosa is an eating disorder typified by refusal to maintain normal weight for age and height. Those with anorexia also have an intense fear of gaining weight (even when significantly underweight); distorted body image (see their stomachs as enormous and protruding when, in fact, they are concave); and in women, the absence of at least three consecutive menstrual periods. There are two types of anorexia nervosa: (a) restrictive type, where the individual does not engage in binge eating and/or purging behavior; and (b) binge-eating/purging type, where the individual engages in binge eating and/or purging behavior.

Those with anorexia nervosa are preoccupied with weight and restrict their food intake in order to achieve their goal of weight loss. They do not see their restrictive eating or weight loss as a problem. Despite their significant weight loss, they often continue to express "feeling fat," even when grossly underweight. As they continue to lose weight, their views of their bodies become more distorted, which reinforces their perception that they need to lose weight. Their struggle with food, dieting, and weight begins to interfere with their life, and they begin to isolate from friends and loved ones, experience a decrease in work/school performance, and often exhibit signs of depression and anxiety. To them, nothing is as important as being thin. They believe that becoming thin is the route to happiness. Sadly, no matter how thin they become, they are never thin enough, and thus, never happy. Their unhappiness and weight loss becomes a vicious cycle. As they further restrict food, and lose weight, they become depressed. Depression leads to a wish for thinness . . . which leads to depression. This is the vicious cycle which ensues.

Signs and Symptoms of Anorexia Nervosa
- weight loss
- feeling fat
- denial of hunger
- excessive exercise
- restriction of calories
- restriction of fats
- restriction of certain food groups
- making excuses why not eating
- cooking for others
- pushing food on others
- preoccupation with food and weight
- fear of gaining weight
- loss of menstrual cycles (amenhorrhea)
- food rituals
- distorted body image

WHAT I LEARNED AS THE MOTHER OF AN ANOREXIC DAUGHTER . . . MAY IT HELP YOU . . .

My daughter's therapist told us treatment would be a roller coaster ride for us, and it was. We reminded ourselves of this warning often. But despite this reminder, we were not prepared, as this ride was unlike any other we had ever been on. On this one, you could not foresee the hills, the valleys, the turns, or the end. There was no sense of reassurance that the ride would end shortly, nor were we aware of whether or not we could withstand the fear we were experiencing.

Teachers, coaches, and friends . . . even a neighbor we did not know, came to us after school started one September to express their concern and shock upon seeing my daughter after summer break. We knew, of course, that she was sick, but because we were so close to her and saw her on a daily basis, we could not see the drastic changes that were so apparent to those who were at a distance. Furthermore, we were "dealing with the situation"; this, I believe, also clouded our perception to some extent.

My daughter had been seeing a doctor every week or two. The therapist she had been working with had stopped seeing her the previous April (approximately five months before we received the numerous messages of concern). Anxiety had made us *blind* to the truth about of my daughter's situation. The therapist's recommendation that my daughter no longer needed treatment falsely reinforced this blindness. We held onto the belief that if she just ate a little more, things would be better.

The stated concerns from others felt both scary and hurtful. We tried to defend ourselves against their intrusion. Ultimately, we listened to what was being shared with us, and learned of our blindness. This breakthrough forced us to make some very difficult phone calls. We began to challenge my daughter's treatment "plan," do our own research for resources, and most difficult of all, confront her more directly. For all of us, the fragile veneer that things were "okay" began to crack (and quickly crumbled).

In October, my daughter began seeing a new therapist. This therapist pulled together a team; they all worked together and had a firm understanding of eating disorders. To this day, our biggest regret is that it took so long to halt the downward spiral. We had wasted two crucial years following a treatment plan which didn't even come close to what my daughter needed. It is hard not to look back at this time without asking "what if . . . " My husband and I find ourselves consoling each other with reassurance that we were doing the best we could at the time; we had entrusted our daughter with professionals, and wanted to believe she was in good hands.

There are always lessons to be learned in life. The lesson I often give to frantic parents in similar situations is to do *more* than you think you need to, and do it *sooner* than you think you need to. Find a team of professionals in whom you can place your trust, and work with them. Interview them! Educate yourself on treatment approaches! Don't merely accept that because they have initials after their names that they are experts! Placing trust in professionals is more difficult than it sounds for parents who are accustomed to making decisions on their own. However, once you have found the team you can trust, it is critical to follow their objective recommendations. As parents, listening to your heart may not always foster appropriate support; trusting the professionals can help you find that appropriate support. Finding a therapist for yourself can help you with the ache your heart feels when you are not able to act on what it is feeling.

Early on, during my daughter's first hospitalization, my husband and I had made a pact. We would not spend valuable time and energy looking back at the "what ifs," the "whys," and the incidents that every parent can recall with absolute clarity when they wish they could do it over and handle it differently. We had done our best. As hard as it was not to look at the losses, the "what might have beens," we knew we could not do that now. We needed every bit of energy and resolve to help our daughter fight the fight of her life, and to help us deal with the gut-wrenching fear of losing her.

There were heart-wrenching decisions to make along the way: medication, hospitalizations, restrictions, consequences for behaviors. All loving parents would like to avoid these decisions. For us, they were made bearable and possible because we developed trust and confidence in a few key people, and made ourselves step back and share decision-making with them. This did not mean blindly following every recommendation made by everyone involved, but it did mean listening carefully and as non-defensively as possible to recommendations, especially when voiced by more than one of the people we trusted.

How do you decide whom to trust? What a difficult yet crucial question. On an outpatient basis, it would seem to be a little easier, as you can develop this through family meetings, ongoing communication, and time (yet our early experience shows clearly the dangers of misplaced trust). When hospitals are involved, this is tough, given the number of people you must deal with, and the speed with which you must work: Inpatient team members include a new doctor and/or therapist assigned with each new admission, partial hospital program team members, a transfer to a completely new hospital. We had to get to know people quickly, just as they had to get to know our daughter quickly. We learned early on that we had to act assertively on her behalf, in order to make sure even more valuable time was not wasted. This involved establishing telephone contact immediately with newly assigned personnel, insistence that they speak with my daughter's outpatient therapist (in order to be brought up to speed), pressing for a meeting as soon as possible to meet face to face, requesting that a new or previous person be reassigned to her if necessary. I can recall when my daughter was moved from a partial hospital program to an inpatient program at the same hospital. The hospital's plan was to assign a new therapist for the several days she would be an inpatient. We were successful in convincing them to be flexible and allow the therapist from the partial hospital program to work with her in order to maintain continuity. Keeping a notebook with key names, dates, decisions, etc., was an important tool (and still is as I try to reconstruct facts from a highly emotional and stressful period of time!) to make it as easy as possible to give an accurate history to each new person who needed it. We also became much more skilled at dealing with the insurance agency, but this is another story . . .

The concept of trust (or rather the lack of it) was also central to our dealings with our daughter and her eating disorder. This was one of the most difficult aspects to accept and deal with.

We could not "trust" her in the areas associated with her eating disorder. This was so difficult to accept as parents, as she had always been so trustworthy in other aspects of her life. In the past, she was always where she had told us she was going; if she said she had no homework . . . she didn't. For a long time, we held on to the false belief that this trustworthiness also applied to her reassurances that she had eaten lunch, that her weight had gone up a pound, that school was fine, and that she was happy. We wanted too much to believe this was the truth and that she

Continued

was getting better. Finding out that we could not trust her (in some fairly dramatic ways, may I add) shocked and scared us. It helped drive home just how strongly the eating disorder was controlling her, and how much danger she was in. It was a terrible feeling to find out the extent of the deception, and still shocks me to this day.

One of the most difficult aspects of the recovery process at first was rebuilding that ability to trust and believe. It has helped us greatly to understand better the idea of the "anorexic voice" within her which was driving her behaviors. We learned how to talk to and support her "healthy voice." Guidance from therapists, both individual and family, were essential to help with this. It was also essential in supporting us as we sought to learn new and healthier ways to interact with her and within our family.

Last weekend, I had the pleasure of running some errands with my daughter. She had been spending the summer living and working in Boston, and was home for the day. One of the stops (at her request) was the grocery store, where she happily roamed the aisles, selecting a wide variety of foods to stock her apartment. I pushed the cart behind her and could not help looking back a couple of years. How many times a similar trip to this same store had left me in tears as I tried in vain to get her to pick out something . . . anything . . . that she would eat! This time, I made no suggestions. Her tastes are different than her dad's and mine, and that is okay. She urged me to try a few new foods that she has discovered. How much we have grown in the past two years! Paying the bill was such a pleasure!

Jackie

Bulimia

Bulimia is an eating disorder in which the individual engages in episodes of *binge eating* (eating a large amount of food in a brief period of time) and *purging* (getting rid of the food).

Binge eating is:

- eating more rapidly than normal
- eating beyond being full
- eating a large amount of food when not physically hungry
- eating in secret so no one knows how much you are eating
- feelings of shame, disgust, and depression following a binge

Purging is the act of getting rid of food eaten, in an attempt to avoid weight gain. Methods of purging include:

- vomiting
- abuse of laxatives
- abuse of enemas
- abuse of diuretics
- excessive exercise
- fasting

Those with bulimia tend to seek treatment more readily than those with anorexia nervosa. In part, this appears to be because they are so troubled by their binge eating and purging behaviors. They don't like these behaviors and they wish they could stop. In contrast, those with anorexia nervosa wish to continue their weight loss and food restriction. They like losing weight and eating very little. They are less likely, therefore, to seek help on their own.

Those with bulimia are disgusted by their bingeing behaviors. They want to lose weight, but they hate how they attempt to do it. Many with bulimia, not only fail to lose weight, because of their binge eating, but, some gain weight. Eventually, weight reduction through purging doesn't work. No matter how much the person purges, purging does not compensate for binge eating.

In other words, purging does not work! This reason alone encourages some with bulimia to seek treatment. One client once summed up her experience with bulimia this way,

"I can't even have an eating disorder right; I am a failed anorexic."

This young woman felt like a failure because she was unable to deny her body food and lose weight despite her frequent episodes of vomiting. Those with bulimia cannot deny their physical and emotional hungers. In an attempt to satisfy these hungers, they binge. Bingeing makes them feel shame, disgust, and fear about weight gain, which leads them to purge.

The shame and embarrassment of bingeing and purging may often bring an individual with bulimia into treatment more often than one with anorexia nervosa who is satisfied with her symptoms (i.e., they do lead to weight loss!).

Because those with bulimia feel such shame, when confronted by a loved one or when asked about their symptoms by a treatment professional, they may deny or minimize their behaviors. They fear others will be disgusted or critical, therefore, they keep secrets even from those who love and care for them. We will address this more later in the chapter in the section entitled What to Do If You Suspect Your Loved One Has an Eating Disorder.

As with anorexia nervosa, there are two forms of bulimia. The first is *purging type*. In this form of bulimia, the individual regularly vomits, abuses laxatives, diuretics, or enemas as the chosen form of weight loss. In the *nonpurging type*, the individual relies on excessive exercise or fasting as the chosen means of weight loss. Not all individuals with bulimia are underweight; thus it is harder to detect than anorexia nervosa. However, it is possible to detect bulimia through signs and symptoms.

Signs and Symptoms of Bulimia
- eating a large amount of food in a short period of time
- feeling unable to stop eating
- purging through vomiting, laxatives, diuretics, enemas, fasting, or excessive exercise
- swollen glands
- broken blood vessels in eyes or on face from vomiting
- teeth marks, scabs, or scars on fingers from using the fingers to induce vomiting
- going to the bathroom shortly after eating
- mood swings
- gastric complaints
- sore throat
- preoccupation with food and weight
- other addictive behaviors (drinking alcohol, smoking, shopping, etc.)

Compulsive Overeating or Binge Eating

Compulsive overeating, or binge eating, is defined as recurrent episodes of binge eating (as described above). The major difference between compulsive overeating and bulimia is that in the former there are no compensatory behaviors; meaning those who compulsively eat neither purge nor fast or excessively exercise. Those who compulsively overeat make excuses to isolate in order to eat. They are ashamed of their eating and wish to hide their behavior. They eat beyond physical fullness, sometimes to the point of illness.

Those who compulsively eat say they do so to fill up an "emptiness" that cannot be satisfied with food. Others speak of eating compulsively to "stuff down" uncomfortable feelings. Although they know the compulsive overeating will lead to feelings of guilt and shame, they cannot stop.

Signs and Symptoms of Compulsive Overeating or Binge Eating

- eating beyond physical fullness
- eating a great deal of food in a short period of time
- eating in secrecy
- inability to stop eating
- weight fluctuations
- yo-yo dieting
- mood instability
- isolating and making excuses in order to be alone with food
- stealing or hoarding food

If you would like to learn more about these disorders, please refer to Chapter 3, What Is Your Relationship with Food?

COMMON MYTHS ABOUT EATING DISORDERS

The following are some common myths and truths about eating disorders:

Myth: Individuals with eating disorders are *doing it* for attention!

Truth: Eating disorders are not something that a person "does." Having an eating disorder is not a conscious choice, nor is it a purposeful bid for attention. Eating disorders are illnesses. These illnesses serve as *coping mechanisms*. Though maladaptive, they are an individual's best attempt at coping with something in his or her life that otherwise feels out of their control. Remembering that eating disorders are not a choice will help you support your loved one on her or his journey to recovery.

Myth: Your loved one "just won't eat," or "just won't stop eating."

Truth: Eating disorders are not a choice. It is important for you to understand that it isn't that she *"won't"* eat or stop eating; it is that she *"can't"* eat or stop eating. She is enslaved by the *eating disorder voice*. This is a voice of hatred and self-loathing. It tells her she must suffer. It tells her she is not worthy of care.

Even though you may feel your loving, supportive voice falls on deaf ears, your loved one needs and craves to hear it. Eventually, we hope she will believe the voices of care, acceptance, and self-respect. Eventually, we hope hers will join the chorus of voices of caring, acceptance, and self-respect. Be patient with your loved one. Help her fight the voice of the eating disorder by being the voice of love, respect, and care. For example, when your loved one cannot eat or cannot stop eating, instead of chastising her or telling her she is not trying hard enough, say something like the following: "It saddens me to see you starving (or overfeeding) your body. Your body . . . your soul . . . all of you deserves good, compassionate care. I want to be the loving voice that reminds you of this because I know the eating disorder is telling you to destroy yourself."

Myth: If your loved one could just lose weight, everything would be okay.

Truth: Eating disorders are not about food and weight. They serve as metaphors for other issues in the person's life. In other words, despite what you may hear from your loved one about losing weight, it is not really weight that is the issue at hand. Food and weight are the symptoms; there is something underneath the food and weight issues that are the *real* issues. Therefore, focusing on food and weight alone is not going to bring about recovery. Recovery will come when your loved one learns more appropriate ways of coping with issues that led to her eating disorder.

Myth: Your loved one will *always* be in recovery.

Truth: It is possible for those struggling with eating disorders to *fully recover*. Food and weight does not need to rule them for the rest of their lives. This is important for you to understand: you need to believe in recovery in order to support your loved one's recovery!

Myth: There is always *a* reason for the development of an eating disorder.

Truth: There are always *many* reasons for the development of an eating disorder. Rarely, if ever, is there only one underlying issue! Eating disorders develop as a result of biological, psychological, and sociocultural factors. Please don't focus on finding *the* cause of your loved one's eating disorder. Instead, be open to the numerous contributing factors that led her toward using food and weight as a form of coping.

Myth: There is nothing I can do to make my loved one recover.

Truth: It is true that you cannot *make* your loved one recover. However, there are things you can do to support your loved one's recovery.

MY SUGGESTIONS FOR FAMILY AND LOVED ONES, FROM ONE WHO SUFFERED

1. Be aware of the people in your life, and if you suspect someone you love has an eating disorder, talk with them about it.
2. Do not assume or accuse!
3. Be aware that they may be in denial and not ready to deal with their eating disorder.
4. Remember that anorexia nervosa and bulimia are very secretive disorders that leave the individual feeling very shamed.
5. Do not baby-sit, follow the person to the bathroom, make the person weigh in, or force-feed the person you are concerned about.
6. Be available to talk and offer support, but know your limitations as a loved one!
7. Recommend a therapist who specializes in eating disorders.
8. Also recommend your loved one meet with a medical doctor.
9. Educate yourself on eating disorders so you can understand what may and may not be helpful.
10. Love unconditionally.
11. Hold the person responsible for his or her decision, but do not place blame or shame.
12. Seek therapy for yourself, even if the person you are concerned about will not seek therapy.
13. If your loved one is in imminent danger, you must push the issue and seek outside intervention.

Jennifer, age 34

WHAT TO DO IF YOU SUSPECT YOUR LOVED ONE HAS AN EATING DISORDER

You have just learned, or you suspect, that your loved one has an eating disorder. *How* you present your concerns to your loved one is just as important, if not *more* important, than what you have to say. How you raise your concern and how you phrase your observation may reinforce denial and shame, or it may provide an opportunity for your loved one to consider (and maybe even talk about) the denial, shame, and other feelings that are contributing to the eating disorder.

Here are some suggestions on how to *gently* confront your loved one in a simple step by step format.

Identifying Your Concerns

Remember your loved one is vulnerable. She will hear your concerns best if you say what you have heard or observed followed by an expression of your concern for her health, safety, and happiness. Here is an example.

> *"I have overheard you vomiting in the bathroom at night when you think I'm asleep. At first I thought nothing of it, but after a month of hearing it almost every night, I have become so worried about you that I had to talk with you about it. I love you, I'm worried about your health, and I don't want you to continue suffering."*

If you have noticed or heard about the following symptoms, you may want to talk about them with your loved one.

preoccupation with food and weight	withdrawal from family and friends
weight loss dizziness	distractibility menstrual irregularities
being cold all the time	gastric complaints/bloating
impulsive behaviors compulsive exercise	food missing moodiness
laxatives enemas	ipecac syrup diet pills
residual vomit in the bathroom	frequent trips to the bathroom after eating
picking at food, without really eating	cooking for others without eating
weight fluctuations	puffy eyes and/or broken blood vessels near eyes
swollen glands and/or puffy cheeks	fatigue excuses why not eating
complaints of muscle cramps	problems with teeth and gums
chronic sore throat	burning in throat/chest
closet or secretive eating	talk of dieting avoiding of activities

Others (please explain): _____

Now, it is important that you do not use this list as a means of attack. Rather, this list will help you clearly define what concerns *you*.

Gathering Resources

Again, confronting a loved one struggling with an eating disorder is a very delicate task! It is important that your strategy be well thought out ahead of time. You will do best, and your loved one will benefit more, if you have learned about eating disorders and identified resources for help before you discuss your concerns with her. In all likelihood, if you are concerned about your loved one, you are going to want her to receive help. Finding this help *before* confronting her could show her you are serious about finding help for her *and you*. You may want to start by contacting your physician, local hospital, or eating disorder hotline/facility. Some useful information could include: local eating disorder support groups, written information, potential therapists, physicians, and nutritionists who specialize in the treatment of eating disorders. Whenever possible, try to gather the phone numbers, professional background, and addresses of these agencies and professionals. If and when your loved one is ready to seek help, this information will facilitate the next step (i.e., getting help). Find out as much as possible about what your loved one can expect when contacting a professional. Getting help can be very scary. The more you know, the more you can help your loved one allay her fears.

Below are spaces to write information that your loved one may want or need.

Therapist's Name: _____
    Address: _____
                _____
    Phone: _____

Therapist's Name: _____
    Address: _____
                _____
    Phone: _____

Nutritionist's Name: _____
    Address: _____
                _____
    Phone: _____

Nutritionist's Name: _____
    Address: _____
                _____
    Phone: _____

Physicians's Name: _____
    Address: _____
                _____
    Phone: _____

Physician's Name: _____
    Address: _____
                _____
    Phone: _____

Support Group: _____
    Address: _____
                _____
    Phone: _____

Support Group: _____
    Address: _____
                _____
    Phone: _____

Whenever possible, you should try to get the name of more than one expert in each specialty area. Providing more than one name to your loved one can help her feel that she has a *choice*. Choice is critical. Your loved one must feel empowered, not controlled.

Understanding the Role of the Eating Disorder

As we stated earlier, eating disorders are coping mechanisms. As you prepare your *gentle* confrontation, think about some possible factors that you believe may be contributing to your loved one's coping via her eating disorder. For example, if you know your loved one has been under great stress, it might be important for you to note this. Your loved one may feel better understood or affirmed if she knows you notice more than her symptoms.

In the spaces below, write anything that you believe may be a contributing factor:

_____   _____   _____

_____   _____   _____

_____   _____   _____

Planning the "Talk"

We have been using the word *confrontation* throughout this section, when we refer to talking to your loved one. Please understand that we want you to confront in the most gentle of ways! That is, we use the term confrontation because you are going to be bringing up a subject that is going to be most difficult for your loved one. Be aware of just how difficult this is going to be for him or her. Try to put yourself in the place of a person who is about to be called on something that is shameful and embarrassing. Imagine someone telling you they know all about the secret you've been keeping. It is a very difficult position in which to be; much more difficult than the position in which you find yourself. Please keep this in mind, as you choose your words—the gentler the confrontation, the better the chance of a positive outcome. Below is a list of things to consider as you strategize your talk:

Timing: Never will there be a good time for a discussion such as the one you are about to have. Still, try to find a time when you will not be distracted. Find a quiet place where you can sit and talk, without the interruption of the telephone or others.

Goals: Consider your goals. Try to be realistic, and keep in mind the probability that you may be met with denial and/or anger. Do not let this deter you from expressing your concerns. You can tolerate your loved one's denial and anger better than her continued suffering or possible death. Remember this!

Presentation: As we stated earlier, *how* you express your concern is almost more important than what your concern is. Whenever possible, try to begin each sentence with "I." For example, you may begin by saying, "I have asked to talk with you because I am concerned about you. Because I am concerned about you I want to share my concerns with you." Your loved one is much less likely to become defensive when you take responsibility for your feelings and experience and keep the focus on "I." If you find yourself talking in "You" statements, she is more likely to become defensive to ward off an attack. An example of a "You" statement is, "You have an eating disorder; I know you have been throwing up after every meal you eat . . ." A gentler way of expressing this same concern might be, "I care about you and that's why I am bringing this up. I am concerned that you may be struggling with an eating disorder. I have noticed that you frequently excuse yourself after meals to go to the bathroom, and I am concerned that you may be doing this in order to purge."

You may want to tell your loved one that you have been reading about eating disorders so you will understand more. You might offer her the books, articles from the Internet, brochures, and pamphlets that you have been reading. You could tell her that you have been gathering information about eating disorders support organizations and professionals in your area that specialize in eating disorders. If she doesn't want this information now, tell her you will keep it for when and if she should ever need it. *Your research shows the seriousness of your concern, as well as the seriousness of your love.*

You may also want to consider writing a letter to your loved one ahead of time to make certain you say what it is you want to say in the gentle and loving way you want to say it. Or you may decide to give her the letter to hold on to after you've finished talking. Although it may take time, a letter of concern from you may eventually empower your frightened loved one to embark on her journey to recovery.

Expectations: Don't have any! Actually, expect the worst. That is, expect that your loved one meets you with resistance, anger, and denial. Prepare for this, and do not get angry in return. Stand your ground, hold to what you have prepared, and allow your loved one to have time to think about your concerns and information. If met with resistance, wait a little while before confronting your loved one again. Give her an opportunity to speak with you, and if this does not occur within a brief period of time (a week or so), check in with her and ask her how she is feeling about the talk you had. Remember, you have nothing to lose by gently confronting your loved one. You, (and your loved one), have *everything* to gain!

HOPE FROM A MOTHER

I would like my contribution to this book to be one of hope . . . a rare commodity when dealing with a family member or friend with an eating disorder. My daughter, Jessica, has been in recovery now for three years. She is living away at college; she has regained the weight she had lost, and she is the most delightful, funny person to be around. Her energy level is over the top! Every time I look at her I thank God, and her therapist, for her ability and courage to overcome this destructive disorder. I have prefaced my remarks with positive ones because I know the guilt, desperation, and fear that you live with every waking moment when your loved one has an eating disorder. I want to assure you that people *can* and *do* recover.

I don't suppose I will ever understand how her eating disorder started. This knowledge is for Jessica and her therapist. Instead, what I have learned through this experience is that I do not have to know "how" or "why." Instead, I have to know "how" to be patient . . . a task that can be terribly difficult when you know life is at stake. I have learned to just be her mom . . . not her therapist or the "food police." I confess that I had made these mistakes initially, but never having dealt with such issues, I was clueless. I grasped at anything I could in an attempt to make my daughter better. I now know that eating disorders are not like medical illnesses; it isn't as simple as taking a pill and getting cured! Anorexia is like an all-white jigsaw puzzle. It takes time and a tremendous amount patience in order to put the puzzle together.

Living with my daughter was frustrating and frightening. My husband and I often felt guilty. Had we not been supportive? What could we have done differently? How could this be happening? What went wrong? It was easy to fall into self-blame, but in doing so, physical and emotional energy was getting lost. There was no time for this; instead we needed to place our energy on whatever was necessary to get Jessica the help that she needed. Our hearts were breaking; we could see our daughter fading away! It took every breath I had, but I managed to get her into treatment.

We were on the right track. Jessica was now under the watchful supervision of a doctor, nutritionist, and therapist. She was being weighed weekly (backwards so she wouldn't know her weight) but, unfortunately, was continuing to lose weight. The risks had increased, and it was time now for my husband and me to agree to an inpatient hospitalization. In her first admission, she weighed 82 pounds, with a body temperature of 95 degrees and a very faint blood pressure. Although terrified of leaving my child in a hospital, I felt relieved to know she was in a place where she would be constantly monitored and receive the medical and psychiatric attention she deserved. Let me tell you how shocked I became when I learned the next day that her insurance company was denying further inpatient treatment! My daughter could die! How could there be any question to the need for serious medical intervention? After hour-after-hour of challenging the insurance company, we were able to have Jessica remain inpatient for a brief period of time. Upon discharge, she was transferred to a partial hospital program.

This hospitalization experience proved to be unsuccessful. Not long after Jessica's discharge, her weight began to drop drastically once again. In hindsight, I believe part of the difficulty with this first experience for Jessica was that she was not in an eating disorders facility. She was hospitalized on a general psychiatric unit; most of the patients struggled with drugs, alcohol, and other psychiatric disorders. I do not believe the hospital had the capabilities of providing a comprehensive eating disorder program given the diversity of patients and so few patients diagnosed with eating disorders.

Continued

Anyway, due to Jessica's weight loss, she was once again hospitalized. This time, she was admitted to an eating disorder unit in a hospital closer to home. This program had a very comprehensive schedule of groups, meetings, and activities. It also provided individual and family therapy, and had strict food regimens. The team of professionals showed respect and genuine care for the patients. This time I felt confident in the program, and with my daughter's recovery. After two weeks inpatient, Jessica was transferred to their day treatment program for another two weeks. Although we talked often by telephone, my husband and I also visited Jessica daily. I had missed Jessica terribly, and still felt uncomfortable with her not being home (despite my comfort with the program). On Wednesdays, we attended family groups in which we learned to understand eating disorders. This helped me to appreciate how difficult my daughter's recovery was going to be.

Once discharged, Jessica continued to see her doctor, nutritionist, and therapist on a weekly basis. This had become her full-time job! Her life was now a combination of school (senior year) and appointments. Her outside activities had been limited, as she was still underweight with a low heart rate. I continued to worry . . . would she be able to have children someday? Would she have cardiac problems? Osteoporosis? The process of recovery was slow and painstaking; I would find comfort in my daughter's willingness to work on her recovery. I believe this kept me going!

Jessica had been working with her outpatient therapist off and on for approximately one year. She had begun to express feelings of frustration and appeared more resistant to meetings with him. When she came to me refusing to go back, I had no option but to intervene. I did not want all her hard work to be for nothing! I wasn't going to make her return to a therapist with whom she didn't want to work, but I also wasn't going to let her be without therapy. We talked, and Jessica was willing to consider working with another therapist.

After much research, I received the name of a new therapist for Jessica. I was uncertain how she would respond, and was delighted after Jessica came home from this first meeting. "She gets it," Jessica said. This was music to my ears! If your loved one doesn't want to work with a particular therapist, listen to her concerns and explore your options. Some patients may use this as an excuse to not get help. For Jessica, I knew she wanted help, and as such I took her feelings about therapy very seriously. I also recommend that you consider confronting your loved one's therapist if necessary. First of all, you are hiring him or her to provide a service for you, and second of all, it is your loved one's life that is in jeopardy. Educate yourself as much as possible on eating disorders. Talk to as many people as you can. Find a support group in your area and talk with other parents and loved ones! The more help and education you get for yourself, the more support you will be able to provide for your loved one.

As time went on, I stopped asking Jessica about her therapy session (I used to ask her after each session, and she would respond by retreating and ignoring me). Instead, I realized that if she wanted to talk to me, she would. I became a better listener by not interfering. I returned to being her "mom"; this is what she needed. She didn't need for me to be her therapist.

Today Jessica's relationship with food doesn't even cross my mind. When someone told me three years ago that she would get better, I was unable to think that far ahead. I wanted it to be the way it is now and have the eating disorder behind us! I smile now when I think of what my daughter has been through—not because I would wish this horrific experience on her, but because of how proud I am of her for overcoming such a battle! My family is whole again, and we enjoy one another's company. In looking back, I can say that my husband and I were not bad parents. Sometimes bad things happen to good people!

                                                                            Judy

HOW TO BE SUPPORTIVE OF RECOVERY

Support for those struggling with an eating disorder varies from person to person. What may feel supportive to one person may not feel supportive to another. For example, Mary finds it supportive if her parents check in with her at the end of the day and ask her how she did with eating that day. Eric, on the other hand, might feel that his parents are being controlling and overprotective if they check in with him. For this reason, it is best if you sit down with your loved one and ask how you can best support her. Support is as individualized and unique as your loved one! There are, however, certain do's and don'ts. Here is a list of suggestions that are useful to remember. Share them with your loved one.

Do's and Don'ts

Don'ts:

1. Don't discuss food, weight, eating habits, or appearance. If your loved one attempts to bring up such discussions, let her know that you are not comfortable having such discussions at this time, and that you do not feel it is a productive discussion to have (based on your concerns for her). Discussion or focus on food, weight, and appearance can be experienced as efforts by another to control or as judgments about the self. Such discussions can also reinforce the focus on food to the exclusion of the underlying feelings and issues.
2. Don't talk about how her body looks, her weight, or dieting, and refrain from making critical comments about your body or anyone else's body.
3. Don't have emotional discussions around mealtimes. Mealtimes should be relaxing and not stressful.
4. Don't become the "food police." Encourage your loved one to develop a meal plan with her nutritionist. Whenever possible, ask to participate in one of these meetings in order to understand how best to support her during meals/snacks.
5. As with #4, don't become your loved one's therapist or physician. Your role is to be her support; it is not your place to be taking professional action. It is your role, however, to take action according to what your loved one and/or professionals deem to be supportive.
6. Don't become critical of your loved one's recovery. If you are concerned about treatment recommendations, seek support from a trained professional, support group, or educational resources.
7. Don't allow yourself to get involved in power struggles around food; you cannot force your loved one to eat! Trying to do so will only result in alienation and frustration.
8. Don't stock your kitchen with foods that are going to contribute to binge behaviors if your loved one is trying to reduce her bingeing or compulsive eating (e.g., gallons of ice cream). Do not stock your kitchen with foods that collude with your loved one's compulsion to cut calories when she needs to gain weight (e.g., no-fat foods, diet foods).

Do's:

1. Do share your concern for your loved one, and your wish to be supportive. Ask how you can best be supportive, and recommend professional support if she is not currently receiving such help.
2. Do educate yourself on the complexity of eating disorders and recovery.
3. Do talk about topics other than food. Your loved one is more than her eating disorder.
4. Do get involved; contact local professionals for education, support groups, and therapy for yourself.
5. Do allow your loved one the opportunity to develop her own thoughts, beliefs, and identity. Do not preach!

6. Do make certain that plenty of "safe foods" are available. Safe foods are those foods that your loved one feels comfortable eating at her particular stage of recovery.

7. Do consider your own relationship with food and your weight. If it's not a healthy one, find help for yourself and acknowledge your difficulties. This will support your loved one's efforts at recovery.

8. Do remember that eating disorders are not a conscious choice! Differentiate between being angry with your loved one, and being angry at the eating disorder.

Recovering from an eating disorder is difficult, but doable. With your help, your loved one's journey to recovery will be a less arduous, less lonely, and less terrifying journey. May you both find your way.

Concluding Your Journey: The Tree and the Web Revisited

You've reached the end of the workbook, but there are two more tasks to accomplish. Look at the tree you drew at the beginning of the workbook. The roots were the causes of the eating disorder, as you understood them. The branches were the purposes the eating disorder served. Draw another tree. Are the root causes the same? Do you see any causes that you didn't see before? Are the purposes the same now as when you started this journey? Are there any new purposes that the eating disorder serves? Could the purposes be better served by something other than the eating disorder?

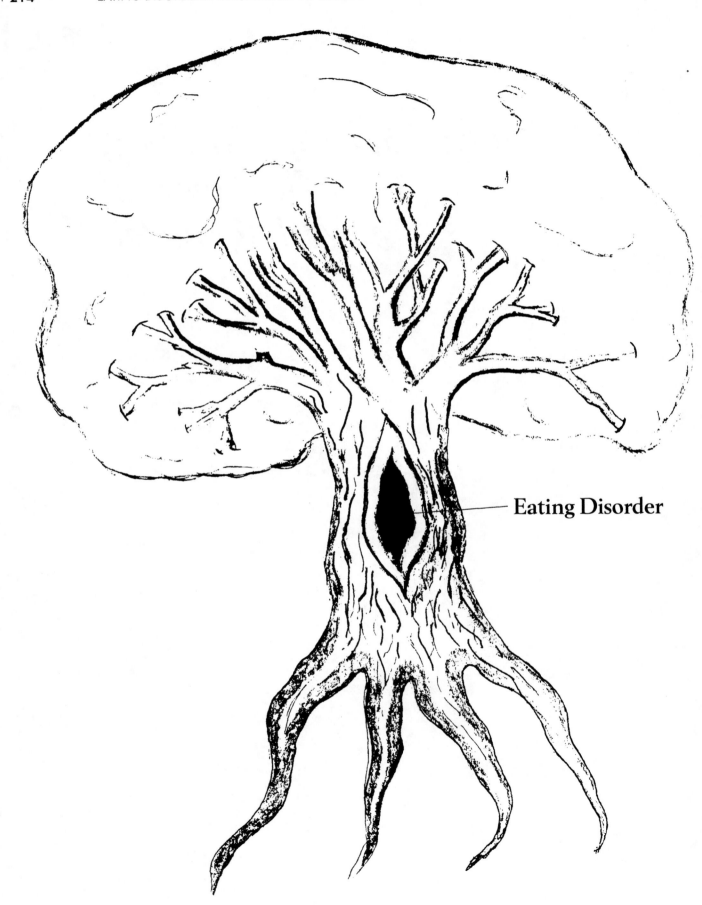

Eating Disorder

Now, look at the web you drew as you began this workbook. This web represented the costs of your eating disorder. Now draw a new web.

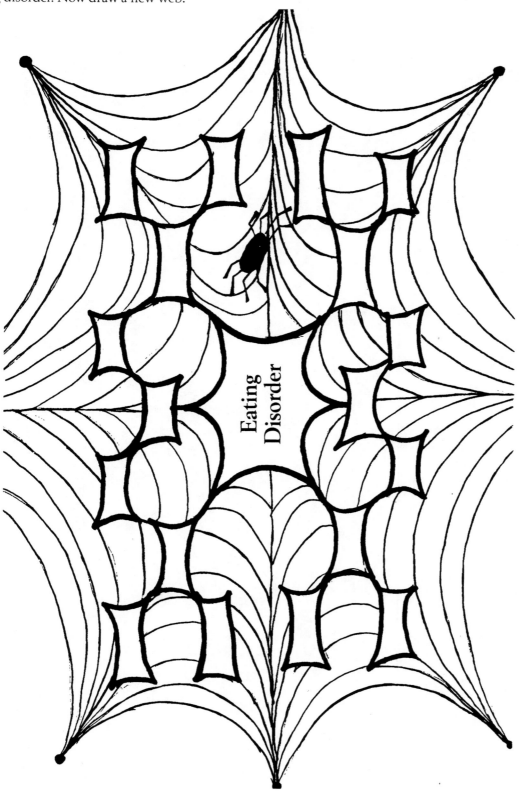

This web represents the outcome of your recovery. What will you attain? What are the benefits? Imagine. Wonder what recovery will look like! May recovery be yours!

Resources and References

Books, Journals, Magazines, and CD-Roms

American Psychiatric Association. (1994). *Diagnostic and statistical manual of mental disorders* (4th ed.). Washington, DC: Author.

Budman, S., & Villapiano, M. (1999). *Nutritional health information CD-Rom for college women.* Newton, MA: Innovative Training Systems.

Bulik, C., Sullivan, P., & Rorty, M. (1989). Childhood sexual abuse in women with bulimia. *Journal of Clinical Psychiatry, 50,* 460–464.

Carlat, D., & Carmago, C. (1991). Review of bulimia nervosa in males. *American Journal of Psychiatry, 148,* 831–843.

Carlat, D., Carmago, C., & Herzog, D. B. (1997). Eating disorders in males: A report on 135 patients. *American Journal of Psychiatry, 154*(8), 1127–1132.

Fahy, T., & Treasure, J. (1989). Children of mothers with bulimia nervosa. *British Medical Journal,* 299, 1031.

Franseen, L., & McCann, S. (1996, Summer). Mind games. *Olympic Coach, 6*(3), 15–17.

Garner, D. & Garfinkel, P. (Eds). (1997). *Handbook of treatment for eating disorders* (2nd ed.). New York: Guilford.

Goldbloom, D. S. (1993). Menstrual and reproductive function in the eating disorders. In A. S. Kaplan & P. E. Garfinkel, *Medical Issues and the Eating Disorders, the Interface* (pp. 165–175). New York: Brunner/Mazel.

Goodman, L. (1992). *Is your child dying to be thin?* Pittsburgh, PA: Dorrance.

Herzog, D. B., Norman, D. K., Gordon, C., et al. (1984). Sexual conflict and eating disorders in 27 males. *American Journal of Psychiatry, 141,* 989–990.

Kaplan, A., & Garfinkel, P. (Eds.). (1993). *Medical issues and the eating disorders: The interface.* New York: Brunner/Mazel.

Knowlton, L. (1995, September). Eating disorders in males. *Psychiatric Times, 12*(9).

Linehan, M. (1993). *Cognitive-behavioral treatment of borderline personality disorder.* New York: Guilford.

Microsoft Corporation. (1993–1997). The judgement of Paris. *Microsoft Encarta 98 Encyclopedia.*

Mondadori. A. (Ed.). (1998, April/May). Fat*Grasso, *Colors 25,* C.P.N 1812 (ABB) 2010, Milano Italia.

Prochaska, J., Norcross, J., & DiClemente, C. (1994). *Changing for good.* New York: William Morrow.

Seid, R. P. (1994). Too close to the bone: The historical context for women's obsession with slenderness. In P. Fallon, M. A. Katzman, & S. C. Wooley (Eds.), *Feminist perspectives on eating disorders.* New York: Guilford.

Siever, M. D. (1994). Sexual orientation and gender as factors in socio-culturally acquired vulnerability to body dissatisfaction and eating disorders. *Journal of Consulting and Clinical Psychology, 62,* 252–260.

Silberstein, L. R., Mishkind, M. S., Streigel-Moore, R. H., et al. (1989). Men and their bodies: A comparison of homosexual and heterosexual men. *Psychosomatic Medicine, 51,* 337–346.

Stambler, M. R. L., Hoover, E., Conneff, T., Matsumoto, N., McFarland, S., & Huziner, M. (1992, January). On the cutting edge. *People Magazine.*

Stein, A., & Fairburn, C.G. (1989). Children of mothers with bulimia nervosa. *British Medical Journal, 299,* 777–778.

Thompson, R. A., & Sherman, R. T. (1993). *Helping athletes with eating disorders.* Champlain, IL: Human Kinetics Publishers.

Vanderlinden, J., & Vandereychen, W. (1993). Dissociative experience and trauma in eating disorders. *International Journal of Eating Disorders, 13,* 187–194.

Villapiano, M. & Goodman, L. (2001). *Eating disorders: Time for change.* Philadelphia: Brunner-Routledge.

Winnicott, D. W. (1958). The capacity to be alone. *The maturational processes and the facilitating environment* (pp. 29–36). New York: International University Press.

Wurtman, J. (1993). *Emotions, overeating and the brain.* Boston, MA: Walden Health Resources.

Yager, J., Kurtzman, F., Lansverk, J., et al. (1988). Behaviors and attitudes related to eating disorders in homosexual male college students. *American Journal of Psychiatry, 145,* 495–497.

Yates, A. (1991). *Compulsive exercise and the eating disorders.* New York: Brunner/Mazel.

Internet Sites

http://www.addictions.net – "Addictions and More"

http://www.anred.com – Anorexia Nervosa and Related Eating Disorders

http://www.cosmeticscanada.com

http://www.depression.com

http://www.diabetes.org

http://www.drkoop.com

http://www.health-net.com

http://www.health.org – The National Clearinghouse for Alcohol and Drug Information

http://www.mayohealth.org The Mayo Clinic

http://www.mhsource.com – Mental Health Infosource

http://www.members.tripod.com/~thecooksbooks/FoodPyramid.html

http://www.mirror-mirror.org

http://www.mrfredfurs.com/twiggy.html

http://www.plasicsurgery.org/mediactr/trends.htm

http://www.plasticsurgery.org/mediactr/99stats.htm

http://www.something-fishy.com/ed.htm

http://www.usoc.org

Index

A

abuse 131–146
action stage 29
addiction 112–114, 119–122
adjustment disorder 158
affirmations 16, 80–83, 108–109, 151–152
alcohol 117–119
Anderson, A. 97, 105
anorexia nervosa 8, 12, 53–54, 68–70, 91, 94–96, 102–103, 105, 174, 197–200, 209–210
Apgar scores 84–86
appearance 78–80
athletics 100–101

B

balance 74
Barbie Doll look 78
belief systems 31–32
binge eating 11, 23–26, 94, 200, 202
biochemistry 160
bipolar disorder 158–159
birth complications 86
birth weight 84–86
Budman, S. 42
body dissatisfaction 78–80, 100
body distortion 77
body image 43, 47–62, 78–80
body roadmap 59–61
Buddha 38
Bulik, C. 134
bulimia nervosa 68–70, 87–91, 94–96, 105, 115–117, 200–201

C

cardiac irregularities 123
Carlat, D. 105
Carmago, C. 105
Christianity 37–38
cognition 9–15
cognitive-behavioral therapy 171
confrontation 207–208
constipation 123
contemplation stage 29
coping mechanisms 17

D

dehydration 14
depression 155–161

diabetes 161–164
DiClemente, C. xv, 28–30
DiDomenico, *not in references* 97
dieting 5–12
diet pills 25, 124
distortion 49
diuretics 25, 124
drug abuse 119–122
dysthymic disorder 158

E

edema 123
education 197–202
electrolyte imbalace 123
emotional abuse 133
emotional hunger 33
emotions 9–15
environment 160
Ewing, John 118
exercise 14, 63–74

F

Fahy, T. 86
Fairburn, C. G. 86
families 195–212
family therapy 171
fasting 39
feelings 105–106
female body 37–38, 41–42
feminist therapy 171
fetal abnormalities 86
food pyramid 18
Franseen, L. 101
friends 195–212

G

Ganesh, Lord 38
gastrointestinal system 13–14
gender differences 96–97
genetics 160
Goodman, Laura 105
Gordan, C. 105
group therapy 171

H

H.A.L.T. 114
Herzog, D. B. 105

Hinduism 38
homosexuality 104–105

I
identity 73–74
infertility 84–86
interpersonal therapy 171
ipecac abuse 125

J
Jesus 38
Joan of Arc 38

K
Keys, A. 10–15
kidney dysfunction 123
Knowlton, L. 105

L
laxatives 14, 25, 122–123
Linehan, M. xvi
liposuction 78
loved ones 195–212

M
maintenance 29
malnutrition 175
McCann, S. 101
measurements 51–52
media 185–194
medication 181–182
metabolism 7–9, 13
Mishkind, M. S. 105
misperceptions 50
Mondadori, A. 38

N
negative self-talk 108–109
Norcross, J. xv, 28–30
Norman, D. K. 105
nutritionist 175–180

O
obsessive-compulsive disorder 147–154
Olympic Coach 101
osteoporosis 8, 90–91
overeating 20–22, 26–28, 44–46, 202

P
personality 160
personality changes 11–12
pharmacologist 181–183
pharmacotherapy 172
physical
   abuse 132
   changes 12–15
   exam 167–168
   hunger 33
physician 166–169
plastic surgery 78
positive self-talk 80–83, 151–152
potential foods 33

precontemplation stage 29
pregnancy 84–86
preparation stage 29
Prince Phillip 42
Princess Diana 42
Prochaska, J. xv, 28–30
professional growth 98–99
psychodynamic psychotherapy 171
psychotherapy 175
purging 13–15, 23–26, 200

R
recovery 17, 211–212
regulated weight 7–9
religion 37–40
resources 205–207, 217–218
restrictive eating 10–15, 19–20
risk foods 33, 35–36

S
safe foods 33
seasonal affective disorder 158
Seid, Roberta P. 42
Semel, George 78
set point theory 7–9, 15
sexual abuse 132, 139
sexual changes 12
sexuality 91, 104–105
Siever, M. D. 105
Silberstein, L. R. 105
social changes 12
social hunger 33
stages of change theory 28–30
Stein, A. 86
Streigel-Moore, R. H. 105
substance abuse 11–129

T
termination stage 29
therapist 170–173
thermogenesis, diet-induced 8–9, 15
thinking, changes in 12
Too Close to the Bone 42
trauma 131–146
Treasure, J. 86
twelve-step programs 114
Twiggy 41

U
underlying issues 1–3

V
Vandereychen, W. 134
Vanderlinden, J. 134
Vedas 38
Venus 38
Victorian period 42
vomiting 13–14

W
Winnicott, D. W. 77
women's issues 75–110